# Latin American Poetry

# LATIN AMERICAN POETRY
## ORIGINS AND PRESENCE

Gordon Brotherston
*Reader, Department of Literature*
*University of Essex*

Cambridge University Press

CAMBRIDGE

LONDON · NEW YORK · MELBOURNE

Published by the Syndics of the Cambridge University Press
The Pitt Building, Trumpington Street, Cambridge CB2 1RP
Bentley House, 200 Euston Road, London NW1 2DB
32 East 57th Street, New York, NY 10022, USA
296 Beaconsfield Parade, Middle Park, Melbourne 3206, Australia

First published 1975

Composition by Linocomp Ltd, Marcham, Oxfordshire
Printed in Great Britain at
the University Printing House, Cambridge

Library of Congress cataloguing in publication data
Brotherston, Gordon.
Brotherston, Gordon.
Latin American Poetry.
Bibliography: p. 213.
Includes index.
1. Latin American Poetry – History and criticism. I. Title.
PQ7082. P7B76    861    75-2734
ISBN 0 521 20763 0 hard covers
ISBN 0 521 09944 7 paperback

*For A.I.B. and A.I.B.*

# Contents

# Acknowledgements

Some of the ideas and passages in this book were first worked out in articles and reviews in *Books Abroad, Comparative Literature Studies, Stand Quarterly* and *The Times Literary Supplement*. I am grateful to the following people for their help and criticism: Ted Berrigan, Michael Black, Leon Burnett, Herbie Butterfield, Richard Gray, Jack Hill and, above all, my wife Gisela. I owe a great debt to Arthur Terry who went through the typescript in its final stages and made many incisive comments on it; and to Peter Hulme who compiled the index.

Acknowledgement is also due to the following writers and publishers for quotation of copyright material: João Cabral de Melo Neto; José Emilio Pacheco; Ediciones Carlos Lohlé (Ernesto Cardenal); Editorial Nascimento (Nicanor Parra); José Aguilar Editora (Manuel Bandeira); Editorial Losada (Alberto Girri, Nicolás Guillén; Pablo Neruda); Editorial Alfa (Carlos Germán Belli); Barral Editores (Octavio Paz).

G.B.

*Wivenhoe*
*September 1974*

# 1. Introduction

In language and politics, Latin America, that part of the world which stretches from the Rio Grande to Cape Horn, is not a single entity and never has been. This fact is of prime importance for understanding the poetry written by Latin Americans, and considerably complicates the task of the critic who wants to discuss it at all comprehensively. At a practical level we cannot rely on the props of standard literary histories or critical studies as we may, for instance, with French or Spanish poetry. Or, if we imagine we can, we are often liable to miss the point. A rewarding study might be made of the obvious or covert search for identity in Latin American poetry, an identity in terms of cultural tradition usually taken for granted in many other parts of the world. This book by no means pretends to be such a study, but rather to keep such considerations alive while giving some account of the nature, history and main works of Latin American poetry.

The actual term 'Latin American' owes its coinage not to some compelling inner sense of origin, but to the designs of French foreign policy in the late nineteenth century. At least until recent years we find scant awareness of a common heritage in Brazil and the Spanish-American republics (and, ironically, still less in French-speaking America), some of whose citizens would still reject the epithet 'Latin American', or as poets would question it. Yet it is not wholly misleading as a description of poetry from that part of the world in Spanish or Portuguese. (French poetry in Canada and the Caribbean is a special case: the first must lie outside our scope, the second is touched on in chapter 2.) For most poets of the sub-continent have accepted not just the Spanish or the Portuguese languages, but the metrics, prosody and much of the literary vocabulary and rhetoric traditionally associated with them, and through them with Latin and the classical world. A sonnet by the Mexican José Manuel Othón (1858–1906) is formally indistinguishable from the Spanish–Petrarchan norm, just as words like 'contempt' or 'rose' have quite similar connotations whether they are found in Pablo Neruda or in Lorca. Indeed, at this level, most battles for cultural separateness, and these have been many, have been fought with weapons supplied by the other side.

To this we might add that from the first days of European colonization, in the sixteenth century, up to the present, there is plenty of evidence of a desire to continue the Latin tradition, not just via the languages of the colonizers, but directly. Partly due to the influence of the Church, and because of centuries of isolation from the rest of the world, Latin long remained an important literary language. The Jesuit Rafael Landívar (1731–93) is recognized as one of the great modern Latin poets; and, as Pedro Henríquez Ureña has remarked, the finest neoclassical poets of the eighteenth century are those who wrote in Latin. Virgil, for example, *the* Roman poet, has been a recurrent model, and not just in poetics. His *Eclogues*, about the innocent pastoral life of the Golden Age, his *Georgics*, about the essential ethic and practice of agriculture, and his *Aeneid*, the epic apology of the Roman empire, have, since Independence, again and again been referred to as moral statements of the first order. Virgil was a touchstone for the Independence poet Andrés Bello, as he was for the Brazilian Mário de Andrade in the 1920s, and has been, more recently still, for the Argentinian Alberto Girri. Indeed in these and other cases Latin has been considered something prior and superior to the Romance languages like Spanish and Portuguese, which derived from it.

When political independence was won in Mexico, Central and South America in the early nineteenth century, under the leadership of such figures as San Martín and Bolivar, the struggle was naturally against the occupying powers. As a result, a good deal of energy was devoted, not least by poets, to proving how little Spain and Portugal mattered culturally. It is here that we first find that concern with an early, unspoilt Latin tradition; and, no less important, with all that the European conquest suppressed and destroyed in America. The Indian heritage that had survived, and had been acknowledged hitherto mainly by priests and a few rare scholars, was suddenly made much of. There was a great literary exhumation of the Toltecs and Aztecs of Mexico, the Maya of Yucatan and Guatemala, the Pipil (related to the Aztecs) of Nicaragua, the Incas and the Quechua and Aymara Indians of the Andes (Peru, Bolivia), the Guarani of Paraguay, their relatives the Tupi–Guarani of coastal Brazil, the Araucanians of Chile, and so on. This rediscovery was by no means universal or consistent. In fact the consequences of it are perhaps only now being fully realized in poetry. But as an event it did suggest the possibility of an alternative cultural tradition, of radically challenging Old World orthodoxy in literary and other ways. For this reason we may fairly associate this voluntary 'Indianism' with the enthusiasm that poets have shown from Independence onwards for consecrating or adopting such American idioms as the gaucho or the Negro dialects (the gauchos being the cowboys of the South American pampas, the Negroes being descendants of African slaves).

So far we have, then, two sets of possible 'origins': that of the 'Latin' languages Spanish and Portuguese, an imported paternal heritage; and that of violated local or 'mother' cultures like the Indian, gaucho and Negro. How attractive and unstable each has proved becomes conveniently clear when we focus on poetry which attempts to deal, precisely, with America, the birthplace, as a source of identity. Significantly enough, almost all of the many attempts to write such poetry have failed, for one reason or another. The one big exception is *Canto general* (1950) by the Chilean Pablo Neruda: a colossal work which by its excellence and felicity allows us better to approach its precedents (which Neruda himself, however, only seldom acknowledged). In both Saxon and Latin American there is undoubtedly such a thing as a tradition of poets obsessed with writing the song of their place, though in the second case they have perhaps been recognized less than they deserve. What at first sight may seem to be a purely formal problem, how a poet defines his place and identifies himself within it, in fact tells us a good deal about the nature of Latin American poetry.

The first part of this book, which takes up the points raised here, does not then, pretend to be a historical survey of the first poetry written in what is now known as Latin America. Chapters 2 and 3, 'Vernacular American' and 'The Great Song of America', are as much thematic as historical, and deal as much with the modern as with earlier periods. Very little was written during the Colonial period, and even during the nineteenth century, that need occupy us; and that little is often more properly considered as a sub-chapter of Spanish and Portuguese literature. Our emphasis is very much on what was and is new in the context of those languages. Consistently, it is taken for granted that the Spanish and Portuguese poetic traditions, even though essential to the beginnings of Latin American poetry, exist in their own right and are to be known about separately; and they are specifically invoked only to enforce a particular point.

If we want to say when, in time, Latin American poetry became independent and something for itself, we must first of all distinguish between Spanish America and Brazil. Although, in relation to Europe and America, Spanish American poetry has at most periods closely resembled Brazilian, historically they are normally considered to have 'come of age' at different moments. In both cases, however, the phenomenon was called by the same name: Modernism (*modernismo*). In Spanish-speaking America this term refers to the prolific flowering of poetry between about 1880 and the First World War, which not just announced an unmistakably American style but profoundly affected poetry in Spain itself. Much of this writing, with its initial debt to nineteenth-century Western literature, chiefly French, may seem to us outdated and boring. But without it Spanish America would have remained heavily dependent, poetically, on Europe. The writers who mattered most to the Modernists, Hugo, the Parnassians and Symbolists, Edgar Allan Poe, also left their mark in Brazil, among the *simbolistas* like Olavo Bilac at the turn of the century. But it was not until the 1920s that the Brazilian Modernists emerged as such, under the influence, in turn, of *avant-garde* movements like Futurism and Surrealism. While given social and economic conditions can hardly be expected automatically to *produce* a given kind of poetry, they can at times appear indispensable, a prerequisite. In this sense the modern 'world city' (*Weltstadt*, to use the German word) of São Paulo was for Oswald and Mário de Andrade and the Brazilian Modernists what Buenos Aires had been in the 1890s for Rubén Darío and the Modernists of Spanish America.

There is little magic in the term Modernism, which has the disadvantage of being widely used to refer to movements in Western literature as a whole. And fully to define what it means in Latin American poetry is probably impossible. Apart from the big difference between Spanish America and Brazil, so much of the detail is diffuse. The two chapters of this book which deal with the subject (4 and 5) are the most historical, and rely most on a recording of that detail as it seemed important to the poets involved. Perhaps part of the difficulty stems from the fact that those poets did not achieve their highest ambitions, innovatory as they were. Darío, or the Andrades, if historically indispensable, recognized an ideal greater than they themselves could embody. This is what the Uruguayan critic José Enrique Rodó seemed to express in his review of Darío's *Prosas profanas* (1896): there he spoke of Modernism as 'a return of the galleons' to Europe, a redressing of the cultural balance between the Old and the New World, at the same time as saying that in Darío, for all his creative energy, we could not yet discern 'the poet of America'.

If writing a history of Latin American poetry before Modernism is uninviting because there is little to say, after that event the same is true for the opposite reason. Spanish American poetry since the First World War, and Brazilian poetry since 1930, are dauntingly rich. And the three chapters of this book which concentrate on this period (6–8) could by no means present a complete picture (if such a thing is ever possible or desirable). We are faced with several major poets, who are both prolific and of international stature, among them a number of women writers of pronounced independence, like the River Plate poets Alfonsina Storni (1892–1938) and Juana de Ibarbourou (1895), and the Chilean Gabriela Mistral (1889–1957), who won the Nobel Prize for literature. We find an intricate interaction with the literature of other cultures: responses to, say, T. S. Eliot, André Breton, Ezra Pound, in a wide variety of poets. We also find, for the first time, numerous internal traditions, a sense of organic growth within Latin American poetry that is subtle in detail: César Vallejo drawing on Darío, for example, but quite differently from Octavio Paz; or João Cabral de Melo Neto drawing on Carlos Drummond de Andrade, who draws in turn on the Brazilian Modernists. And so on.

To make some sense of this it seemed a good idea, first of all, to dwell on two poets whom only the most parochial could refuse to acknowledge as great: the Peruvian César Vallejo, and Pablo Neruda. These two have, independently, received far more critical attention than any other Latin American poet. They both began to write when heavily conscious of Modernist precedent. After a period of intense introspection in the 1920s they struggled to express a larger communal self. Because of this, and of the high quality of existing commentaries on their work, I have chosen to compare them in detail in what has turned out to be the longest chapter in this book.

The main disadvantage of spending so long on Vallejo and Neruda is obviously that contemporaries or near contemporaries of theirs, important in their own right (the Mexicans Ramón López Velarde, José Gorostiza, Xavier Villaurrutia, for example), go barely acknowledged. To attenuate this tendency, in chapter 7 Octavio Paz is discussed as much for his criticism as for his poetry. He proves a convenient if contentious guide. He has gone deeply into the poetry of his country (Mexico), his sub-continent (notably in a brilliant essay on Darío), and beyond, and has borne out his discoveries in his verse, in the phases of a vivid intellectual development. But he has also ignored whatever failed to fit into his notion of tradition at any given stage. In this he may be fairly compared to T. S. Eliot, equally fundamental and provocative in his interpretations of English-language poetry.

In the final chapter I try to suggest that the co-ordinates of Spanish American and Brazilian poetry are today perhaps closer than they ever have been. The emergence of Latin America as not just a geographical but a nascent political area, if not part of a controversially-named Third World, has been reflected in poetry, not least in a concern with what poetry is and should do in these circumstances. The choice of poets discussed will unavoidably seem wilful (the Nicaraguan Ernesto Cardenal, the Peruvian Carlos Germán Belli, the Chilean Nicanor Parra, the Brazilian João Cabral de Melo Neto and the Argentinian Alberto Girri). At best, some idea may be had of their work both for what it is, and as a series of modern responses to those recurrent problems of origin and identity.

In sum, much of the emphasis of this book is on historical definition. It starts and ends by asking: what is 'Latin American' poetry anyway? In the space available clearly not every relevant poem could be mentioned (I should have enjoyed, for example, talking about the work of such writers as Jaime Sabines, Pablo Antonio Cuadra, Antonio Cisneros, Enrique Lihn, to mention only a few). At the same time I hope that the poems which are discussed (in most cases at some length) appear to be respected as such, as intricate accomplishments in their own right, which we should be the poorer for ignoring.

# 2. Vernacular American

In Latin American poetry, the metropolitan, or inherited European, tradition has persistently found itself in conflict with others distinct from it. First among these is the Indian tradition. For the vast oral and written literatures of the original Americans were far from totally extinguished by the European conquest, and 'classical' literature from the Pre-Columbian period has increasingly made its presence felt. Second, there is the native-born or creole (*criollo*) tradition, based on local dialects within Spanish and Portuguese that have often been considered languages in themselves, especially around the time of Independence. Third, the speech peculiar to the descendants of millions of African slaves in the Caribbean and Brazil has nurtured a poetic idiom of its own. None of these other traditions can be said to have posed a serious threat to Latin hegemony, at least for very long (though the desire in certain poets to preserve that hegemony at all costs could itself be thought paradoxically American). But to the degree that the very question of identity (poetic or other) has become unsurer, the force of 'marginal' traditions of this kind has been stronger, and any account of the poetry of Latin America does well to start by reckoning with them. What is at stake is not writing which depicts or is simply *about* Indians, creoles or Negroes, like the Uruguayan José Zorrilla de San Martín's famous epic *Tabaré* (1888), for example. Our concern is the more radical impingement of what those people had and have to say poetically, of their different poetic languages, on that of Latin America.

I

The first book known to have been printed in America was bilingual: a work of Christian doctrine of 1539 composed in Spanish and Aztec (or Nahuatl). Like many other such works which circulated in what are now Mexico, Guatemala, Peru and Brazil, this manual had an immediate missionary purpose. But the fact that bilingual or wholly Indian texts were published at all, into the late seventeenth century and even longer, on a large scale, indicates the strength of Pre-Columbian linguistic survival, and a certain European respect for it. Indeed, Spaniards and Portuguese were prepared to learn native languages not just functionally but, precisely, for literary ends. Sor Juana Inés de la Cruz (1651–95), the 'tenth muse' of colonial Mexico,[1] and José de Ancheita (1530–97), the 'father' of Brazilian poetry, turned to the Indian languages of their adopted countries as easily as they did to Latin when composing poems of their own. This for example is Anchieta's recasting of a traditional Tupi–Guarani chant:

> Come great chiefs
> stir from afar
> I too bring
> my people to dance
> I surrender them into your hands

Ou tubixa katu/mamo sui nde reka/Xe abe xe anameta/aroporasei seru/nde pope imeengatu.[2]

Quechua, the language of the Incas, became the vehicle of a full-length verse drama, *Ollantay*,[3] composed in colonial Peru by an anonymous writer who was clearly familiar with both the native heritage and the conventions of Spanish Golden Age literature. Others, with or without native help, went so far as to translate important works of European literature into American languages (Calderón's plays, Aesop's *Fables*, Racine's *Phèdre*), contributing to their literary strength and status.

Over the centuries the principal Indian languages (Nahuatl, Maya, Quechua, Tupi–Guarani) have undoubtedly declined. But they have far from disappeared from oral and written literature, and have continued to fascinate and 'win over' poets in Latin America. Like a considerable number of Andean writers, the Peruvian José María Arguedas reserved for Quechua his most deeply-felt rhetoric, in his hymn to Tupac Amaru, for example, which closely echoes Inca prayers:

> Come down to earth, Serpent God, breathe into me;
> put your hands on the tenuous web that covers my heart;
> give me your strength.

Uraykamuy Amary, samayniykita urpuchiway; sonqoypa llikanpi makikta churaykuy; kallpachaway.[4]

In the realm of folk song, artists like the Chiriguanos in Paraguay (still a bi-lingual state),[5] and the Chilean Violeta Parra (sister to

Nicanor, see p. 182) in her Araucanian lyrics, have helped to keep traditional literature alive in their original tongues. However a full account of compositions of this order, as of compositions by the prolific native Indian writers who after the conquest used trans-criptions of their languages and old scripts into the Roman alphabet, belongs to the history not of Latin but of Indian American literature. Here, our interest is how these unex-tinguished native modes have affected Spanish and Portuguese poetry written in America.

Only with the movement towards Independence, and as the cultural relativism expounded by Vico and his disciple Boturini[6] filtered into Latin America, did the syntax and prosody charac-teristic of Indian verse begin to be much respected for themselves. For all their Indian interest, colonial poets like Sor Juana, Anchieta and the anonymous author of *Ollantay*, sensed no professional reason why native verse should not be made to conform to Latinate conventions. By them, Nahuatl, Tupi and Quechua are made to rhyme, something they had never done before, and to scan (though two ancient songs, recently echoed in Shaffer's *Royal Hunt of the Sun*, do survive unscathed in *Ollantay*). So it is hardly surprising to find that, when they 'imitated' native poetry in Spanish and Portuguese, these writers moved formally a long way from their sources. Towards the end of the eighteenth century however a new sensitivity emerged. Arguably the first piece of 'free verse' in Spanish is a poem published in 1778 by Granados y Gálvez as an example of the artistic genius of ancient Mexico (said by Boturini to equal that of the Greeks). He presented the piece (as did W. H. Prescott after him) as a lyric by Nezahual-coyotl, the poet king of fifteenth-century Texcoco.[7] It cannot be claimed to be that unequivocally; but the presence of native thought and form in the poem is unquestionable. A better-known example from this historical period would be the 'hymn', osten-sibly modelled on Inca originals, which crowns the celebration of the victory of Junín in 1824 by the Independence poet José Joaquín Olmedo.[8] And at this same time at a humbler level, the *yaraví*, a traditional Quechua verse-form often accompanied by the *quena* (flute) and strangely forlorn in tone, began to emerge in Spanish in the work of Mariano Melgar. Once established, this and other forms of Quechua poetry flourished in the last century and still to some extent in this, and appeared, for example, in the work of Gabriela Mistral, the Peruvian Juan Gonzalo Rose[9] and others.

Independence in Brazil resulted in nothing less than a school of 'Americanists',[10] who were influenced in turn by Herder's enthusiasm for a literature of the people deriving from the unlettered and more 'primitive' elements of the nation ('Die Wilden'). The local force of this movement caught even the cosmopolitan Machado de Assis. His *Poesias Americanas* (1875) came as a tribute to the poems published under that same title thirty years previously by Antonio Gonçalves Dias. Indeed, Machado's praise of the novel *Iracema* by José de Alencar (1829–77), as the tale of a native bard in a style like the speech of those peoples accords so ill with his customary urbanity that it would seem ironic, were it not for the history of his own affection for literary tenets most uncompromisingly expressed by Alencar:

Knowledge of the native language is the best criterion for the nationality of the literature. It gives us not just the true style but the poetic images of the savage, the modes of his thought, the tendencies of his spirit, and even the smallest particularities of his life. It is at this source that the Brazilian poet must drink; it is from it that the true national poem, such as I imagine it, will emerge.[11]

It was Alencar who took the literary consequences of this programme furthest. He started by wanting to write a verse epic, *Os filhos de Tupã* (Tupã being a major deity of the Tupi–Guarani who once dominated large areas between the Amazon and the River Plate). Gonçalves Dias had had similar ambitions for his unfinished 'Os timbiras. Poema americano' (1848), but had come no nearer to fulfilling them; lines from the 'Introdução' effectively form its epitaph ('Oh that I could, o warrior, repeat for a single moment the voice of your songs'). But while Gonçalves Dias's despair of ever finding that voice led him to scientific research (in 1857 he published a *Dicionário da língua tupi*), Alencar stayed with literature and looked for other forms of expression. Rejecting as too civilized the 'linguagem clássica' of 'Os timbiras', and the Indian style of poets like Gonçalves de Magalhaes and Araujo Pôrto Alegre, he ended up writing three novels or *lendas* in poematic prose: *O Guarani* (1857), *Iracema* (1866, an anagram of America) and *Ubirajara* (1874).

The grander hopes of the Americanists were disappointed

because the Brazilian language they concentrated on, Tupi, was all but dead by then, and because they themselves remained unmitigatedly bourgeois in all their pretension to authenticity. The overtly cannibalistic intent of certain Tupi songs (highly praised by Montaigne),[12] which so embarrassed them, did however actually stimulate the Brazilian Modernists in the 1920s who were associated with the review *Antropofagia*: Oswald de Andrade, Raul Bopp and others. In a manifesto poem published in *Antropofagia*, referring not just to Brazilian poetry but to a whole life-style, Andrade said, not altogether flippantly: 'Tupi or not Tupi, that is the question' (see p. 86).

Generally, Latin American poets of this century have hardly been playful in referring to Indian literatures. Indeed, the political and cultural reasons for wanting to rescue the expression of oppressed and sometimes nearly extinct peoples have become increasingly intricate and urgent. Significantly, they have been analysed with most confidence by Marxist critics like the Peruvian Juan Carlos Mariátegui. In any event, those who have most persistently drawn on American Indian traditions in the twentieth century have done so, like their contemporaries in the United States and Canada, out of political conviction. Even the Guatemalan Miguel Angel Asturias, who operated in unashamedly dilettante fashion in several of his 'Maya' poems and lyric dramas, making mere ornament of ritual phraseology, has shown himself elsewhere to be notably 'committed' (for example in his introduction to his important anthology of pre-Columbian poetry in Spanish translation).[13] The poematic opening of *Hombres de maíz* (Men of Maize, 1949), with its rhythmic repetitions, its numerous Indian words (explained in a glossary) and set poetic phrases, its cyclical paragraphs and distortion of sequential time, illustrates how Asturias formally tried to enter the Maya–Quiche mind (in this case, that of the hero Gaspar Ilóm). By making Ilóm both someone immersed in the ancient poetry of his language, and the victim of an economy alien to him, he urges that the Indian heritage, in all its 'formal' detail, has been wrongfully denied in America.

This would certainly be the point of Ernesto Cardenal's recent *Homenaje a los indios americanos* (Homage to the American Indians, 1969), a verse collection which incorporates whole passages of their poetry as a vindication of cultures widespread over

the original America. Cardenal, it is true, can often rely dis-
appointingly on secondary sources and push favourable readings
of his own too hard.[14] His response to the *Cantares mexicanos* (a
sixteenth-century manuscript of Nahuatl lyrics) is vitiated from
the start by a reluctance to admit fully the original context of the
lyrics, the martial and homosexual rites that informed them as
song. Specifically, his reworkings of poems by Nezahualcoyotl
are less sensitive than Granados y Gálvez's and sooner recall the
Biblical tone of W. H. Prescott's 'translations' of them in the
*Conquest of Mexico*, and the pious versions made by nineteenth-
century poets like José Joaquín Pesado.[15] Little remains of the
Aztec sense of poetry as *xochicuicatl*, 'flower-song' (where the
element *xo*-suggests growth and excitement) and of their distinct
lyric modes (the *icnocuicatl* or 'orphan-song', the *yaocuicatl* or
'war-song', and so on). Elsewhere Cardenal is more successful,
especially when he makes a collage of his own and Indian verses
(a practice which he learned from Pound's *Cantos*). This can have
the striking effect of 'emptying' his Spanish and creating resonance
between his voice and that of the ransomed text (see p. 175). '8
Ahau' directly evokes the prophecy chants of the Yucatec *Books
of Chilam Balam*, which in turn derive from ancient origins not
just in the Maya tongue but in Maya script, in pre-Columbian
codices like the Dresden and carvings on the stone of numerous
stelae. The first person he uses is subtly defined to include also
strangers like himself and his reader:

> En palabras pintadas está el camino
> en palabras pintadas el camino que hemos de seguir.
>     Mirad la luna, los árboles de la selva
>             Para saber cuándo habrá un cambio de poder.
> ¿Qué clase de estela labraremos?
>         Mi deber es ser intérprete
>                 vuestro deber (y el mío)
>         es nacer de nuevo

The road is in depicted words, in depicted words the road we shall
follow. Look at the moon, the trees of the jungle to know when there will
be a change in command. What type of stelae shall we carve? My duty is
to be an interpreter; your duty (and mine) is to be reborn.

In the Andean area, conscious of Arguedas's and perhaps
Cardenal's example, poets have felt a similar urge and mission.
The Bolivian Pedro Shimose asks a Quechua-speaking friend:

'Decipher the stone for me, your ancient law, give it to me', and enforces his point by setting Inca liturgy into his own:

> Es justa y necesaria mi alegría.
> Barro en mi talón partido de tanto y tanto caminar.
> Anduve por la patria Pacha-Mama, mamahuakay-
>      chaquita.
>      Pacha Mama, suma yujra churita.
> (Tierra-Madre, conserva mi existencia.
> Tierra-Madre, da a las mieses tu esencia.)

My happiness is just and necessary. Clay in my heel split from so much walking. I walked through the land Pacha-Mama, mamahuakay-chaquita, Pacha-Mama, suma yujra churita. (Mother-Earth, preserve my existence. Earth-Mother, give to the crops your essence.)[16]

In Mexico, perhaps the most complex and agonized of Latin American national cultures from this point of view, poets have increasingly paid attention to their scantily acknowledged Indian past. More locally involved than Cardenal, with his continental view, they have also been stimulated by the *Cantares mexicanos* and other manuscripts, translated into Spanish by Angel María Garibay. But in Mexico the crucial factor was the Revolution of 1910 and after, which had a more obvious and immediate effect on the fine arts, notably Diego Rivera's indigenist murals. The literary repercussions of this cultural upheaval in Octavio Paz and other Mexican poets are discussed in chapter 7.

It would certainly be going too far to compare the secular silencing of American Indian languages by a foreign imperial idiom with that of Old English by the French-speaking Normans before its historical re-emergence. But the sense of a poetic heritage to be redeemed has powerfully stimulated poets, significantly in predominantly Indian areas, to be less singly 'Latin'.

## 2

This modern respect for another, 'maternal' tradition, evident also in the work of such major poets as the Peruvian César Vallejo, was, then, purposefully awakened with Independence, when the father-fixation of the Colonial period was challenged politically. In those heady days avenging zeal led even to the proposal that the descendants of the royal Incas should become the constitutional monarchs of the vast territories of Great Columbia once they were liberated (that is, Latin America plus the lands like California seized by the US in the early nineteenth century). But in practice the creoles exposed that racial prejudice against the Indian (seriously challenged only in quite recent years) which had made half-Indian ancestors of theirs scorn their mother tongue and want to be wholly white. For example, in the address which accompanies the Inca hymn in Olmedo's poem on the Junín victory, the Inca (implausibly enough) was made to renounce power in favour of the creoles. When it came to the test, in the early nineteenth century, the native-born populations of Latin America largely chose to adorn their newly-won political independence with poetry in a creole, and not an Indian, idiom. Rather than revive or adopt Indian tongues they preferred to hope that they would acquire their own, in a process whereby their versions of Spanish and Portuguese would come to differ as much from those languages as they in turn had come to differ from Latin. With the exception of the gaucho, native of the River Plate area (Argentina, Uruguay and Southern Brazil), they found no one to sustain that dream.

The gauchos, akin to the plainsmen (or *llaneros*) of Venezuela and in certain respects to the cowboys of the West, were one of several groups in South and North America who, being of mixed ancestry and living for centuries in relative isolation, had evolved a distinctive style of life and speech. (They were keenly observed by Darwin's evolutionist eye.)[17] And the question has often been asked, why they should have affected Latin American poetry when others did not. The point made by Borges and Bioy Casares[18] certainly stands: that although the gaucho was rural his style penetrated deeply into the towns of the River Plate region. For a 'civilized' and literate creole to adopt gaucho style was not a huge or awkward affectation. A gauchesque poem like Estanislao del Campo's *Fausto* (1866), which records the reactions of two gauchos to a performance of Gounod's opera in Buenos Aires, no doubt betrays and relies on facetious amusement at their ineptitude; at the same time it exists as a serious *translation* of European into local value and phrase.

Perhaps a more important stimulus to the glamorous if unenduring vogue of the gauchos' idiom was the fact that they themselves played a crucial role in the wars of Independence from Europe, and in ensuing national conflicts. The first verse

generally acknowledged as gauchesque was penned in the very
heat of battle: Bartolomé Hidalgo's rousing *cielitos* and patriotic
dialogues. In what might be called poetic bulletins ostensibly
composed by gauchos themselves, Hidalgo captured the sentiments of gaucho fighters in their language, and reported on
military successes on a continental scale, celebrating for example
San Martín's entry into Lima (1820). His verse form may have
been the old octosyllabic, with assonance or rhyme on even lines,
of the archetypically Spanish *romance*; but the vocabulary,
grammar and tone are recognizably American:

> Cielito, cielo que sí
> todo era humor y alegría
> andaba mandando juerza
> toda la mujería

*Cielito, cielo que sí,* all was humour and gaiety, all the women were giving
us strength.

The first line is entirely folk, and untranslatable; *juerza* (*fuerza* in
Spanish) and *mujería* are Americanisms. Chronologically, Hidalgo
was succeeded by Hilario Ascasubi, who contributed many verses
to publications like *El Gaucho en Campaña* (The Gaucho on
Campaign), which emanated from Montevideo around 1840.
Ascasubi went on, however, to elaborate this style in larger works,
notably *Santos Vega*, which began appearing in instalments a
decade later.

At some length, Santos Vega tells of life on a gaucho *estancia*,
authentically in so far as it presupposes rather than describes local
customs and speech. Critical reaction to it in the River Plate
countries was extravagantly enthusiastic, just because it seemed
to satisfy creole demands for cultural separateness. It was confirmed that here, at last, was a work which came from the heart of
the people, which was 'foreign to the language of Spanish literature', untranslatable even, and which would be the Homeric
antecedent of their 'own' literature.[19] Musical accompaniment
typical of the gaucho, and his characteristic *payada*, or sung dialogue, had provided the beginnings of a new genre, just as the
idyllic singing matches of the Dorians in Sicily had been the origin
of the pastoral eclogue. But a certain ambiguity undercut this
enthusiasm right from the start. 'Enlightened progress' urged by
several parties in Argentina and Uruguay (urbanization, railway
networks, mass immigration from Europe, new types of agricul-

ture and the introduction of barbed wire) was or would soon be putting an end to the gaucho. Critics candid enough to admit this finished up trying to have it both ways: to retain the gaucho as a profoundly national creature in Herder's terms, a poetic origin, and to eradicate him for being politically retarded. The roots of this conflict, manifest in Domingo Sarmiento's famous study of 'Civilization and Barbarism' in *Facundo* (1845) went very deep; from it issued the last and greatest example of gauchesque poetry, *Martín Fierro*.

José Hernández's work was published in two parts in the 1870s. The first especially brings to a high pitch the author's indignation at Sarmiento's presidential treatment of the gauchos: his cynical undermining of their existence in the name of progress, and his wholesale conscription of them to fight Indians (as late as that) in the frontier wars. The poem is spoken, or sung, in the first person by the gaucho Martín Fierro, who grimly struggles for survival in an increasingly hostile environment. Taking his guitar he quickly establishes an unmistakable presence:

> Yo no soy cantor letrao;
> mas si me pongo a cantar,
> no tengo cuando acabar
> y me envejezco cantando:
> las coplas me van brotando
> como agua del manantial.

I'm not an educated singer; but if I start to sing I never stop and grow old singing: verses spring from me like water from the source.

In a dialect and a courageous tone much admired by Che Guevara he tells of the misfortunes crowding in on him, driving him to a murderousness he would sooner have avoided. As in the best tradition of gauchesque poetry, landscape and custom are always implied or presupposed, everything being recorded from his point of view. His phrases and gestures record a whole other world, for which the immense *payada* in part 2 between El Moreno and Fierro serves as a kind of requiem. Perhaps the most telling stanzas of the poem come quite near the beginning of the first part when Martín Fierro reflects on life as it used to be, as if aware of it as an irrecuperable golden age:

> Aquello no era trabajo,
> más bien era una junción;
> y después de un güen tirón
> en que uno se daba maña,

pa darle un trago de caña
solía llamarlo el patrón.

Pues vivía la mamajuana
siempre bajo la carreta;
y aquel que no era chancleta,
en cuanto el gollete vía,
sin miedo se le prendía
como guérfano a la teta

That wasn't work, it was more like a party; and after a good stretch of it skilfully done the boss would call you for a swallow of *caña*. ¶For the flagon lived always under the cart and anyone who had his wits about him, as soon as he saw the neck, grabbed it like an orphan the tit.

As with Ascasubi, the speech is markedly American (*junción* for *función*, *güen* for *buen*, *vía* for *veía*, and so on). Mamajuana is a compellingly gaucho word. It derives from the same source as 'demijohn', and in imperial Spain was, appropriately, *damajuana*, 'dame Joan'. On the pampas, through a phonetic change which corroborates precisely the mammalian yearning of the whole stanza, it (or she) became *mamajuana*; the intimate sustenance of an 'orphaned' America, now moribund.

Early this century Leopoldo Lugones and others took to referring to *Martín Fierro* as a national epic,[20] the fulfilment of the promise of *Santos Vega*, comparable in all respects with the great, supposedly national, epics of Europe (*The Cid*, *The Song of Roland*, and so on). Their claims stick no better than those of Ascasubi's admirers, worse in fact, since as hero Fierro waxes and perishes in conflict not with some alien foe or infidel but, himself an outlaw, with his fellow countrymen. At best *Martín Fierro* is the poem of the gaucho part of several nations, in an idiom that has now apparently been reduced to the folkloric and the quaint. It may have exposed a common allegiance in Argentinians as different from each other as Borges and Che Guevara. But the idiom which gave this and other gauchesque poems birth has vanished with those who spoke it, disowned too soon and too drastically by the very Latin Americans who might have made of it a poetry of 'their own'.[21]

## 3

A further poetic tradition of Latin America, which in origin is no more Latin than a Quechua *yaravi*, and which in this century especially has flourished in ways denied to the gauchesque, derives from the black populations of the Caribbean and of the north and west coasts of South America. Working chiefly as plantation slaves these people kept alive, over centuries, rituals and songs of African origin; as in the Confederate States these were the source of a distinctive Afro-American music and poetry.

The first Negroes in Latin America to become literate and write poetry committed themselves single-mindedly to dominant tastes, putting their folk culture behind them. The Parnassian poems of the Brazilian João de Cruz e Sousa ('O pure white Forms, light Forms of moonlight, snows and mist') testify to this to the point of apparent parody. In Cuba, Gabriel de la Concepción Valdés ('Plácido') concurred in white sentiments of the nineteenth century to the extent of writing a fashionable ballad on the fall of Moctezuma. On occasion tunes from closer to home did make themselves heard, in verse that did not pretend to high poetic status. Luis Gama, a slave from Bahia, spoke wrily of himself as 'negro o bode' (an unflattering slang word for Negro), while in Colombia Candelario Obeso forcefully lamented in Negro dialect the travails of his condition.[22] But only in this century, more precisely, after the catastrophe of the First World War and the awakening of urgent European interest in Africa, did black poetry, *poesía negra*, conceptualized as such, become a recognizable idiom.

'Black' poets of Negro, mulatto or even largely white origin, have ranged from the occasional and folkloric to the heavily political. Many were first stimulated simply to capture African rhythms in Spanish and Portuguese verse. In the 1920s countless rumbas were composed in the Caribbean, Brazil and as far away as the River Plate cities, poems which evoked the music of the Yoruba and other cultures, the sacred *ekue* (the ritual Avakua drum), *palos*, and small drums like the *bembe*, the maracas and the bongo. Often 'black' sounds with no semantic meaning in Spanish or Portuguese would be recorded for little more than the sake of the exercise. 'The Tambo', by the Uruguayan Juan Julio Arrascaeta, has the incessant refrain: 'son, congo tambo bo'. Chanted phrase and drum beat mark the steps of a consciously 'primitive' adventure, at a time when Lorca was exploring the *canto hondo* of Andalusia, and when jazz rhythms and diction were making themselves felt in English-speaking America,

through Langston Hughes and others. Efforts were made to consecrate not just the detail but whole poetic forms which corres-
ponded to Negro music. Pointed and faintly sardonic 'contributions' to the courtly love tradition were made in 'Madrigals' like
this one by Nicolás Guillén:

> Tu vientre sabe más que tu cabeza
> y tanto como tus muslos.
> Esa
> es la fuerte gracia negra
> de tu cuerpo desnudo.

Your belly knows more than your head and no less than your thighs.
That's the strong black grace of your naked body.

The body of the Negress, preferably dancing, came positively
to bewilder some, as a reservoir of spontaneous sensuality drained
long ago in whites. Emilio Ballagas (who edited two important
anthologies of *poesía negra*)[23] and Luis Palés Matos made of her
a creature too transcendental to be contained in a racial idiom. She
became 'the night of this night', too vast to be named; 'all the sea
and earth' of the Caribbean, a 'free and limitless immensity'. To
exalt her Palés Matos resorted to the Song of Songs and, more
frantically, to Wagner ('black Walküre'). Such hyperbole could
hardly be sustained 'from the inside') and belongs only marginally
to black poetry, like several contemporary paeans to specifically
'Ethiopian' beauty. Perhaps the sagest response to all this was
made by Alejo Carpentier, who began his career publishing several
pieces of this sort, only to forget them quietly later.[24]

The most vivid poem to emerge from the Negro cult in Brazil
in the post First World War period was also about a woman, 'That
negress Fuló' ('Essa negra Fuló'), who throughout it is invoked
in a series of rhythmic chanted refrains. The author, Jorge de
Lima, serves black love less blindly however, being still the cir-
cumspect heir to his grandfather's sugar plantation. The poem has
a certain fairy-tale quality and the time is indefinite, ritualized.
Relationships between whites and blacks (elaborately studied in
Gilberto Freyre's monumental work of the same period *Masters
and Slaves, Casa grande e sengala*) are astutely caught in a series
of addresses to Fuló in her own terms by others and by the
narrator, and in folk verse recited by Fuló herself. She eventually
usurps the white wife when the master takes her off to whip her

for stealing and is presumed to make love to her. At this point there is more than a hint of the salaciousness which brightens other writing of the period, Lins do Rêgo's autobiographical novel *Plantation Lad* (*Menino de engenho*, 1932), for example. But while Lins do Rêgo wrestles with guilt for his past excesses with black girls, Jorge de Lima would sooner say all is well with the very verve of his idiom. He thus avoids a potential racial 'problem' (had Fuló and her master exchanged sexes the situation would have been a lot stickier) with the kind of indigenous music which enriches a work like *Black Orpheus*, or the bossa nova, both creations of the younger poet Vinícius de Moraes.[25] This is not to say that Lima or his contemporaries were socially unaware. But interestingly enough such protest against injustice as they did make comes very much from a 'higher' plane: 'Hey negro! Hey negro!/The race that exploits you exploits out of boredom, negro!'[26] The indignation is as it were on the Negro's behalf, and scarcely stands comparison with the powerful racial voice which developed in the Caribbean,[27] notably in the poetry of the Cuban Nicolás Guillén.

In the 1930s Guillén began his long career with three collections which may echo and be echoed by contemporaries like Ballagas, Palés Matos and Ramón Guirao,[28] but which speak in an idiom far surer than theirs. In these terms the best is probably the first, *Motivos de son* (Motives of *son*, 1930; *son* being a kind of black sound), which is very brief but unrivalled as black poetry untainted by folklore or indulgence. Each of the poems is spoken by or to someone who knows what it is like to be black in a city like pre-Revolutionary Havana. Yet this knowledge does not spoil their style or presuppose an unreal politicization. In fact the music, dialect and tone of the people Guillén knew themselves generate a black world, just as the finest passages of *Martín Fierro* themselves generate the world of the gaucho. There is certainly no false solidarity. In the poem 'Sóngoro cosongo' (untranslatable sound words which became the title of Guillén's next collection) someone ruefully reflects on the indifference of his *negra* now that he has no money. The fact that he is caught still in the rhythm of her body, and verbally recreates it, serves to suggest a complexity of relationships wholly lacking in, say, 'rumba' poems by Tallet or Ballagas. Guillén's ironies can be savage to the point of apparent disownment:

Por qué te pone tan bravo
cuando te dicen negro bembón,
si tiene la boca santa,
negro bembón

Bembón así como ere
tiene de to;
Caridad te mantiene,
te lo da to.

Why do you get so fierce when they call you black blubber-mouth, if your
mouth is so holy, black blubber-mouth? ¶Blubber-mouth just as you are
you've got everything; Charity keeps you, gives you it all.

Guillén's necessarily complex commitment comes out brilliantly
when he mocks a certain 'Vito Manuel' for having pretended to be
smarter than he is.

La mericana te buca,
y tu le tiene que huir:
tu ingle era detrai guan,
detrai guan y guan tu tri . . .

The American woman is looking for you, and you have to get away: your
English amounted to: try one, to: try one and one two three.

The trick of spelling out Vito Manuel's street-seller's pronuncia-
tion of English words has its humour and involves us in a kind
of neighbourhood joke: this may be hard on the person laughed at
but in the last analysis is not detached. Then comes the bantering
advice that he should not 'fall in love ever again' without learning
more English to defend himself with. This does not preclude the
'interpretation' that the Cuban black and mulatto should be wary
of their exploiters, here emblemized by a randy lady tourist from
the US. Yet nothing in the poem cannot be referred to an immediate, if subtle, situation. This is true of all the poems in *Motivos
de son* ('Get yourself some money', for example, spoken by a
hungry wife, seeing luxury all around her). In them, Guillén performs the notable feat of regularizing a dialect, giving it literary
status and making of it the vehicle of a distinct consciousness.[29]

The next collection, *Sóngoro cosongo*, is decidedly more ambitious. It opens with a rousing piece entitled 'Llegada' (Arrival),
spoken in the first person plural. The exhortation is clear, to sweep
away the last vestiges of the civilization Spengler and others announced was in unalterable decline. At first ('Here we are! The

word comes to us wet from the forests'), the 'we' could be heard
as the collective voice of the people in *Motivos de son*, now turned
positive and enthusiastic. But by the end it is clear that a spokesman has the word ('Hey, comrades, here we are!), and is addressing the reader on behalf of the group. That Guillén was moving
out of the coherent and powerfully-evoked world of his first book
is made clear in his 'Ode' to a Cuban boxer punching out a living
in the rings of the US. He matches the sad spectacle of the futility
of this man's 'black jack aggression' with wholesale assertion of
black values:

> Y ahora que Europa se desnuda
> para tostar su carne al sol,
> y busca en Harlem y en La Habana
> jazz y son,
> lucirse negro mientras aplaude el bulevar
> y frente a la envidia de los blancos
> hablar en negro de verdad.

And now that Europe strips to toast its flesh in the sun, and goes to
Harlem and Havana for jazz and *son*, it's fine to show off being black to
street applause and before the envy of the whites to speak true Negro.

Guillén doubtless modulates his attitude: he is amused by the
boxer's 'precarious' English as he was by Vito Manuel's, and
there is a similar underlying sympathy in his ironic congratula-
tions to the boxer for being so good at 'eliminating fat under the
sun'. But the boxer has nevertheless become palpably emblematic,
a 'modern elastic ape', seen from the outside.

It is a short step from *Motivos de son* and some poems in
*Sóngoro cosongo* to the *négritude* of French-speaking Caribbean
and African poets, or to modern black writing in the US by
Eldridge Cleaver, LeRoi Jones and others. But Guillén did not
make it. By the time he came to publish *West Indies Ltd* in 1934
his black poetry had clearly separated into the political on the one
hand and the folkloric on the other, to the mutual disadvantage of
both. A poem like 'Sensemayá', a chant for killing a snake, which
relies heavily on rural survivals of African magic, can be electrify-
ing in performance. But it remains a precious re-creation, connected with Afro-Cuban reality only in the preterite or past tense. In
his political pieces, like the long title poem of *West Indies Ltd*,
blacks turn out to be only one of several peoples in the Carib-

bean ('Here there are whites and blacks and Asiatics and Mulat-
toes'), for whom the common enemy is the dollar:

> Aquí están los servidores de Mr Babbit.
> Los que educan sus hijos en West Point.
> Aquí están los que chillan: hello, baby,
> y fuman Chesterfield y Lucky Strike.

Here are the servants of Mr Babbit. Those who educate their sons at
West Point. Here are those who scream: hello baby, and smoke
Chesterfield and Lucky Strike.

Location and identities are notably vague, and the plight of the
blacks ceases to be specific or even very remarkable. Correspondingly Guillén abandons the black idiom he had so successfully
established, except in short interludes assigned to a neighbourhood character John the Barber. In fact, under the guise of a more
structured political awareness, Guillén if anything plays on a new
racial nerve, as a Spanish-speaking *antillano* ('Antillean'), which
is what he calls himself in the lapidary last lines of 'West Indies
Ltd'. Not just the economy but the language of the Anglo-Saxon
descendants of Francis Drake become an ominous threat, to be
resisted by Hispanic and Latin culture. Though he appeals for
sympathy to French-speaking Haiti, Guadeloupe and Martinique,
he leaves unsaid what black Jamaicans should feel about this.
Identifying as much (in speech, more) with his other Spanish
ancestry in the 'Balada de los dos abuelos' (Ballad of the Two
Grandfathers) he comes close to that vision of the Caribbean as
the Mediterranean of the New World, expressed with such persuasive passion by the Cuban novelist Alejo Carpentier (once his
Negro phase was over). Of course this is not to suggest that
Guillén ceased to write good poems: his protest (1948–51) at the
murder of Jesús Menéndez is perhaps his finest. But simply
that they no longer belonged to the tradition of black poetry in
Latin America.

A remarkable fact about Guillén is that, although he never
wholly became a poet of *négritude*, he did at one point have some
influence in the French-speaking Caribbean, especially Haiti,
which freed itself from US occupation (1915–34) the same year as
*West Indies Ltd* was published. The Republic of Haiti, which
became independent of Europe before the rest of Latin America in
1804, is of course unique is being the only autonomous black state
of America, to the extent that the term 'creole' there, as in the

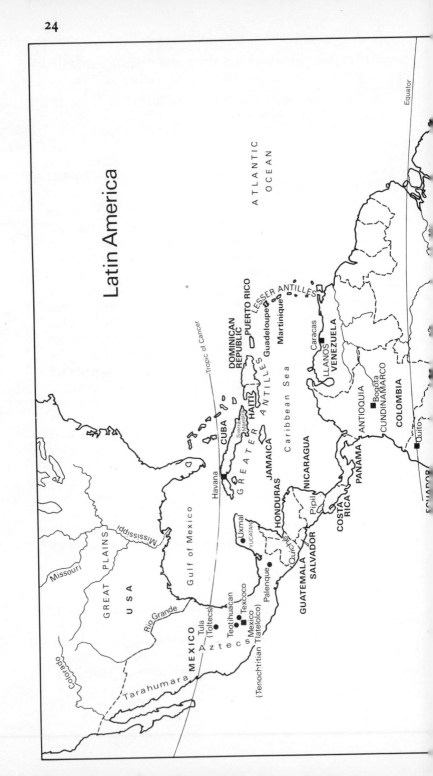

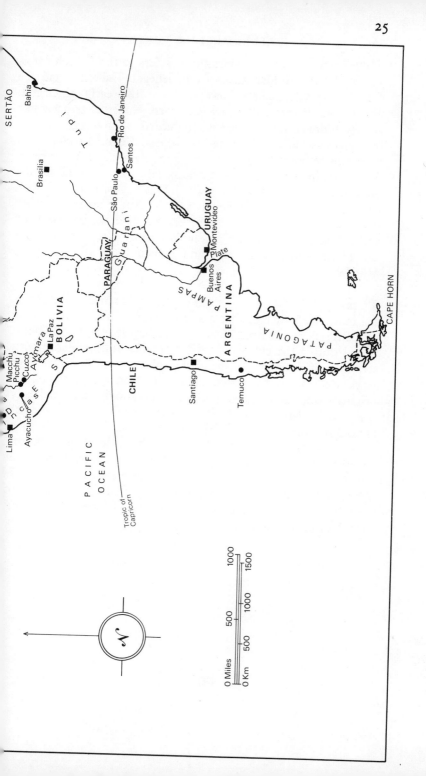

islands Guadeloupe and Martinique, refers to the French patois spoken by the former slaves from Senegal, Dahomey and the Congo. Written poetry, however, from the early nineteenth century on, has generally been in French. Nonetheless poets like Aimé Césaire of Martinique have succeeded in conveying a powerful racial sense within that language. Indeed, Césaire's *Cahier d'un retour au pays natal* (1956) shows him to be altogether less Latin American, in any sense, than African. His yearning is all for the other native continent in the east, and his closest kinship is with poets like Léopold Sedar Senghor of Senegal. Though his work (like that of René Depestre and others) has been widely translated and published in Castro's Cuba he has firmly placed the heart of his 'Third World' in Africa, as in the poem 'Pour saluer le Tiers Monde'.[30]

To pretend that the main origin of 'Latin American' poetry was not indicated by that epithet would be fanciful. Yet the hegemony of 'cultured' and 'correct' Spanish and Portuguese, hardly questioned during the colonial period, has since Independence been seriously challenged by poets of the subcontinent in a variety of ways. Such poets have attempted to ransom the poetry of the original America in translations and imitations which radically question the language of its conquerors, or have deliberately enhanced the vernacular of the gaucho or the Negro. Though none of the resultant idioms can be said to have developed into an American tradition in its own right, their presence has been more deeply felt or more widespread than the few examples discussed above might indicate. To this extent our prejudice in going on to consider poems that are more obviously Latin by tradition will be, then, that of their authors.

# 3. The Great Song of America

From Independence to the present, Latin American poets have recognized the challenge of writing on a continental scale, of creating a 'poem of America', though few have met it fully. And the work of those few has been fraught with the kind of problems faced by poets in other parts of the continent. How and where can a poet find moral or even geographical identity in America and how can he personally relate to it? Given the nature of American experience, is a form like the epic possible at all? And so on. It is fair to say that answers to these and similar questions, in poems and criticism by Latin Americans, form less of a conscious tradition of endeavour than they do in English-speaking America. There is little to compare with that idea of work in progress which links Whitman, Pound, Williams and Olson.[1] Indeed, would-be 'major' Latin American poets are characterized by an apparent disregard of precedent. Nevertheless a chain of responses exists. In form, perspective and diction the only major continental poem of twentieth-century Latin America, Neruda's *Canto general*, unmistakably takes further the achievement of the New World Modernists (Rubén Darío, José Santos Chocano) and of poets of Independence like José Joaquín Olmedo and Andrés Bello.

I

The first instalment of Bello's *América*,[2] hardly a cryptic title, appeared in 1823. The second followed three years later, together with the announcement that the author did not think he was up to his original ambition. The reasons for this modesty demand our attention as much as the brilliance of those parts of the poem that were published. Born in what became Venezuela, later a Chilean citizen, and an intimate of the Independence leaders, Bello was fully alert to the difficulties of being American. Never ceding that loyalty he strove to reconcile it with the classical sense of priorities in culture and literature that he had developed as a humanist of profound erudition. During his years in London in the 1820s, when he was writing *América*, he mixed freely with the exiled Spanish opponents of the despotic Spanish King

Fernando VII (who was equally the enemy of independent Spanish Americans), and was impressed by their creed of romanticism in literature and liberalism in politics. Yet sympathetic as he may have been to their intolerance of 'authority', the spectre of anarchy and fragmentation in America never ceased to haunt him. (He would not have disowned the arguments of Matthew Arnold's *Culture and Anarchy*.) While as a literary critic he censured slavish imitation of classical models he continued to recommend study of those very models to those younger poets of Spanish America whose obsession it was to portray the various regions of the New World with as much linguistic peculiarity as possible. He translated several Latin and neoclassical poets (Virgil, Horace, Pope, Delille) and cast his own verse in the classical moulds of Spanish: the two fragments of *América* are *silvas*, unrhymed verse of 11 and 7 syllable lines with consciously Latinate overtones. Yet within these formal limits he concentrated his whole attention on speaking as an American. Perhaps his position emerges most sensitively in his works on language, his *Ortología y métrica de la lengua castellana* (Orthology and Metrics of the Castilian Language, 1835), and his *Gramática de la lengua castellana destinada al uso de los americanos* (Grammar of the Castilian language destined for the use of Americans, 1847) which proposed revised spellings and other changes widely accepted in South America. Summarizing his ideas he said in the introduction to the second work:

I think it important to keep the language of our forefathers as pure as possible, as a providential means of communication and a fraternal bond between the various nations of Spanish origin scattered over the two continents. But it is not a superstitious purism I am recommending. The prodigious advance of all the sciences and arts, the propagation of thought and culture, and the political revolutions all demand daily new signs to express new ideas; and the introduction of new words taken from foreign and the ancient languages now no longer offends us when it is not obviously unnecessary, or when it does not reveal the affection and bad taste of those who attempt in this way to embellish what they write.

'Fraternal bond' could not be a more apt or revealing phrase. For, in conceiving *América*, his main problem was after all to establish a central point of authority from which to speak. In his terms he certainly needed it to compose the epic he doubtless aspired to, the highest form appropriate to the high task in hand.

In the opening instalment, the prolonged 'Alocución a la Poesía' (Allocution to Poetry), he wishes for the voice of 'algún Marón americano', 'some American Virgil', and later on fondly invokes Ercilla's epic of the conquest, *La Araucana*. Indeed, in scale and tone the 'Allocution' anticipates a work of epic proportions:

> Divina Poesía,
> tú de la soledad habitadora,
> a consultar tus cantos enseñada
> con el silencio de la selva umbría,
> tú a quien la verde gruta fué morada,
> y el eco de los montes compañía;
> tiempo es que dejes ya la culta Europa,
> que tu nativa rustiquez desama,
> y dirijas el vuelo adonde te abre
> el mundo de Colón su grande escena.

Divine Poetry, you, inhabitant of solitude, taught to match your cantos with the silence of the shady forest, you, for whom the green cave was a dwelling and the echo of the hills company; it is time that you leave now cultured Europe, which disregards your native rusticity, and steer your flight to where the world of Columbus opens to you its great scene.

Taking his cue from the first lines of the *Aeneid*, he soon asks Poetry to sing the heroes and deeds (*hechos*) of the wars of Independence. Names of the Liberators and their battles succeed each other as in a roll of honour that will consecrate the dead and those contemporaries active in creating new America, the Great Columbia ('from the Missouri to Cape Horn') whose outer boundaries had still to be drawn.

The list culminates in San Martín, who is however left unnamed as his glory and vision are left for 'another occasion'. The poem breaks off, as if before the kind of awareness which that other great Liberator, Bolivar, expressed once victory was won in remarks like: 'to govern America is impossible', 'to serve the Revolution is to plough the sea' and 'the duty of every honest American is to emigrate'. Precisely when the pressure for historical meaning reaches a climax Bello cannot meet it. The beginnings and the immediate past of Latin American 'fraternity' could not so easily be shaped into the collective consciousness presupposed by the *Iliad*, or by Camoens's Portuguese epic the *Lusiads*, let alone by a single hero like Aeneas. Too much was disparate, or inadmissible, or absent. In this interpretation Bello's criticism of his contemporary Olmedo has added point. Olmedo celebrated Latin American Independence most notably in his long poem 'La Victoria de Junín. Canto a Bolívar' (1825).[3] Like Bello, he was in part anxious simply to register for the first time the names of numerous generals and captains from all parts of the continent; but he didn't shrink from trying to give historical shape to the whole. To this end he 'selected' the battle of Junín as his nominal subject, though in practice he spent much time narrating that of Ayacucho, which in fact has subsequently come to seem more significant. Indeed he used the common epic device of foretelling the outcome of this later battle, in full detail, emphasizing the grander view. The 'prophecy' is delivered by the last Inca himself, Huayna Capac, who, after Junín, appears out of the sky to address the creole troops. His perspective is thus sanctioned by a paternal authority that is conveniently ancient (though as we noted earlier when it 'came down' to immediate political decision the poor Inca had voluntarily to renounce power in favour of the 'fraternal' creoles, who even then were effectively grouping themselves into a collection of mutually hostile national states). Bello was not alone in remarking that these literary devices of Olmedo's were too transparent as such. Knowing the sentiments of the Indians who under Tupac Amaru had risen against creoles and Spanish in 1780 (the original *tupamaros*), Bolivar found the Inca's self-effacement preposterous. More important here, he concurred with Bello in finding that in any case the authority proposed by 'our Homer'[4] (as he dubbed him) was unconvincing and that the poem lacked all unity. Bello's admirable discrimination and sense of the probable are witnessed by the very fragmentariness of his *América*. Unlike Olmedo, and unlike a near contemporary in the United States, Joel Barlow, author of the failed epic *The Columbiad*, he respected his classics too much to make of them the commander of a reality which on this scale he suspected was beyond their control.

In his two fragments Bello tries to establish that Latin Americans had at least something holding them together, first by sharpening the edge of the military conflict. The Spaniards are greedy, cruel beyond belief, treacherous, and wholly ignoble, even compared with adventurers like Pizarro. The creoles, the opposite of all these things, are fired by ideals that raise them above self-interest. Bello was by no means a democrat but he warmly conceded that the cause of Independence was also a popular one, supported by commonfolk ('el inexperto campesino vulgo'), and by women. Hardly emulating Bartolomé Hidalgo's gauchesque enthusiasm on this last point, and with small loss of dignity, he still recognized a situation 'where even the fair sex share with the men the hard work and the danger of war'. Above all, the Americans (a term used insistently throughout) were emboldened and vindicated by the fact that they were fighting for a better *place*: the land they lived in and which became so important to the idea of an American epic. That is, they were both defending its innocence against European rape and wanting it to be named and mature.

According to Bello the best days of America's life were those of her innocent childhood, a golden age like that of Hesiod and of the pastoral eclogue:

> Allí memorias de tempranos días
> tu lira aguardan; cuando, en ocio dulce
> y nativa inocencia venturosos,
> sustento fácil dió a sus moradores,
> primera prole de su fértil seno,
> Cundinamarca; antes que el corvo arado
> violase el suelo ni extranjera nave
> las apartadas costas visitara.
> Aún no aguzado la ambición había
> el hierro atroz;

There memories of early days await your lyre; when Cundinamarca gave easy sustenance to her inhabitants, happy in sweet idleness and native innocence, the first stock of her fertile breast; before the curved plough violated the soil, or strange ships visited these distant shores. Ambition had not yet edged atrocious iron.

The 'strange ships' were of course Columbus's: a sinister intrusion on virgin America. Bello freely proposed that the heroes of Independence, the Liberators, were actually *avenging* the offence consequent on it. 'The shades of Atahuallpa and Moctezuma,' he says, 'now sleep sated with Iberian blood'; the upstart Spanish will not for long 'usurp' the kingdom of the sun. Of course, it was out of just such sympathies as these that the Indianist cult sprang, in early nineteenth-century politics and literature. In his 'Allocution' Bello contributed to it himself by showing that the poetry of America's golden age is an 'amorous *yaravi*', or an Indian creation myth like the one of Bochica and Huitaca, which he retells over twenty lines (honestly acknowledging his source in Humboldt).

Bello was certainly prepared to admit the loss of American innocence as a sexual metaphor. In lines which uncannily antici- pate Neruda he speaks of 'the first genital vigour' ('el vigor genital primero') kept intact in unspoilt America, where the adjective evokes both the luxuriance of Eden, genesis manifest, and sexual inviolacy. But he does not for an instant insist on the horror of European rape in this sense, and mainly avoids the 'dishonoured mother' complex which afflicts the work of so many Latin Ameri- can poets. Part of the reason for this is simple and altogether crucial: the golden age, earthly paradise, could not have been expected to last in America or anywhere else in the world. He follows Judeo-Christian belief in suggesting that the ease (ocio) of the innocent becomes the sloth (desidia) of a wiser mankind. But more important than the Bible were the classics, from Hesiod, who spoke of man's need to uncover by work riches hidden by Jove, to the resounding phrase that serves as an epitaph to the golden age in the first Georgic: 'labor omnia vicit inprobus'. Man was destined to work the earth, to violate the land, less because of his Fall than because only this way could 'necessity' be avoided and that intellectual advance be continued which began with the sailor's and then the farmer's knowledge of time through observ- ing the heliacal risings of stars and constellations. The dominant moral positive of Bello's América is not native (Indian) innocence, but what he pointedly calls the 'valor latino' which must succeed it. His ideal is the Rome of the consuls, where politics and agri- culture were not mutually inimical and where virtue was directly proportional to man's ability to work his land. With a possible smile he hints that this ethic may be especially appropriate to his continent because of a certain 'innate blandness dormant in the American breast'.

If Bello found he could not match the epic Virgil he surely identified the more with the Georgics. The second fragment of his poem, 'La agricultura en la zona tórrida' (Agriculture in the Torrid Zone), elaborates, in part quotes, a stanza of the first, on the only subject he felt able to proceed with satisfactorily. Leav- ing San Martín unsung for ever, he exhorted fellow Americans to forget heroism, and to repair the havoc of war as good farmers, to plant, irrigate and fell forests. Tactfully he does not dwell on what this must mean for the Indians: they may become the evanescent creatures of countless romances (of which W. H. Hudson's *Green Mansions* is perhaps the finest) but are soon forgotten here:

> Huyó la fiera; deja el caro nido,
> deja la prole implume
> el ave, y otro bosque no sabido
> de los humanos va a buscar doliente ...

The wild beast fled; the bird leaves its dear nest, leaves its unfeathered brood, and sorrowfully seeks another forest unknown to humans ...

Bello's American Georgics, his most powerful and coherent writing, stand at the beginning of a long tradition in its own right, which includes such works as Gregorio Gutiérrez González's *Memoir on the Cultivation of Maize in Antioquia* (1881), and Leopoldo Lugones's *Secular Odes* (1910).[5] They amounted to an inspiring and safe statement of early Latin virtue, against which the Spanish would seem imperial and vicious, and rightly expelled from American land.

Bello was doubtless aware that in the full Latin span the *Aeneid* succeeded the *Georgics* as surely as these succeeded the pastoral eclogue: that the Rome of the consuls had not proved static or stable. And it is possible that he gave up the epic aspiration announced in the 'Allocution' for reasons other and more humane than those we have suggested so far. Nowhere does he wish American man to do more than throw off the foreign yoke, does he suggest he might dominate others. That the American farmer should always 'suspect' the sword comes in marked contrast to the imperial injunction to Aeneas: 'tu regere imperio populos, Romane, memento' (you, oh Roman, remember to rule peoples by dominion), and, for that matter, to the spirit of many national anthems which the separate states of Latin America learned to sing at each other. 'Latin valour' should provide a dynamic up to the stage of agricultural plenitude, and no further.

However, he thought and wrote all this in London, in the heart of a civilization that flagrantly exploited the fact that other parts of the world strove for or were condemned to this modest principle. 'The countryside is your heritage', he says somewhat brusquely to his fellows across the sea: 'enjoy it'. And: 'You love freedom? Then dwell on the land.' Of course Virgil's *Georgics* are replete with such advice. But it is matched by that idea that intelligence and industry must inexorably 'develop' and, in any case, what Virgil had to say there about the 'land' did not have to be applied to Rome as a political and economic entity. Though Bello came 'back' to the *Georgics* in *América* he was still left with the commitment emblazoned in his original title. And in the part of the poem he persisted with, the ideal of rural Latin valour could not too perversely also be interpreted as an invitation to others to exploit. That his Lombard Street and City friends could read his lush description of American produce as an investor's brochure heightened the difficulty of his own hope and ambition as a Latin American in his poem. The *Georgics* may have allowed him to proceed with a further 373 lines of the poem but they aggravated sooner than solved the problem of his own relationship to his subject: the 'American material' he urges Poetry to come and get.

At first, in the 'Allocution', Bello's position may best be described as virtual. He speaks always to Poetry, listing what it might choose as subject matter. Asking where the muse shall reside in America he sweeps panoramically over the River Plate, the valleys of Chile, the waterfalls of Colombia, the cactus of Mexico, and the Andean peaks near Quito, then believed to be the highest in the world. But even that chance of focus and perspective is passed over. In presenting possible subjects to the muse he moves ceaselessly from one item to another, the series being no more than potential. The second fragment is likewise an address, but to America's torrid zone and then its inhabitants. Since this is something more defined and substantial than 'Poetry', he could less easily avoid revealing an attitude towards it and became involved in the questions of commitment or indifference, participation or 'selling out', that we have just mentioned. Significantly he is at his best when he establishes an American reality strong enough itself to embody attitude, in noun and verb. In the second stanza of 'Agriculture', the 'self-plagiarism' (as some have called it) from the 'Allocution', he presents the natural products of American soil in a characteristic 'series', within the second person address. The poet's position is delicately assured by this repeated 'tú' as nowhere else in the poem:

> Tú das la caña hermosa,
> de do la miel se acendra,
> por quien desdeña el mundo los panales;

> tú en urnas de coral cuajas la almendra
> que en la espumante jícara rebosa;
> bulle carmín-viviente en tus nopales,
> que afrenta fuera al múrice de Tiro;

You give the beautiful cane where the honey is refined, for which the world disdains the honey comb; you, in coral urns, curdle the nut that brims in the foaming chocolate cup; living crimson seethes in your nopals [cactus used to feed the cochineal beetle] that affronts Tyrian purple.

American abundance is matched by her generosity, and she can hardly 'help' outdoing the Old World. But still, her fertility is not wanton or unconscious. The skill implied in the verb 'curdle' is now drawn out in a set of verbs in which plants themselves become the kind of mentor Bello profoundly wished to be:

> Para tus hijos la procera palma
> su vario feudo cría,
> y el ananás sazona su ambrosía;
> su blanco pan la yuca;
> sus rubias pomas la patata educa;
> y el algodón despliega al aura leve
> las rosas de oro y el vellón de nieve.

For your sons the lofty palm rears its various fief, and the pineapple seasons its ambrosia; its white bread the *yuca*; the potato educates its blond apples; and the cotton plant unfolds on the light breeze roses of gold and fleece of snow.

'Exotic' growth, originally named (*ananas*, *yuca*), authors its produce, is itself fully incorporated into the georgic process, in a series of brilliantly chosen verbs: *criar*, to create and bring up; *sazonar*, to season in time and taste; *educar*, to lead out and instruct; *desplegar*, to unfold and develop. These seven lines superbly achieve his yearned-for conjunction of classic with American value. His expression is so apt and resonant as to banish the problems of perspective and identity which hover over most of the poem: he could hardly be more in his language. Then, as if emboldened by the success, he daringly broadens the definition of the 'you' addressed to include both American origin and the observer of it, the turning point being in the verb *desplegar*, which further means 'to flaunt':

> Tendida para ti la fresca parcha
> en enramadas de verdor lozano,
> cuelga de sus sarmientos trepadores

nectáreos globos y franjadas flores;
y para ti el maíz, jefe altanero
de la espigada tribu, hincha su grano;
y para ti el banano
desmaya al peso de su dulce carga;

Stretched out for you in branches of lush green, the fresh *pasionaria* droops from its climbing tendrils orbs of nectar and striped flowers; and for you maize, haughty chief of the spiked tribe, swells his grain; and for you the banana plant swoons under the weight of its sweet load.

Luxuriance, 'for you', waxes to the point of embarrassing husbandry and his georgic code. As the identity of his addressee begins to split he is put out of the process and the phrase. Sexual display ends in a swoon before the charge (*carga*) of American produce explicitly becomes the load (also *carga*) to be freighted away, with Bello as the middleman, again between the two worlds of innocent and exploiter.

2

Compared with the work of most Americanists, Bello's poem, fragmentary as it is, excels in sustained intelligence and observant sobriety. In fact, apart from the Indianizing efforts of Gonçalves Dias and his contemporaries in Brazil, few serious attempts were made to write poems of a continental scope in Latin America until the end of the nineteenth century. Then, the Spanish American group of poets known as the Modernists began to react vigorously against the nationalism which had engulfed the grander ideas of Independence in their respective countries of origin. The most prominent among them, Rubén Darío, considered himself more a citizen of the continent than a national of his native Nicaragua, or of the states he formed deep attachment to (Chile, Argentina). Bello's desire for a 'fraternal bond' manifests itself anew in their brotherhood (an English word they sometimes used), though the situation they found themselves in had changed considerably.

The quatercentenary, in 1892, of the Discovery elicited a number of occasional poems from Latin Americans. One, quite clearly spoken, was Darío's 'A Colón' (To Columbus),[6] whose 'poor America', whose 'beautiful hot-blooded Indian virgin' was said now to be pale, convulsive and hysterical. Seeing perpetual warring between brothers and nothing but blood and ash on the fraternal fields, Darío hints it might have been better had the 'strange ships' never arrived ('Would to God that the once intact waters had never mirrored the white sails'). Yet just before this he says that iron race of great Castile was no less noble than the Indians they encountered. The poem is in fact itself made convulsive by conflicts of loyalty, the sense of being internally undermined and the haunting suspicion of racial inferiority. A 'disastrous spirit' possesses Columbus's land. Darío does not commit the heresy of saying that poor native, half-Spanish Americans should never have fought to be independent; but he does say that they cannot cope with their own treachery and fratricide (Judas and Cain), that the language of Cervantes and Calderón is being vilified by Americans who perhaps did not know what was happening when to the sound of trumpets 'we gave ourselves laws, disdaining kings'.

The defeat of Spain by the US in 1898 removed most vestiges of Latin American resentment against the old fatherland. Though through part of the nineteenth century the US had been held up as a model of enlightened progress (notably in Argentina, by Sarmiento and others), the Mexican war and the annexation of Texas, the arrogance of John Hay *et al.* at the Pan-American conference of 1889–90 and the large-scale investment that accompanied it, and finally the devastating assault on Spain and the appropriation of Cuba and Puerto Rico, powerfully encouraged Latin Americans to define themselves within the continent of Walt Whitman's americanos. Spaniards, Bello's vicious imperialists, came to be regarded with sympathy, even affection. The changing mood was clearly visible in the reception given to José Enrique Rodó's discourse 'to the youth of America', *Ariel*, at the turn of the century. Though little in the essay has to do with ethnic culture it was voraciously read as an indictment of the 'anglo-yankee' race and a celebration of its Spanish–Latin opponent.[7] By the time Darío came to write his 'Salutación del optimista' in 1904, Latinity had swelled from being Bello's careful cultural preference to full-blooded racial and political enthusiasm.

Appealing directly to the heroic Virgil, the rousing hexameters of Darío's 'Salutation' sang of a great future ahead:

Inclitas razas ubérrimas, sangre de Hispania fecunda,
espíritus fraternos, luminosas almas, salve!
Porque llega el momento en que habrán de cantar nuevos himnos
lenguas de gloria.

Illustrious fertile races, fecund blood of Hispania, fraternal spirits, luminous souls, hail! Because the moment is coming when tongues of glory shall sing new hymns.

Spurning the despondency he himself had earlier expressed, and warning of the danger of the northern eagle, he wished that the old virtue of his audience (he first read the poem in Madrid) might be felt by Americans, giving them hope. The ancient fathers who began the saga with their 'triptolemic work' by ploughing the earth and thus started, georgic, on the ascending path to Roman empire, are now asked to preside over the rise of Latin empire in America, and to crown with laurels the Hispanic progeny of the 'Roman wolf'. Darío knew that the political and economic reality of Latin America supported such ambition far less than it had Bello's more modest and carefully limited hope. Correspondingly he invokes cataclysmic change, not cultivation, and allows himself to be swept up (as Bello never did) in strongly Latinate oratory ('ínclitas', 'Hispania', etc.), as if to drown the inner groan of convulsive half-Indian America.

The most remarkable thing about 'Salutation' is that in it Darío contrives to refer to the Spaniards from a position of apparent strength. In part this is because they had so recently been defeated, but it is also a mark of the cultural self-confidence vis-à-vis the Spaniards, if not anyone else, which the Modernists inspired with their huge rejuvenation of Spanish verse (discussed in the following chapter), and their evident influence on Spanish writers at the turn of the century, a phenomenon grandly described as 'the return of the galleons'. Indeed, at their most confident Darío and his Latin American contemporaries wanted the best of both worlds. As the direct heirs to the conquistadors they insinuated a closer claim than the Spaniards to Hispanic glory, at the same time as arrogating to themselves the highest grandeur of their maternal past: the resplendent courts of MesoAmerica and the majesty of the Inca. Bello, as we noted, was hardly a democrat: the Modernists in a continental mood actively silenced grassroots America singing the 'heroes' of both the Spanish and the Indian past. American aristocratism had already spiced the preface to Darío's highly-influential verse collection of 1896, *Prosas profanas*.

I detest the life and the time in which it was my lot to be born; and I cannot salute the president of a republic in the idiom I should sing to you, oh Elagabalus, whose court – gold, silk, marble – I remember in dreams . . .

(If there is poetry in our America it is in old things; in Palenque and Utatlan, in the legendary Indian, and in the sensual, refined Inca, and in the great Moctezuma with his golden throne. The rest is yours, democrat Walt Whitman.)

This attitude was reinforced, less flippantly, a few years later in his address to Theodore Roosevelt. There Darío distinguished between the noble (if ingenuous) tradition of his America, that had ancient roots in Bacchus and the regal Nezahualcoyotl, and the deceptive egalitarian simplicity of its future invader, the US. Yet only a few years later again he saluted the eagle of the north as the only live force in the continent, the one capable of the Olympian tasks in hand, which Whitman (he now claimed) would himself dearly have liked to sing.[8] In practice Darío focused on the continent only in oratory, in a series of exhortations issuing from contradictory hopes, but always as rhetorical overlay on an immediate 'disastrous' reality. His very self-questioning, which after the Pan-American Congress in Rio in 1906 led to the first modern poem by a Latin American (his 'Epistle' to Lugones's wife), effectively prevented him from being more that 'poet of America' that Rodó had wanted him to be.[9]

Without Darío, however, there would have been little impetus to the movement at the turn of the century known as *mundonovismo*, represented for us by the Peruvian José Santos Chocano. In his main collection of 'New World' verse, *Alma América. Poemas indo-españolas* (America Soul. Indo-Spanish Poems, 1906), Chocano would strike a pose reminiscent of his friend Darío, notably in the face of Whitman's seething democracy, or of the style of political commitment urged by José Martí[10] who died fighting for the independence of Cuba from Spain (not won until 1898). Chocano's fawning to Spanish nobility is little short of nauseating, as for that matter is most of his biography. But over all it is hard to find anything in his poems amounting to an attitude, an oratorical stance, or for example even the stoic decadence in Darío's phrase: 'The rest is yours.' This is so despite the fact that Chocano is the most blatantly egoistic of poets. He didn't shrink from the largest anouncement: 'I am the primitive soul of the Andes and the forests', for example; or, addressing Spain, 'I have given you the Sun of my mountain and you have given me the Sun of your standard'. Again, in the sonnet 'Símbolo' (Symbol):[11]

Y así soy, en la pompa de mis cánticos regios,
algo Precolumbino y algo Conquistador.

Soy épico des veces;

And this I am in the pomp of my royal canticles, part Pre-Columbian and
part Conquistador. ¶I am twice epic.

And so on. As a whole, and despite pages of bombast, *America
Soul* does perhaps deserve to be considered epic. There is a tire-
less ambition to speak of the whole continent. The native flora
and fauna are surveyed in various sets of poems (some of the
sonnets being notably close to Leconte de Lisle), as are creole
'types' like the gaucho and the *llanero*. Similarly, the great
moments of American history are related in episodes or condensed
in heroic figures like Cuauhtemoc and Pizarro, all without animus
and with a view to totality.

When Chocano consciously embarked on a full scale epic, the
vast projected *Hombre Sol* (prompted by the centenary celebra-
tions of Ayacucho), he managed only one barely readable canto.
Though he planned and described in detail the themes and action
of the remaining five, he never reflected for a moment on the
possibility, in the first place, of such an American epic, or on
what form might be appropriate to American experience. He
lacked both Bello's modest discrimination and Darío's oratorical
verve. And having a vast ego as the core of his poetry he lacked too
the faculty of a Whitman, venturing in and out of reality around
him in 'Song of Myself'. If Chocano succeeds, in *America Soul*,
it is because he simply lets go on a series of American topics, his
moments being the luck of an all-encompassing 'I' devoid of
personal reserve, 'celebrating' itself without inhibition. The extent to which his best verse flowed straight from him is abundantly
clear in his 'Savage Ode' ('Oda salvaje'), a powerful, near-inco-
herent piece written shortly after *America Soul*.

'Savage Ode' was composed, appropriately, somewhere off
shore; 'from the sea' he repeatedly salutes his American goal,
'the forest of my primitive ancestors, the tutelary goddess of the
Incas and the Aztecs'. Being thus unbounded in space he ranges
over 'the road of the Americas', picking out details of its vegetable
and animal life, and of its peoples, as he had done (though in
separate poems) in *America Soul*. But here he also plunges deeply
into the dark unsung heart of the continent, in a transmigratory
dream:

Vuelvo a ti sano del alma,
a pesar de las civilizaciones enfermas:
tu vista me conforta,
porque al verte, me siento a la manera
de los viejos caciques,
que dormían sobre la yerba
y bebían leche de cabras salvajes
y comían pan de maíz con miel de abejas;
tu vista me conforta,
porque tu espesura de ejército me recuerda
de cuando, hace novecientos años,
discurrí a la cabeza
de veinte mil arqueros bravíos,
que, arrancándose del éxodo tolteca,
fueron hasta el país de los lagos y de los volcanes,
en donde el chontal sólo se rindió ante la Reina,
y de cuando trasmigré al imperio armonioso
del gran Inca Yupanqui, y le seguí, por las sierras
a las vertientes de Arauco,
en donde con alas de cóndor nos improvisábamos tiendas;
tu vista me conforta,
porque sé que los siglos me señalan como tu Poeta,
y recojo, del fondo alucinante
de tus edades quiméricas,
la voz con que se dolían y exaltaban,
en sus liras de piedra,
los haraviccus del Cuzco
y los Emperadores Aztecas.

I return to you healthy in soul, despite sick civilizations: the sight of you comforts me, because on seeing you I feel like the old *caciques* [Indian chiefs], who slept on the grass and drank wild goat's milk and ate maize bread with bees' honey; the sight of you comforts me because your massed forest reminds me of when nine hundred years ago I roamed at the head of twenty thousand savage bowmen, who leaving the Toltec exodus went to the land of the lakes and volcanoes, where the Chontal surrendered only before the Queen; and of when I transmigrated to the harmonious empire of the great Inca Yupanqui and followed him through the mountains to the source of the Arauco, where we improvised tents with condor wings; the sight of you comforts me, because I know that the centuries designate me as your Poet, and I gather, from the hallucinatory depths of your chimerical ages, the voice with which on their lyres of stone the *haraveks* of Cusco and the Aztec emperors grew plaintive and passionate.

Moving like this first from over-civilized Europe to a pastoral Golden-Age America, Chocano follows just the course which Bello had begun his 'Allocution' by marking out, as he no doubt was aware in then claiming to be designated as the continent's

Poet. The massed forest ('espesura de ejército') which greets him there prompts him, however, not to Georgic cultivation but extravagant fantasy. His ethic, unrestrainedly egoistic as ever, puts him at the head of primitive conquest, a position quite appropriate to his own in poetry. His transmigration as a warrior to a mysterious native past is undoubtedly more exciting than Darío's moves in that direction, in the sonnet to the Araucanian hero 'Caupolicán' (1890) or in the long narrative 'Tutecotzimí' (also 1890, but first included in *El canto errante*, 1907), who was the leader of the Nahuatl-speaking Pipil who conquered Nicaragua some centuries before the Spaniards arrived. It can be fairly claimed that before Chocano no Latin American had attempted to assimilate the Indian past with quite such bold intimacy as this.

Yet, almost as if the dream had been a lapse, in the following stanza he suddenly forgets those lyres of stone, and the hallucinatory power of the vision they once expressed: he switches to formal address, implicitly from some distance, and to an exterior decorum that recall, respectively, Bello (again) and the Parnassians ('Yours is the jaguar who leaps . . . yours the puma who weaves cunning strategies . . .' etc.). Further he indulges in the kind of sterilely ingenious 'one-off' images which mar so much of his verse: 'Yours the boa that resembles an interminable arm incised in the shadows by a Dantesque axe'. Nevertheless, however momentary his responsibility for it, the greater vision remains recorded on the page, and anticipated that of the Latin American whom this century at least would 'designate' as its poet: Pablo Neruda.

## 3

Neruda's great American work, *Canto general*,[12] was first published in Mexico in 1950, though he began it a decade before and added to it afterwards. His main stimulus to a major poem of this kind was given him in the late 1940s when the Chilean Communist Party (which he joined in 1945) commissioned him to compose a new history of that country. Soon afterwards his violent conflict, as a senator, with the national president González Videla, resulted in a long pilgrimage which took him as far as the Urals. Unable to finish the poem as it had been planned he made of it something yet more ambitious; and this, with all its imperfections, amounts to the grandest profession of American faith by a Spanish-speaking citizen of that continent.

Of the fifteen sections of the poem (each a canto in itself) the first five fit most obviously into a historical and ideological design. We move from the earliest America, as yet unnamed continentally (1), which he himself would know through the remains of the Inca city Macchu Picchu (2), to the chronicle of Conquest (3) and of Liberation (4), and to the betrayal of that Liberation (5). Neruda's view here both coincides with and differs sharply from that of his predecessors. As for them, the first America was paradise; 'a green uterus' of rivers, plants, animals, and of men who had barely learned to speak or name themselves, let alone work their environment. These he addresses as 'pastoral brothers', now quite preterite, over and done with. The Zapotec flowers are simply scented shade, and the singing of the Guarani is in the past tense. Faced with this massive absence he determines to find a centre for both it and himself, in the most genital part of the land, paradoxically seeking out an umbilical link with virgin America. Through the 'terrible tangle of the lost forests' from which Chocano never re-emerged, he ascends to Macchu Picchu, the mysterious abandoned city in the Andes, first discovered by the modern world as late as 1911. Macchu Picchu becomes the mother of those who built her and of those like him who would now be reborn as their heirs. He approaches this 'mother of stone' asking to be accompanied by American love ('sube conmigo, amor americano'), a phrase which, curiously enough could derive as well from the Inca's speech in Olmedo's Ode as from Whitman.

In *Canto general* the Conquistadors again violate, rape, spoil, outrage, torture and all but destroy original America. But as before, and 'despite wrath' at their behaviour, Neruda credits them with an advance in humanity that is seen to be just as 'necessary' as it was by Bello: an unavoidable if rude awakening. The final poem in canto 3, brief and allusive as it is, registers that, despite the daggers, light came to Indian America with the Conquest, virginal 'Asia' surrendering to the more 'advanced' Europeans:

> Asia entregó su virginal aroma.
> La inteligencia con un hilo helado
> fue detrás de la sangre hilando el día.

El papel repartió la miel desnuda
guardada en las tinieblas.

Asia surrendered her virginal aroma. Intelligence with a frozen thread
came after the blood threading the day. Paper spread out the naked honey
kept in darkness.

By the fourth part of the work, however, Neruda's divergence
from literary precedent, already manifest, quite eclipses his con-
sistency with it. For the liberators of his America are by no means
identical with the heroes of Independence. In fact the very concept of Independence as it had been understood hitherto disappears entirely in his verse, along with the complex and un-
resolved problems it had entailed. With Neruda liberation is
something much older and much more recent, stretching from
Cuauhtemoc's valiant resistance to Cortes in 1520 to the founding
of the Chilean Communist Party by Recabarren, and Prestes's
rebellion in Brazil in this century. Between these events stand
figures as diverse as Las Casas, the Araucanian Lautaro (who
displays an odd similarity with Hiawatha),[13] Tupac Amaru,
Lincoln, Martí, Zapata, Sandino, as well as some to the cham-
pions of Latin American Independence in the nineteenth century.
Neruda's treatment of these last brings home his disagreement
with standard histories and intimates the coherence he would
wish for his own. Instead of military prowess and sundry lists of
creole generals, and instead of the patriarchal, part-Hispanic part-
Indian, tradition espoused as an alternative by Darió and Chocano,
we are given mass virtue: the persistent and sometimes unconscious struggle for an America of the people. Like Whitman
(who he claimed taught him to be American) he would turn to
his advantage the very difficulty of subjecting Americans to paternal authority, vindicating them in their myriad being. In this view
even the Spanish epic poet Ercilla, in the most confident days of
conquest, is shown to be impotent before his 'material':

> Deja, deja tu huella
> de águila rubia, destroza
> tu mejilla contra el maíz salvaje,
> todo será en la tierra devorado.

Leave your blond eagle trace, destroy your cheek against the wild maize,
everything will be devoured in the land.

The first 'hero' of Independence that he sings is Bernardo
O'Higgins, who, foreign to pomp and nobility, is presented first

of all as a 'son of love', one who carries in him the 'popular'
strength of illegitimacy and abandonment. So deeply does Neruda
immerse himself in the people, thus understood, that the consciously aristocratic leanings of a figure like Darío seem not so
much vicious as amusing (at his ease in the house of President
Balmaceda, Darío is fleetingly noticed as 'a young Minotaur with
his head wrapped in river mist').[14] At the same popular level
Neruda establishes a bond from the first between European invader and Indian victim in human want: both know the prime
reality of hunger and exploitation. Fame and honour were the
spur of few of America's discoverers:

> El hambre antigua de Europa, hambre como la cola
> de un planeta mortal, poblaba el buque,
> el hambre estaba allí, desmantelada,
> errabunda hacha fría, madrastra
> de los pueblos, el hambre echa los dados
> en la navegación, sopla las velas:
> 'Más allá, que te como, más allá
> que regresas
> a la madre, al hermano, al Juez y al Cura,
> a los inquisidores, al infierno, a la peste.
> Más allá, más allá, lejos de piojo,
> del látigo feudal, del calabozo,
> de las galeras llenas de excremento.'

The old hunger of Europe, hunger like the tail of a mortal planet, peopled
the ship, hunger was there, decrepit, vagrant axe of cold, step-mother of
peoples, hunger throws the dice on board, puffs the sails: 'On, on, or
I eat you, on, on, or you'll return to your mother, your brother, the Judge,
the Priest, the Inquisitors, hell, the plague. On, on, far from the lice, the
feudal lash, the dungeon, and the shit-filled galleys.

In many points of detail Neruda can be seen echoing artists before him with similar politics, Mayakovsky for example. His
picture of the lonely mechanical Cortes is transcribed from the
Mexican muralists (Diego Rivera[15] and David Siquieros in fact
illustrated the first edition of *Canto general*). And into his saga
of liberation he intercalates popular songs, from the Mexican
Revolution, or the *cueca* from Chile, in the way Nicolás Guillén
did in his 'West Indies Ltd'. But the larger vision in his, or at
least first expressed by him.

Whatever difficulties Neruda may have had in making his
vision coherent, in attributing to his various liberators a common
cause and allegiance, were in large measure obviated in the fifth

canto, 'La arena traicionada' (The Sand Betrayed). There a common enemy, at least, is sharply defined, an opponent less ambiguous than the Conquistadors whose arrival was residually necessary, as we have seen. After initial and uncertain notes on such 'tyrants' as Dr Francia of Paraguay, and the Argentinian Rosas (now, incidentally, abhorred far less by Latin American Marxists), Neruda issues into angry denunciation of the havoc wrought in America specifically by the capitalists of Europe and above all, the US. The traitors are those who connived with these interests, middle-men who sell their lands and people for private gain, protected diplomatically and if need be militarily by power that is foreign to the extent that it wants only to exploit. Whatever Neruda's simplifications of the situation are, and they are often gross, and however much the politics of the Cold War determine the detail he emphasizes or ignores, this canto greatly strengthens his 'general' argument and first intimates the depth of his personal interest in it. With invective of lacerating intensity he reviews the behaviour of such figures as the Cuban Machado, the Guatemalan Estrada (Chocano's patron), the Venezuelan Gómez, and the Chilean González Videla, his persecutor. Using the strongest weapons of the satirist, he then addresses poems to the source of the evil, entities such as Standard Oil, the Anaconda Copper Mining Company, and the United Fruit Company:

> Cuando sonó la trompeta, estuvo
> todo preparado en la tierra,
> y Jehová repartió el mundo
> a Coca-Cola Inc., Anaconda,
> Ford Motors, y otras entidades:
> la Compañía Frutera Inc.
> se reservó lo más jugoso,
> la costa central de mi tierra,
> la dulce cintura de América.
> Bautizó de nuevo sus tierras
> como 'Repúblicas Bananas',
> y sobre los muertos dormidos,
> sobre los héroes inquietos
> que conquistaron la grandeza,
> la libertad y las banderas,
> estableció la ópera bufa:
> enajenó los albedríos,
> regaló coronas de César,
> desenvainó la envidia, atrajo
> la dictadura de las moscas,

When the trumpet sounded everything was ready on earth, and Jehovah handed out the world to Coca-Cola Inc., Anaconda, Ford Motors, and other entities: the United Fruit Company reserved for itself the juiciest bit, the middle coast of my land, the sweet waist of America. It rechristened its lands 'Banana Republics', and on top of the sleeping dead, the unstill heroes who won greatness, freedom and banners, it set up a comic opera: it alienated choice, bestowed Caesarean crowns, unsheathed envy, brought in the dictatorship of flies.

To close this section he turns again to González Videla, heaping on him insults of exhaustive detestation. He concentrates in this figure the treachery of the continent and suggests that only by squashing this 'rat' will his people again recover their destiny.

In this fifth section of *Canto general*, then, Neruda begins to identify the story of the continent with his own, the likeness of the two becoming ever clearer as the poem develops. At first he, Neruda, is virtual, shadowy and anonymous, when he searches for obscure umbilical origin in Macchu Picchu or when he only alludes to the hated father's presence in images of Conquistadors, blond, bearded and surprisingly often named Reyes[16] (the paternal name Neruda disowned). With time the struggle between 'orphaned' or bastard Americans, of 'disastrous birth', and their treacherous exploiters is increasingly incorporated into his personal history as it is into theirs. He thus prepares for the daring gesture of Canto 6: 'América, no invoco tu nombre en vano' (America, I do not invoke your name in vain), where he takes on the continent, matching himself with it. By contrast with what has gone before the poems here are remarkably disparate, and lack all obvious 'theme'. They are personal memories ('Winter in the South, on Horseback'), the description of a particular place like Santos ('On the Coast') or Patagonia, a comment on a time of life ('Youth') or a moral quality ('The Crimes'), or the image of a given hero ('Varadero in Cuba'). Yet in context they generate and are generated by a centre of energy, and feel like short stabs from it. The American soul which Bello held back except as an educator, and which Chocano's schizophrenia prevented him from knowing wholly, is manifest in the way Neruda describes himself in the next to last poem in the Canto: 'I am, I am surrounded by days, months, waters that only I know, by hooves, fish, months that I establish.' In the perhaps not altogether successful last poem he further describes this 'I':

América, no invoco tu nombre en vano.
Cuando sujeto al corazón la espada,
cuando aguanto en el alma la gotera,
cuando por las ventanas
un nuevo día tuyo me penetra,
soy y estoy en la luz que me produce,
vivo en la sombra que me determina,
duermo y despierto en tu esencial aurora
dulce como las uvas, y terrible,
conductor del azúcar y el castigo,
empapado en esperma de tu especie,
amamantado en sangre de tu herencia

America, I do not invoke your name in vain. When I subject the sword to my heart, when I put up with the leak in my soul, when through the windows a new day of yours penetrates me, I am and I exist in the light that produces me, I live in the shade that determines me, in your essential dawn I sleep and awake sweet like grapes, and terrible, a conductor of sugar and punishment, soaked in sperm of your kind, suckled on blood of your inheritance.

The remaining sections of *Canto general* (7–15), though consistent in themselves, have overall a similar disparateness in appearance. Some deal with himself and his country: the 'Canto general de Chile', once the extent of the poem (7), his flight from González Videla ('The Fugitive', 10), a miners' strike in Punitaqui (11), a 'New Years Carol for the Country in Darkness' of 1949 (13). The others range from poems to, and ostensibly by, ordinary people ('The Land is Called John', 8), an appeal to the common people of the US ('Let the Rail-Splitter Awake', 9), letters and odes to other writers ('The Rivers of Song', 12), to the more overtly comprehensive final statements 'The Great Ocean' (14) and 'I am' (15). This second group of cantos interacts with the first (1–5) through the isthmian invocation of America, to the extent that no part of the poem can work properly in isolation from the rest. When first expressing the time and space of America, in a sequence readily relatable to 'objective' history and geography, from pre-Columbian days to the present, and from 'the peace of the buffalo to the whipped sands of the final land', Neruda, as we noted, persistently indicated his own interest in them. The 'personal' approach to Macchu Picchu, for example, is later echoed in a highly lyrical elegy intercalated into section 3 between 'accounts' of what was done by the 'cruel pig' Pizarro. The possible truth of such accounts in themselves is further integrated into the poet's own by being referred to a continuous present. Within the 'broad' scheme countries and places are arranged at random, in patterns of the conjuring mind; chronology is effortlessly inverted or ignored (Francia precedes Rosas, González Videla surfaces repeatedly at unexpected moments). And events are often announced like news, in the manner of Brecht, flashes of an actual reporter: 'They are coming over the Islands', 'Now it's Cuba', and so on. Neruda thus enhances his claim to be speaking for the people when by that is understood an ever-present and widely-spread consciousness.

By canto 6 Neruda has achieved a first-person presence, within which the 'separate' phenomena of the rest of the poem can be contained and enlivened. As in the classic epic the acts and attitudes of individual characters, the miners of Punitaqui, González Videla, implicate the whole cast, though the 'essential dawn' Neruda guards in himself is now no longer drawn out comprehensively into geography and history. In this sense he himself can act as another such 'character', the 'hero' if there is one. Like Whitman celebrating himself, he makes of his 'I' the designator by turns of the people ('soy pueblo') and of a personal biography. He may deliberately narrow his persona for a moment with phrases like 'I am going to tell you a little story', only for us to discover a few lines later that the story (*historia*) has indeed again become history. At the end, almost as a tour de force, in his last will and testament, the most 'individual' of acts and disposals of property, is incorporated a larger message, his small death, as he put it, becoming the 'huge death' that defines the continent in space and life, also after he has gone.

It would be hard to exaggerate Neruda's achievement as an American poet, and his great work, dividing the century, will surely come to seem one of the major poetic contributions to it in the Spanish language. Yet there are moments in *Canto general* which are inadequate for just that generality of vision, and belie a vestigial uncertainty in the poet's created self which in turn issues from his being, once again, a *Latin* American. With his creed of liberation, betrayal and solidarity he unquestionably overcame the dilemma of 'independence' that had thwarted his predecessors. But he was not always equal to the enormous psychic effort it demanded. A clear indication of delimited scale comes in the canto 'Let the rail-splitter awake', despite its rousing title.

Here he forces entry into the heart of the enemy camp, willing himself a beloved corner near the Colorado River as a foothold. From there he fraternally addresses the US Veteran of the Second World War, who comes back to his simple home, only to find it plagued with unwelcome guests: racists, all powerful capitalists, inquisitors into 'un-American activities'. But very soon he is warning North Americans as a whole not to try and spread their empire further (Greece, China, Nicaragua, Puerto Rico, Peru, Cuba), because they will be implacably resisted at every step: 'If you touch this wall you will fall burnt like factory coal'. In fact the passion of this admonishment contrasts astoundingly with the ensuing suggestion that none of this should happen, that the woodcutter should awake to make life in the US less corrupt and more peaceful ('Let the young white and the young black march singing and smiling against the walls of gold, against the manufacturer of hatred'). And his reveille is further muted by rhetorical modesty on his own part:

> Yo aquí me despido, vuelvo
> a mi casa, en mis sueños,
> vuelvo a la Patagonia en donde
> el viento golpea los establos
> y salpica hielo el Océano.
> Soy nada más que un poeta: os amo a todos,
> ando errante por el mundo que amo:

I say goodbye here, I go back home, in my dreams, I go back to Patagonia where the wind lashes the stables and the Ocean sprinkles ice. I'm nothing more than a poet: I love you all, I go wandering through the world I love.

This nomadic disclaimer cannot but alert us to that problem of moral and geographical identity otherwise resolved or suppressed in the poem. For earlier he had striven to incorporate the people of the US into his general song, and to find a fraternal bond with them: 'you are what I am, what I was, what we should protect, the fraternal substratum of purest America, the simple men of the roads and the streets'. Thus he would share his essential dawn with the woodcutters and rail-splitters, Lincoln's heirs. To do this he worked his way from Colorado River out, drawing constantly on Whitman's sense of a vast unconscious landscape, and in it the minutiae of daily life. Yet in a move ultimately reminiscent of Rodó's suppression of Whitman in *Ariel*, Neruda does not invoke that poet directly at this point or openly credit the US with

keeping his faith alive at home. Indeed Neruda appeals directly
for the voice of his 'deep brother', and the weight of his 'buried
chest', to sing not the US at all, but the reconstruction of Soviet
Russia after the war, which he views from his high point in the
Urals ('From here I see extensive zones of man, the geography of
children and women, love, factories and songs, schools', and so
on). Whitman's voice is made here not to awaken his sleeping
*camerado* at home but to swell the chorus of defiance from abroad.
Neruda thus tacitly relinquishes his prospecting, from Colorado
out, for a pure America from pole to pole, and settles back into an
attitude towards and against the US, from somewhere else. When
the party line is most firmly drawn, that is the Urals; when it
softens, he subsides rapidly right down to Patagonia, the 'extreme
south of America'. From one or other place, his popular American
voice being thus delimited, he resorts to the kind of oratory Darío
used to conceal an absence or plurality of position.

Yet more radical than this divisiveness between Latin and
Saxon America (which Neruda elsewhere certainly overcame,
notably in the urgent unpunctuated flow of 'Wind of Lincoln') is
that between Latin and Indian America, which despite everything dogs *Canto general*. A Spanish-speaking American whose
culture in childhood and adolescence was substantially western,
Neruda endeavoured to unveil the original America in Macchu
Picchu, in the second canto of the poem. Doing this he showed
he was wholly alert to the dangers of fetishism, of 'kissing the
stones' for their sake only. He would always wish the city to invoke those who once inhabited it, the dead of a single abyss, the
vanished common folk. Denouncing their possible suffering and
praising their skill he says furthermore, in the most revealing line
in the section, that he would speak for them:

> Yo vengo a hablar por vuestra boca muerta.

This can mean 'I come to speak on behalf of your dead mouth', or
'through' it. In either case it is clear that he would be the Indians'
spokesman, in the absence of live witnesses. He has already asked
the River Willkamayu, in vain, 'what language do you bring to
the ear', and has interrogated the stones themselves for information. Given the presence of over a million Quechua speakers in
the Andean area, who are aware of the Inca past, choosing to enter
a 'dead' city like Macchu Picchu must seem no less of a subterfuge

than his description, in the first canto, of Guarani (the main
language of Paraguay) as a language of the past. Neruda's evasion
of the live Indian part of the American people appears even
stranger in view of his own quotation of Tupac Amaru's Quechua
as an epigraph to the canto of the Liberators.

Neruda has been widely criticized for indulgence of Indian
America, for forgetting the blood-thirsty imperialism that was
practised there long before Columbus arrived. It might just as
pertinently be remarked that he sells the Indians short, saying
that the conquest was needed to shed intellectual light, when in
fact the Maya had even reckoned the phases of the moon more
accurately than their contemporaries in Europe. But in any case,
although Neruda would continuously deny or denigrate his paternal Spanish heritage, it is in the vocabulary and images of just
that heritage that he is constrained to interpret the very heart of
his indigenous America.

> Pero una permanencia de piedra y de palabra:
> la ciudad como un vaso se levantó en las manos
> de todos, vivos, muertos, callados, sostenidos
> de tanta muerte, un muro, de tanta vida un golpe
> de pétalos de piedra: la rosa permanente, la morada:
> este arrecife andino de colonias glaciales.

And yet a permanence of stone and language upheld the city raised like
a chalice in all those hands: live, dead and stilled aloft with so much death,
a wall; so much life, a blow of stone petals: the everlasting rose, our
home: this reef on Andes of glacial colonies.

As Robert Pring-Mill has pointed out,[17] such imagery is 'part of
the general Catholic heritage of South America', and of an extended frame of reference in the poem. Some of the commonest
words in Neruda's language (rose, blood, chalice, stone), far from
having their Roman cultural origins and their semantic identity
challenged (as they were by Vallejo), effectively silence whatever
'popular' voice may have spoken from the Andean survivors of
Macchu Picchu.

Ultimately this leaves Neruda in the same dubious position as
those poets before him who were anxious to avenge their maternal
line without knowing much about it: an ignorance which in turn
has traditionally indicated deep psychological reasons for thinking of America's cradle as 'disastrous'. For all his desire that
America may awake and grow in a popular spirit of professedly

orphaned brothers and comrades, he is still caught up in the anger of sexual shame and continues a radical ambiguity towards the Indian 'race'. He shares too that compensatory fantasy of an Indian father nobler and more potent than the relentlessly effective European fecundators of the American womb. In the very first poem of his work Neruda reaches out for him: 'I looked for you, o father of mine, young warrior of darkness and copper.' This imaginary warrior forebear (discussed at length by Jung with reference to North America),[18] closely resembles Darío's Caupolicán (also invoked later by Neruda), Chocano's Toltec bowman, and even recalls the potency of Bello's maize: 'haughty chief of the spiked tribe who swells his grain'.

At one point, going beyond anything anyone had expressed before him, Neruda takes the consequences of this fantasy, to produce verse of spine-chilling ferocity. This is how he describes how he and other Liberators ate Pedro Valdivia's heart, after drinking his blood:

> Entonces, de la tierra
> hecha de nuestros cuerpos, nació el canto
> de la guerra, del sol, de las cosechas,
> hacia la magnitud de los volcanes.
> Entonces repartimos el corazón sangrante.
> Yo hundí los dientes en aquella corola
> cumpliendo el rito de la tierra:
>   'Dame tu frío, extranjero malvado.
>   Dame tu valor de gran tigre.
>   Dame en tu sangre tu cólera.
>   Dame tu muerte para que me siga
>   y lleve el espanto a los tuyos.
>   Dame la guerra que trajiste.
>   Dame tu caballo y tus ojos.
>   Dame la tiniebla torcida.
>   Dame la madre del maíz.
>   Dame la lengua del caballo.
>   Dame la patria sin espinas.
>   Dame la paz vencedora.
>   Dame el aire donde respira
>   el canelo, señor florido.'

Then, from the earth made of our bodies, was born the song of war, of the sun, of the harvests, up to the size of the volcanoes. Then we shared out the bleeding heart. I sank my teeth in that corola fulfilling the rite of the earth: 'Give me your cold, wicked stranger. Give me your great tiger courage. Give me your wrath in your blood. Give me your death so that it follows me and takes fear to your people. Give me the war that you brought. Give me your horse and your eyes. Give me the twisted darkness. Give me the mother of maize. Give me the horse's tongue. Give me the fatherland without thorns. Give me conquering peace. Give me the air where the cinnamon breathes, flowered lord.'

These lines rush like electric from the savage to the tender. Flesh consumed, Valdivia, the foreign father, is hated and loved at the same time, as in many ancient American rites. As a frame of reference for the work this functions markedly better than the crypto-Christian and ecclesiastical imagery imposed on Macchu Picchu, and arguably as a more primeval or interestingly surreal version of it. Such expression lies closer both to Neruda's sense of America and to his own propensities as a poet.

Standing as near to the end of *Canto general* as 'The Heights of Macchu Picchu' does to the beginning, the 'Great Ocean' canto in large measure answers it and expresses most successfully the vision of the whole poem. The sea may incidentally be Chile's realm, the arena of its own imperial aspiration (Easter Island, the Antarctic). But much more important, it is the analogue of American genesis and growth. The sexual metaphor of conquest and necessary awakening, so brutal and unacceptable, so keenly felt by Neruda, in the historical cantos at the start of the poem, is here taken to ultimate depths, where violence and impregnation, rape and shame need not be denied as part of life.

> Estrella de oleajes, agua madre,
> madre materia, medula invencible,
> trémula iglesia levantada en lodo:
> la vida en ti palpó piedras nocturnas,
> retrocedió cuando llegó a la herida,
> avanzó con escudos y diademas,
> extendió dentaduras transparentes,
> acumuló la guerra en su barriga.
> Lo que formó la oscuridad quebrada
> por la substancia fría del relámpago,
> Océano, en tu vida está viviendo.

Star of swelling waves, mother water, mother materia, invincible marrow, tremulous church raised on the mud: life in you felt nocturnal stones, drew back when it came to the wound, advanced with shields and diadems, extended transparent rows of teeth, accumulated war in its belly. That which the darkness, broken by the cold substance of lightning, formed, Ocean, in your life is living.

As in the terrible absorption of Valdivia Neruda does not exult in retribution (certainly not vengeance) but tempers this awesome view into life's intimacy with supreme tenderness, his marvellous quality as a poet. This leaves the way open for one of the finest poems in the book, 'La noche marina', which closes the ocean sequence, where Neruda, lover of life 'soaked in sperm', opens himself as totally to the sea and its huge potency as Whitman did to his land and its people:

> Quiero tener tu frente simultánea,
> abrirla en mi interior para nacer
> en todas tus orillas, ir ahora
> con todos los secretos respirados,
> con tus oscuras líneas resguardadas
> en mí como la sangre o las banderas,
> llevando estas secretas proporciones
> al mar de cada día, a los combates
> que en cada puerta – amores y amenazas –
> viven dormidos.
>          Pero entonces
> entraré en la ciudad con tantos ojos
> como los tuyos, y sostendré la vestidura
> con que me vistaste, y que me toquen
> hasta el agua total que no se mide:
> pureza y destrucción contra toda la muerte,
> distancia que no puede gastarse, música
> para los que duermen y para los que despiertan.

I want to have your simultaneous forehead, to open it in my inside to be born on all your shores, to go now with all the breathed secrets, with your dark shielded lines in me like blood or banners, bringing these secret proportions to the sea of every day, to the combats which at every door – loves and threats – live asleep. But then I shall enter the city with as many eyes as yours, and I shall uphold the garment you clothed me with, and may they touch in me right to the total water that is not measured: purity and destruction against all death, distance that cannot be spent, music for those who sleep and for those who wake.

# 4. Modernism and Rubén Darío

The literary movement in Spanish known as Modernism began in the last decades of the nineteenth century and ended with the First World War. Beyond this bald definition the term remains contentious. Because of its undoubted American origins the Spanish have tended to play down its importance and to enhance, at its expense, peninsular traditions of their own (the 'Generation of 98' for example).[1] Because of the undoubted social callousness of many Modernists, other critics have wanted also to reduce its scope, to see it as a pretty but inconsequential bourgeois escapade.[2] As far as Spanish American poetry is concerned the fact stands that before the Modernists there was little worth reading (beside the limited 'Independent' successes of Bello, Olmedo, Heredia and others, and beside efforts in doomed local idioms like the gauchesque), and that it was partially thanks to them that the great poets of this century, Vallejo, Neruda and Paz, were able to find their voice.

The term (*modernismo*) was first used by the Nicaraguan poet Rubén Darío in 1888, the date of his collection *Azul* . . . Two years later he spoke of the 'new spirit which today quickens a small but proud and triumphant group of writers and poets in Spanish America: Modernism'.[3] From then on his prefaces and articles are dotted with references to the 'new way of thinking and writing in Spanish', and to 'the liberating movement' which it fell to him to initiate in America. While most of the Spanish Americans he assigned to this group accepted his account of it, some did not, either because, having preceded him, they had more complex notions of its origins, or because they objected to what it seemed to stand for. José Asunción Silva, for example, both a national of the highly conservative state of Colombia and a revolutionary in prosody and in tormented self-expression who committed suicide at thirty, developed independently of other Modernists. Unlike them he familiarized himself not just with contemporary French writing, but with literature in German, and in English, which he spoke well ('Nocturno', 'Día de difuntos' and other innovatory poems by him owe much to Poe's verse experiments). At the same time he tended to play down his modernity by finding precedents for it in Spanish literature, and not just in Bécquer but in writers as unlikely as the neo-classicist Iriarte. Deeply divided as he was, he devoted a good deal of energy to satirizing the modernizing efforts of those he called the 'Rubén Daríacos'.[4]

As if aware of this kind of eventuality (he responded directly to critics only three times during his life), Darío in fact never insisted on the '-ism'; and he strongly discouraged others from imitating him. He said literary politics disgusted him, and was able to say this precisely because of his desire, not that what for want of another name was called Modernism should exist against or instead of anything else, but that Spanish American poetry should at least exist. Though he may never have expressed it fully in his poetry, in this sense Darío lived and travelled in the name of a continental ideal, after his apprenticeship in his native Nicaragua and other Central American states. Those he knew, often at an admittedly mundane level, in Santiago de Chile, Havana, Buenos Aires, Mexico and even Spain, respected this quality in him. In a juvenile epistle to Ricardo Contreras (who like Francisco Gavidia encouraged his early reading of French literature), he asks with near-pathetic anticipation: 'For here, in our land, is not poetry beginning to awake?'[5] Still after the success of *Azul* . . . and (grudging) recognition from the traditionalist Spanish critic Juan Valera, he put the will for the birth and flight of poetry in America before the need to be rid of the dominant prosodic and other conventions of Spanish, though in subsequent criticism it is this second wish which has most often been equated with Modernism.

Only in this way can Darío's colossal enthusiasm for Victor Hugo be properly understood. (He is hard to take today for many of the reasons that Hugo is.) Wholly aware of his circumstances, he aimed at 'a secular legend'. He arrogated to poets, a frail and fratricidal tribe in America, the sacred fire and the noble voice: the right, above all, to be. Doubtless he knew many other nine-teenth-century French poets[6] as well as Hugo and frequently echoed the Parnassians and the Symbolists. But not at the cost of committing himself to a narrower view of poetry. One looks in vain in his poems for the consciously restrictive practice of a Gautier or a Mallarmé. The ambiguous and evanescent Verlaine is sung in diapason, as the 'liróforo celeste',[7] master of the Olympian instrument of poetry. And if he appeared closer to the Parnassians than to the Symbolists, then it was primarily to Leconte de Lisle, the West Indian admired for his 'vast inspiration':

> Tú tienes en tu canto como ecos de océano;
> se ve en tu poesía la selva y el león;
> salvaje luz irradia la lira que en tu mano
> derrama su sonora, robusta vibración.[8]

You have in your song oceanic echoes; the jungle and the lion can be seen in your poetry; wild light radiates from the lyre which in your hand pours out its sonorous, robust vibration.

At least as a young Modernist he would, then, reserve for poetry the grandest statements. 'El coloquio de los centauros' (The colloquy of the centaurs), the most robust poem of his supposedly 'decadent' collection *Prosas profanas* (Profane Prose, 1896), amounts to a total philosophy, wholly of the order of Hugo's 'Le Satyre', in *La Légende des siècles*, which deals with the origin of the world, human progress and other such subjects. For his part in Darío's colloquy Abantes says:

> Himnos a la sagrada Naturaleza; al vientre
> de la tierra y al germen que entre las rocas y entre
> las carnes de los árboles, y dentro humana forma,
> es un mismo secreto y es una misma norma;
> potente y sutilísimo, universal resumen
> de la suprema fuerza, de la virtud del Numen.

Hymns to sacred Nature; to the belly of the earth and to the seed that among the rocks and the flesh of the trees, and within human form, is the same secret and is the same norm: potent and most subtle, a universal summary of the supreme force, of the strength of the Numen.

This insistence on germination and new birth recurs in Darío's writing: as much as a 'philosophy of life' it was his programme as a Modernist. However ingenuously or bombastically expressed, it served to distinguish him crucially as an American from the European Decadents, whose spiritual home was Paris, the 'capital of the nineteenth century'; and from those Spanish American Modernists like José Asunción Silva or Julián del Casal who felt unable to extricate themselves from European culture. For the Decadents saw themselves at the end of a cultural line and had a horror of progeny, an attitude quite different from that of Darío's cry in the preface to *Profane Prose*: 'When a muse gives you a child, let the other eight be pregnant.' Of course European Decadence, specifically that sense of being *fin de siècle*, was a more complex business than a contrast of this sort might suggest. This is true even of such works as J. K. Huysmans's *A Rebours*, whose hero, Des Esseintes, embodied to perfection the modish qualities of aboulia, neurasthenia and social perversity. Yet on essential points we find Darío agreeing with a simplistic contemporary censure of the Decadents and other late nineteenth-century artistic groups: Max Nordau's *Degeneration*. Not that Darío accepted Nordau's whole thesis (which was in any case outrageously self-contradictory) of the pathological decline of modern European culture, paralleled only by the 'putrefaction' of Latin culture at the end of the Roman empire. But by agreeing with even part of it he showed that he wanted Modernism to be, indeed, a new birth in a new world.

As something like an 'awakening' in Spanish American poetry became recognizable, in the late 1880s and early 1890s, Darío more or less conscientiously acknowledged others responsible for it. In José Martí he saw the man who had tried to alert 'our America' to self-awareness not least in literature, in the chronicles that he had sent in the 1880s from New York to newspapers in Caracas, Buenos Aires and other Latin American cities.[9] Just because he knew Spanish literature so well, having studied in Madrid, Martí was better able to judge what Spanish Americans might learn from the French and US writers he introduced to his public. The brilliant and novel prose in which Martí said all this itself profoundly affected that genre and left its mark on the stories in *Azul* . . . His poems were perhaps less innovatory and only two short collections, *Ismaelillo* and *Versos sencillos* (Simple Verses) were not posthumous. But again Darío clearly echoed him, and caught his 'virile simplicity' in poems in *Profane Prose*. The figures of Martí and Darío have often been opposed to each other, in critical debates about the meaning and worth of Modernism which are not altogether to the point here. Certainly, ideology did distinguish them, though it might be noted that as a Modernist Darío was closer to him than were Silva or Martí's compatriot Julián del Casal. Darío was clearly disturbed by Martí's implacable desire to rid Cuba of Spanish tutelage. True to his belief in the prime, demiurgic power of the word[10] and language, and anxious not to fragment Hispanic coherence, he glossed over Martí's death at the hands of the Spanish in 1895,[11] as we have suggested. And this caution is perhaps more eloquent than anything else of why he was not able to become the 'poet of America', for all his genesial idealism as a Modernist.

During his stay in Mexico Martí had worked with other young writers there in the cause of a nascent Spanish American literature, and to give Spanish the 'grace and elegance' he felt it lacked. First among these was Manuel Gutiérrez Nájera, who publicly embarked on a 'system'[12] of cultural cross-fertilization (in its way a bizarre continuation of the politics of the days of the emperor Maximilian, Napoleon III's protégé in Mexico). To this end he translated the French Romantics and Parnassians, and later (1894) founded the Modernist *Revista Azul*, where Martí published one of his last poems. He spoke French perfectly, though his knowledge of that culture remained as literary as Darío's was when he wrote *Azul*... in Santiago de Chile. In any account of Modernism Gutiérrez Nájera is very much at its origins, as both prose writer and poet. Beyond the Spanish solemnity of his first verse, and a certain Musset-like sentimentality elsewhere, he wrote poetry in Spanish as it had never been written before (to adapt Unamuno's later remark about Darío). For José Emilio Pacheco, the first Modernist poem in Mexico was Gutiérrez Nájera's 'La Duquesa de Job' (1884). The tone is conversational, from one to another just as familiar with the fashions of the Mexican capital, and is the opposite of portentous. Gutiérrez Nájera obviously delighted in snobbish modernity: the 'duchess' has Louis Théo eyes, is dressed better than Hélène Kossut's clients, is Paul de Kock's grisette. With his *noms de plume* he took this tendency to self-parody, as 'Monsieur Can Can' or the duchess's 'Duque Job' (the name of a Parisian comedy of 1859). He was original in suggesting that he knew what 'culture' was, that he was modern and familiar enough with the language and tastes of the capital of the nineteenth century (as Paris has been described by Walter Benjamin) at the same time as being part of another reality. For the 'duchess' is local, a working girl with her room in Mexico City and her Sundays off. Her attraction and complex presence are well caught in the phrase 'trasciende a Francia', which can mean she both savours of France and goes beyond it. The paradox implicit here might be understood as fundamental to the whole Modernist effort both to catch up with and transcend the poetry of France (the modern substitute for Spain); and Darío himself did not find a better way of focusing on the poet's everyday reality until mature poems like his 'Epistle' to Leopoldo Lugones's wife. But Gutiérrez Nájera had the drawbacks of his fashionable intelligence, and the poem emanates, with curious prematurity, a smugness that was anathema to Darío. In fact, though he knew him no more directly than Gutiérrez Nájera, Darío drew much more heavily on another of the Mexicans, a near-contemporary of them both, Salvador Díaz Mirón, who was altogether more Hugo-esque in stance and tone. For Darío, Díaz Mirón's unchained verse rang like the hooves of a herd of American buffalo, while his ideal of Art expansively covered mountains and plains.[13] As a Modernist, Darío (and indeed Díaz Mirón) may with time have modified his idea of poetry. But at the origins of the movement he was primarily interested in enthusiasm on a large scale, breath enough to give all Spanish America poetic life.

After these diverse and partly obscure beginnings in the 1880s, the story of Modernism becomes much more that of Darío's own poetry and of his presence in cities like Havana, Buenos Aires and Madrid. His time in Havana, on his way to and from Europe in 1892, was extremely brief but noteworthy because of his contact with Julián del Casal. The Cuban Casal differed greatly from Martí in everything but his short life and his professional concern with literature. But Casal, a highly accomplished poet, was a self-styled decadent who could forget the falseness of his position only in art. He lamented the continuing subjugation of Cuba to Spain,[14] yet was fascinated by the high social style of 'elegant Havana', the name indeed of the periodical many of his poems were published in (*La Habana elegante*). Like his beloved Des Esseintes (the hero of Huysmans's *A Rebours*) he did not want, by actually going there, to prick his 'great illusion' (to see Paris). In a way unavailable to poets of the nominally independent nations of Latin America he felt deeply implicated in Old World culture, and transmitted it into art – 'my ideal museum' is one of his titles – in just the fashion advised by the French Decadents, and by the Parnassians before them. His translations of the Parnassians (Théophile Gautier, José-Maria de Hérédia)[15] in his first book *Hojas al viento* (Leaves to the Wind, 1890) show him learning to reduce life to art as he would in his own verse, notably the sonnets of *Nieve* (Snow, 1892). A tropical storm, in all its raw might, is made into a cameo: the sea 'paralyses' its waves under the lightning which in turn 'traces' its mark on the horizon ('Paisaje de verano', Summer Landscape). His sonnets from Gustave Moreau's paintings, or at least Huysmans's account of them (the first of their kind in Spanish), closely follow the injunctions of Gautier's 'L'Art', making of poetry something best understood in analogy with other more explicit arts. This he took into a specifically decadent need for artificiality in poems like 'En el campo' (In the Country) with its bored monorhymes and a title as mocking as Havana *Snow*.

> Tengo el impuro amor de las cuidades.
> Y a este sol que ilumina las edades
> prefiero yo del gas las claridades.
>
> . . .
>
> Mucho más que las selvas tropicales,
> plácenme los sombríos arrabales
> que encierran las vetustas capitales.
>
> . . .
>
> Más que el raudal que baja de la cumbre
> quiero oír a la humana muchedumbre
> gimiendo en su perpetua servidumbre.

I have the impure love of cities. And to this sun which illumines the ages I prefer to light of gas. Much more than tropical forests, the sombre quarters in old capitals please me. More than the torrent descending from the summit I want to hear the human multitude groaning in perpetual servitude.

Multiple irony of such lucid perversity was shaped in him by his predicament as a citizen of a doomed European empire.

His poems to María Cay, a beauty of Havana society, who also attracted Darío, are a far cry from those of Gutiérrez Nájera to his 'duchess'. In 'Kakemono', a portrait of her in Japanese dress, like her he turns to the artificial and the exotic out of a need for distraction. Bored with 'reigning' by natural beauty, she dresses and makes up, a process described with near-morbid detail which is that of his 'Kakemono', or verse portrait ('With the dark feather of the swallow put at the edge of the hot perfume pan, you extended the arch of your eyebrows'). Her perfected image fascinates him profoundly but cannot rid him of 'glacial sadness' any more than his poetry can, as time and nature, finally unsuppressible, remind him of his futility. In Casal's company Darío wrote two *sonetillos* (sonnets of 8-syllable lines) to the same lady ('Para una cubana' and 'Para la misma') which confirm a new respect for the detail of the Cuban's artistry, but by no means full commitment to it. The fact that the woman's artificial beauty is incidental precipitates no despair. Indeed, 'mysterious and cabbalistic', she anticipates the inalienable feminine presence who accompanies him in 'Divagación', one of the best poems of *Profane Prose*.

This collection emerged from a capital city of very different atmosphere, Buenos Aires, where Darío spent the years 1893–8. If Modernism can be said to have had coherent expression as a movement, then this period in the city that Darío called cosmopolis would be it. In the company of poets like Ricardo Jaimes Freyre, Leopoldo Díaz, Leopoldo Lugones, and Alberto Ghiraldo,[16] and in contact with critical minds as sharp as Paul Groussac's, Darío found an atmosphere congenial to his endeavour, made evident in the several reviews they founded and contributed to: *Revista de América*, *La Biblioteca*, *El Mercurio de América*. There he made in earnest the formal experiments through which Modernism changed and enriched the prosody of Spanish, together with Jaimes Freyre, who later wrote a treatise on the subject, and Lugones, who began his career in Buenos Aires with a collection, *Las montañas de oro* (The Mountains of Gold, 1897), notable for its free use of the silva form and of lines composed of rhythmic units of a set number of syllables, freely combined. This last had been José Asuncíon Silva's innovation in his 'Nocturno', also used by Darío in his 'Marcha triunfal' (1895). In 'El reino interior' Darío used alexandrines of unconventional caesura and accentuation interspersed with lines of different length, together with startling enjambment ('paralela-/mente'). The dedication of this last poem to Eugenio de Castro pointed to his interest in the prior experiments of the Portuguese poet, whom he discussed in an important lecture of this period,[17] and in an essay in *Los raros*.

This book of essays, first published in Buenos Aires in 1896, stemmed from his obituary and other contributions to the newspaper *La Nación*. Like Verlaine's *Les Poètes maudits* of the previous decade, it amounted to a general statement of principle, by both omission and inclusion. Leaving aside one or two courtesy pieces, and an odd preoccupation with the salacious publications of Kistemackers in Belgium, we find an attempt to understand late nineteenth century art and society on a grand scale, through figures like Ibsen and Poe, and Max Nordau, critic of Western 'degeneration'. With the huge exception of Hugo, dead for a decade, Darío also dealt with those French writers who had helped him, among others, to bring about 'the rebirth of the Spanish language in America': Leconte de Lisle, Lautréamont (another American by birth at least), Verlaine, and, anticipating a growing fondness for the *école romaine* in France, Moréas and Tailhade. Among fellow Spanish Americans he dwelt on only two, Augusto de Armas and Martí, both Cubans who took to different extremes tendencies inherent in Modernism. After early efforts in the manner of Casal, Augusto de Armas actually went to Paris, and furthermore began to publish in French. Darío favourably compares his ease in that language with that of Swinburne and Rossetti, and pronounces him a representative 'of the unity and strength of the Latin soul, whose centre and focus today is luminous France'. By contrast Martí of course is the great New World continentalist. Just as he played down Martí's military martyrdom, so Darío omitted from *Profane Prose* (of the same year) poems which defined him, Darío, too closely as an American: the address to Columbus discussed in a previous chapter, and sagas of the Indian past of Central America first included in *El canto errante* (1907). Striving still for the large statement in the style of the 'Colloquy of the Centaurs' he made a virtue of not foreclosing any possibilities, of keeping options open in the limbo of an America still not quite ready to be itself. The confidence necessary for such an attitude comes through strongest in his remarkable preface to *Profane Prose*, where he speaks of Buenos Aires as cosmopolis, and of the future.

His confidence suffuses most of the collection, notably poems like 'Era un aire suave', 'Divagación' and 'Del campo'. By its title this last obviously evokes Casal's 'En el campo', to which it is a response. Darío starts in the opposite direction to the Cuban, leaving the pleasures of the city for the 'green triumph' of the pampa. But this is no folk or regionalist gesture: rural Argentina is addressed playfully ('Field, good day!') and its glories are soon referred to the attraction of fashionable Buenos Aires streets like La Florida. Local folk culture has none of the suppressed power it had for Casal, and by the close Darío cheerfully has the dearest creole legend, the gaucho, ride off into the sunset:

> De pronto se oye el eco del grito de la pampa;
> brilla como una puesta del argentino sol;

y un espectral jinete, como una sombra cruza,
sobre su espalda un poncho, sobre su faz dolor.
   —«¿Quién eres, solitario viajero de la noche?»
   —«¡Yo soy la Poesía que un tiempo aquí reinó:
yo soy el postrer gaucho que parte para siempre,
de nuestra vieja patria llevando el corazón!»

Suddenly the echo of the pampa's shout can be heard; it shines like the
setting of the argentine sun; and a spectral horseman passes by like a
shade, a poncho on his back, pain on his face. 'Who are you, lonely
traveller of the night?' 'I am the Poetry that once reigned here: I am the
last gaucho who leaves for ever our old fatherland, taking its heart!'

But Darío, incredibly enough, does not seem arrogant usurping an
old national tradition like this. He brings the poem off, with its
fluent alexandrines, by suggesting the imminence of something
new, a broad excitement emanating from a capital more aspirant
than Gutiérrez Nájera's, and certainly free of the elegant im-
potence of Havana.

   *Profane Prose* ranges boldly in time and space, summoning at
will the cultures of the world he knew of (from his Larousse, some
unkindly suggested): the Versailles of Watteau; 'old' Spain;[18]
Venice and Florence; Cleopatra's Egypt; the Far East; the world
of Germanic myth assembled by Wagner. As for this last 'location', these years of the Modernists were distinguished by a kind
of nordic extravaganza, stimulated perhaps by the long hours they
spent in the beer hall known as Auers Keller. Darío's poems are
dotted with references to Wagner: the singer of Lohengrin and
the swan; the friend of Ludwig II (above Verlaine's aspersions);[19]
the full-blooded confidant of Augusta Holmes, whose originality
would not fit the pattern Judith Gautier had made for it in France.
The massive fantasies in Lugones's *The Mountains of Gold* again
linked modern Germanic culture with surviving poetic myth, in
this case 'Nebulosa Thule', while Ricardo Jaimes Freyre's first
and only important collection *Castalia bárbara* (1897 and 1899)
announced in its title a source other than the *castalia clásica* of
Spanish poetry prior to the Modernists ('*castalia*' was a spring on
Mount Parnassus, sacred to the Muses). The title of course evokes
Leconte de Lisle's *Poèmes barbares*; but Jaimes Freyre's excursions, with the freedom of the verse and the pure energy of their
subject, insist more fiercely on the arbitrariness of any given
mould. Here his 'Walhalla' (which barely retains assonance on

even lines and where breath groupings defy the basic octosyllabic unit):

> Vibra el himno rojo. Chocan los escudos y las lanzas
> con largo fragor siniestro.
> De las heridas sangrientas por la abierta boca brotan
> ríos purpúreos.
> Hay besos y risas.
>                               Y un cráneo lleno
> de hidromiel, en donde apagan
> abrasados por la fiebre, su sed los guerreros muertos.

The red hymn vibrates. The shields and lances clash with a long sinister din. Through the open mouth of the bleeding wounds purple rivers burst. There are kisses and laughter. And a skull full of mead, where, scorched by fever, the dead warriors slake their thirst.

Much the same brand of 'barbaric' verse had been retailed in Leopoldo Díaz's *Poemas* (1896): 'Las Walkyrias', for example, has many of the features of the poem quoted above. All this could be seen as a conscious testing of limits, an exultation in new possibilities. As a single example of the mood and practice of the Modernists at this period must come Darío's 'Divagation'.

It is easy enough to list the settings and locations of this pilgrimage, which Darío conceived in a hotel in Buenos Aires in 1894. And this has often been done, with due note of Darío's cultural catholicity, his exoticism, the literariness of his references, and so on. Much more important are the inflexions of his conversational tone, the ease with which he not only moves through space and time but effectively denies a normal understanding of them, and the rhetorical persuasion which leads to the ecstatic close. An American writing in Spanish, he shakes off the weight and claims of history while recognizing it and wanting its glamour, his own position being assured by nothing but errant energy. He starts from a 'here' defined only by the intoxicating presence of someone else:

> ¿Vienes? Me llega aquí, pues que suspiras,
> un soplo de las mágicas fragancias
> que hicieran los delirios de las liras
> en las Grecias, las Romas y las Francias.

You're coming? Since you sigh, a breath reaches me here of the magic fragrances that would make the delirium of the lyres in the Greeces, the Romes and the Frances.

With this sigh we are immersed in the scent of Olympic ambrosia, ritual Bacchic gestures and laughter which loosen the fixity of the Termini, the boundary guardians of antiquity. Then, in a manner characteristic of Darío, we emerge into narrative: Diana is seen looking for Adonis. For a modern reader, such a transition, skilfully affected as it is, feels abrupt, and without full involvement in Darío's driving enthusiasm, curiously dated: it is deeply eloquent of his attachment to Hugo and of his apparent desire not to be restricted to setting or mood as the Parnassians and Symbolists understood them. After only two stanzas, however, we revert to the gentle interrogation of the opening: 'Do you like to love in Greek?' His own assertion, that he prefers the Greece of France to the Greece of the Greeks, is in parenthesis, a device which importantly modifies what otherwise would be a parody of modernity ('Verlaine is more than Socrates; and Arsène Houssaye outdoes old Anacreon'). After an asterisked pause, Darío proposes a series of locations: Florence, with another brief narrative, though this time in parenthesis; Germany, and the white wine of the Teutonic grape; Spain, gold and purple, and, with its carnation, red like Florence. Another asterisk and: 'Perhaps exotic loves ...?' Darío's companion now herself becomes the source of fascination in a variety of guises. So far he has been her solicitous guide, proposing scenarios appropriate to the excitement she creates, at first with 'outside' actors, admitting to his own preferences and insinuating their prior familiarity with each other (in Paris, he has remarked, are love shrines where she joins her fresh lips to his). While his presence as a skilled poet is submerged ('I'll madrigalize near your lips'), imagined realities gain force for themselves, only to be merged into the being of the woman herself. As Gautier's princess she is asked to love him 'in the sonorous Chinese of Li-Tai-Pe'; and then still more directly:

> Amame japonesa, japonesa
> antigua, que no sepa de naciones
> occidentales:

Love me Japanese woman, Japanese woman of old, who doesn't know about western nations.

As the poem spreads in space and time it gathers in intensity, and time spent in any one guise shortens. From the conversational, and then the imperative, the tone moves up with the mood:

> O negra, negra como la que canta
> en su Jerusalén el rey hermoso,
> negra que haga brotar bajo su planta
> la rosa la cicuta del reposo. . .

Oh black, black like the woman sung in his Jerusalem by the beautiful king, Negress who under her foot makes the rose and the hemlock of quiet bourgeon. . .

The final three stanzas are among the more glamorous Darío wrote (thanks in part to their echoes of the *Song of Songs* by that 'beautiful king' Solomon). Darío has moved the poem back and forward in time, and outwards in space, holding ever closer focus on given moments with rhetorical skill, and 'comes through' to a new consciousness, the waking-dream magic of the last 5-line stanza:

> Amor, en fin, que todo diga y cante,
> amor que encante y deje sorprendida
> a la serpiente de ojos de diamante
> que está enroscada al árbol de la vida.
>
> Amame así, fatal, cosmopolita,
> universal, inmensa, única, sola
> y todas; misteriosa y erudita:
> ámame mar y nube, espuma y ola.
>
> Sé mi reina de Saba, mi tesoro;
> descansa en mis palacios solitarios.
> Duerme. Yo encenderé los incensarios.
> Y junto a mi unicornio cuerno de oro,
> tendrán rosas y miel tus dromedarios.

Love, at last, that may say and sing all, love that enchants and leaves surprised the diamond-eyed serpent coiled round the tree of life. ¶Love me thus, fatal, cosmopolitan, universal, immense, unique, single and everyone; mysterious and erudite: love me as sea and cloud, foam and wave. ¶Be my queen of Sheba, my treasure; rest in my solitary palaces. Sleep. I shall light the censers. And by my unicorn horn of gold, your dromedaries shall have roses and milk.

In this poem it would be as irrelevant to reduce Darío's 'exoticism' to the erotic as it would be to invest his journey with precise political significance. In conjuring prior and established cultures he made a virtue of the absence of origin, term and identity. His huge limitation is of course that operatic sense of culture which marks this 'first stage' of Modernism, the total absence of a recognizably real world. But effectively converting his solitary

palaces into the scenario of a Weltstadt, he was creating a potential, a margin of movement, even if, as Rodó lamented, he did not
specify it to become 'the poet of America'. The special power of
the poem can be measured well if it is compared with one in part
inspired by it and which is perhaps the most expressive of what
Modernism became in Spain. This is Manuel Machado's
'Eleusis',[20] like 'Divagation' a movement through various cultures
and times inspired by a feminine presence. She, however, from the
start has to be followed, to be brought back from the places that
successively claim her:

> Se perdió en las vagas
> selvas de un ensueño,
> y sólo de espaldas
> la vi desde lejos. . .
> Como una caricia
> dorada, el cabello,
> tendido, sus hombros
> cubría. Y al verlo,
> siguióla mi alma
> y fuése muy lejos,
> dejándome solo,
> no sé si domido o despierto.

She was lost in the vague forests of a dream, and only from behind did
I see her from afar. . . Like a golden caress, her loose hair covered her
shoulders. And on seeing her my soul followed her and went very far,
leaving me alone, I don't know whether asleep or awake.

The poet is and is taken so 'far' away that conversation is never
practicable. She goes back over the evolutionary map, traversing
regions returned to us as 'trophies' by the Parnassians: the
German iron age, classical Greece, Celtic gold, stone age menhirs
to the cradle of civilization and then the dark chaos that preceded
it. In other words, spatial and temporal dimensions are as fixed
as they were generally for nineteenth century Europe, something
one could become aware of but hardly throw off or wholly transcend. In the final lines the function of imagination, of the denial of
the frontier between waking and dreaming, contrasts sharply, in
this respect, with that of Darío's, as Machado is left alone with
fantasy:

> Siguió; y a lo lejos,
> perdióse en las selvas
> oscuras del sueño,

> dejándome solo,
> no sé si dormido o despierto.

She went on; and far off she was lost in the dark forests of sleep, leaving me alone, I don't know whether asleep or awake.

When he came to Madrid and established himself there in the first years of this century, Darío had the kind of disturbing prestige enjoyed by Pound and Eliot in London not long afterwards. An account of his effect on peninsular poets, and of Modernism in Spain, lies outside our scope, happily so since the subject remains polemical still,[21] though few would deny that he inspired not just Manuel Machado but his brother Antonio, Juan Ramón Jiménez, Gregorio Martínez Sierra, Ramón del Valle-Inclán, and many others. As far as his own writing is concerned, his experience of Spain urged him, perhaps for the first time, to self-definition within and against an environment. His next collection, *Cantos de vida y esperanza* (Songs of Life and Hope), published in Madrid in 1905, gives us a new reflective and explicit mode, as well as oratorically 'American' pieces like the 'Salutation of the Optimist' and 'To Roosevelt', discussed in chapter 3. In the poem which opens as follows, for example, he delimits the range of the 'Colloquy' ('for you . . . thought is in the sacred seed') and still more of 'Divagation' by admitting a given and unalterable situation:

> Carne, celeste carne de la mujer! Arcilla,
> – dijo Hugo –; ambrosía más bien, ¡oh maravilla!
> La vida se soporta,
> tan doliente y tan corta,
> solamente por eso:

Flesh, celestial flesh of woman! Clay – said Hugo; ambrosia rather, oh marvel! Life, so painful and so short, can be tolerated only because of this.

The way he transferred his immense rhetorical subtlety to the purpose of intimating something that 'might have been' becomes quite clear in his 'autumnal sonnet' to the Marquis of Bradomín (i.e. Valle-Inclán):

> Marqués (como el Divino lo eres), te saludo.
> Es el Otoño, y vengo de un Versalles doliente.
> Había mucho frío y erraba vulgar gente.

El chorro de agua de Verlaine estaba mudo.
Me quedé pensativo ante un mármol desnudo,
cuando vi una paloma que pasó de repente,
y por caso de cerebración inconsciente
pensé en ti. Toda exégesis en este caso eludo.

Marquis (like the Divine one [i.e., Sade] you are that), I salute you. It's autumn and I come from an ailing Versailles. It was very cold and ordinary people were wandering about. Verlaine's water jet was mute. ¶I remained thoughtful before a naked marble statue, when I saw a dove suddenly pass by, and through a case of unconscious cerebration I thought of you. All exegesis in this case I avoid.

The very pretence that he does not want exegesis, philosophy after rather than before the fact, poignantly serves to point up his involvement in it. The novel alexandrine (with its quietly forced shift of caesura) which tells us of his unconscious cerebration presupposes a sober regress to a position where 'life' and 'hope' can indeed be conceptualized as such, and contemplated from a distance. Other poems in this collection ('Lo fatal' and the Nocturne that begins 'You who auscultate the heart of the night') announce a black pessimism in dualist contrast with the enthusiasm of before, in what might now be more accurately termed his pan-eroticism.

Of course, Darío's spiritual history should no more be equated with his expressive powers as a poet than it should with the history of Modernism as a whole. This collection, like El Canto errante (1907), contains some of his most accomplished poems. And by the time he died, in 1916, poor, sad and disoriented, Spanish American poetry was incomparably richer than it had been when he was born.[22] Guillermo Valencia had reflected maturely on the achievement of his compatriot and predecessor in 'Leyendo a Silva' (Reading Silva); and José Santos Chocano had propagated his mundonovismo. Before renouncing Modernist 'aestheticism' and striving for sincerity (with dubious results), Amado Nervo was liberated by the skill of 'Divagation' to write poems like 'Edelweiss'. In the River Plate countries the sonnet had acquired unprecedented subtlety at the hands of Julio Herrera y Reissig, and of Leopoldo Lugones in Crepúsculos del jardin (Twilights of the Garden, 1905). A subsequent collection of Lugones's, Lunario sentimental (Sentimental Lunary, 1909) drew on the more recent discovery of Laforgue, like Eliot's Prufrock (compare especially 'Claro de luna' with 'Conversation galante'),[23] and in turn was an important stimulus to the Mexican Ramón López Velarde, a poet of highly intelligent self-exploration. In José Emilio Pacheco's words, López Velarde 'splendidly closes Mexican Modernism and, at the same time as Tablada, converts it into modernity, a foundation stone of our contemporary poetry'.[24] From an early association with Gutiérrez Nájera's *Revista Azul*, José Juan Tablada went on to compose haikus, and then calligrammes in the style of Apollinaire, and to make poetry out of the language of modern media, as indeed did Darío in his newspaper poem 'Agencia':

> ¿Qué hay de nuevo?... Tiembla la tierra.
> En La Haya incuba la guerra.
> Los reyes han terror profundo.
> Huele a podrido en todo el mundo.
> No hay aromas en Galaad.
> Desembarcó el marqués de Sade
> procedente de Seboím.
> Cambia de curso el gulf-stream.

What's new?... The earth quakes. In The Hague war is brewing. Royalty is seriously afraid. The whole world smells bad. There are no aromas in Galaad. The Marquis de Sade disembarked, arriving from Seboim. The gulf stream is changing course.

One of the best poems of Darío's second period[25] (and of the second stage of Modernism as a whole, in so far as one can generalize about that), is his 'Epistle' to Leopoldo Lugones's wife. There he describes, to her, another divagation, but a 'real' one this time: his own journeying from Antwerp to Buenos Aires, Rio, Paris and Palma, Mallorca, in 1906. His letter belongs to a distinguished poetic tradition in Spanish, which began with Garcilaso's epistle to Boscán in the sixteenth century, but is remarkable even within it. He can invoke shared understanding: 'My Brazilian dithyramb is a dithyramb that your husband would approve. *Arcades ambo.*' Or, in Mallorca: 'Sometimes I go down to the market (Quite Coppée, isn't it?).' Or, relying precisely on this sense of intimacy, he can indulge in what he will then call, in gracious retreat, 'mucha poesía': agonized questionings into the meaning of his life, laments for the way his idealism has been undermined by overwork and ill-health, and by exploitative friends, and now appears unreal in prosaic modern reality. The degree to which his private letter is in fact a poem for itself, or

for any one else, can be measured in an amusing aside like the
following:

> Las mallorquinas usan una modesta falda,
> pañuelo en la cabeza y la trenza en la espalda.
> (Esto, las que yo he visto al pasar, por supuesto.
> Y las que no la llevan, no se enojen por esto.)

The Mallorcan girls wear a modest skirt, a kerchief on their heads and a
plait on the back. (That is, those I've seen passing by, of course. Those who
don't should not feel upset.)

In alexandrines more supple than any written in Spanish before,
he ranges from the conversational to the public, from place to
himself, from persuasive optimism to melancholic aside, in ways
which Apollinaire was only then beginning to do in French. And
just as 'Zone' presupposed the evolution of French poetry in the
nineteenth century, so Darío's epistle could hardly have been
written without the prior fact of Modernism.

He opens in light vein, with a couplet in French and a deliberately weak pun in Spanish:

> Madame Lugones, j'ai commencé ces vers
> en écoutant la voix d'un carillon d Anvers . . .
> Así empecé, en francés, pensando en Rodenbach,
> cuando hice hacia el Brasil una fuga . . . ¡de Bach!

Thus I began, in French, thinking of Rodenbach, when I made a 'fugue'
to Brasil. . .of Bach!

Still standing back from the poem proper, he says that in Rio (at
the Inter American Conference) he 'was going to' make verse out
of the beauty of that place. In fact he only talks *about* the gold and
sapphire, the love and the dream, vaguely aware of being in a
false position: 'I panamericanized with a vague unease and very
little faith.' For the moment he avoids this tension by that intimate
appeal to the pastoral convention (*arcades ambo*) mentioned
above. In the second section, however, the very power of Brazil,
as a phenomenon for itself, 'so fertile, so great, so rich, so beautiful'
precipitates deep despair about his old ambitions as a poet. Defen-
sively, he makes a point of honour of his own ceaseless need to
work ('I have squeezed the cerebral udder so often that I'm in a
bad way') and suggests that being a poet was simply much easier
for someone with Garcilaso's advantages. But it is only in the
following section, back in Paris, the 'real' Paris that balefully

complements the cultural illusion of the Modernists, that he goes
beyond sarcasm to self-reflection of this order:

> Y me volví a París. Me volví al enemigo
> terrible, centro de las neurosis, ombligo
> de la locura, foco de todo surmenage,
> donde hago buenamente mi papel de sauvage
> encerrado en mi celda de la rue Marivaux,
> confiando sólo en mí y resguardando el yo.
> ¡Y si lo resguardara, señora, si no fuera
> lo que llaman los parisienses una pera!...

And I went back to Paris. I went back to the terrible enemy, centre of
neuroses, navel of madness, focus of all *surmenage*, where I obediently
play my part as *sauvage* closeted in my cell in rue Marivaux, trusting
only in myself and defending my ego. If I only could defend it, señora,
and weren't what the Parisians call *une poire* . . .

In one interpretation it was just the naïvety exposed in this outburst, and what he calls 'my damned sentimental vision of the
world' (with its attendant aestheticism), that had made his poetic
adventure possible in the first place. Yet, thus curtailed, the
movement of 'Divagation' survives, and indeed is poetically enhanced, notably when he moves on again, to the island of Mallorca.
Sections 4 to 6 are masterful for the way they present a place and
him in it, and for the integration of narrative and mood, immediate
reality and literary consciousness. The gourds and turnips in the
market offer material to 'Madame Noailles and Francis Jammes
alike', exotic and domestic. In his villa he says he keeps a Christ
and a mauser, as the poet Nervo was reputed to, stating and
alleviating his solitude. His initial description of the island, in the
Catalan of Jacinto Verdaguer, as 'la terra dels foners', the land of
the slingers, insinuates a metaphor that later emerges to prime
importance for his understanding of himself. But prior to that
(in section 5), standing before the house of the great medieval
figure Ramon Lull, he opens into eulogy which implicates him
profoundly. In the suppressed and then marginal glory of Cata-
lonia and Mallorca, in the 'sublime exile' of Lull, 'the brother of
Dante', he finds, quite exceptionally, something like a term, a
paternal fixity, a notion of origin at least by analogy.

> mas Ramón Lull es el limosnero de Hesperia,
> injerto en el gran roble del corazón de Iberia,
> que necesita el Hércules fuerte que le sacuda
> para sembrar de estrellas nuestra tierra desnuda.

But Ramon Lull is the alms-giver of Hesperia, grafted on to the great oak of the heart of Iberia, that needs strong Hercules to shake it to sow our poor naked land with stars.

As no one else, Lull embodies a world culture that did not have a Castilian root, and rescuing and ransoming him is altogether akin to the effort of becoming, himself, something else as an American. But as he implies, in one or other case, it may not be he who performs the Herculean task.

The oscillation of his moods, persistent since the opening, becomes noticeably stronger in the long penultimate section (6), where the poem encompasses its widening subject by yet more nervous association. A storm brews up, so boats seek shelter : why can't others take refuge there from 'their Babylon, their Tyre, their Babel'. One who has done is of the type of Jean Orth, an archduke of the Austrian empire who one day renounced all his titles, all the weight of the old world, and disappeared completely. With another quick association he tells us that the air in Mallorca favours all the arts and invokes Santiago Rusiñol, the painter who had inspired the *Festes modernistes* there in the 1890s. But as if that 'programme' were too easy he thinks immediately of 'la literata' George Sand's prior visit there with 'poor Chopin'. There follows this confession (which gave Octavio Paz the touchstone for his essay on Darío, 'El caracol y la sirena'):

¡Oh qué buen mallorquín me sentiría ahora!
¡Oh cómo gustaría sal de mar, miel de aurora,
al sentir como en un caracol en mi cráneo
el divino y eterno rumor mediterráneo!

Hay en mí un griego antiguo que aquí descansó un día
después que le dejaron loco de melodía
las sirenas rosadas que atrajeron su barca.
Cuanto mi ser respira, cuanto mi vista abarca,
es recordado por mis íntimos sentidos:
los aromas, las luces, los ecos, los ruidos,
como en ondas atávicas me traen añoranzas
que forman mis ensueños, mis vidas y esperanzas.

Mas ¿dónde está aquel templo de mármol, y la gruta
donde mordí aquel seno dulce como una fruta?
¿Dónde los hombres ágiles que las piedras redondas
recogían para los cueros de sus hondas?...

Oh what a good Mallorcan I should now feel myself to be! Oh how I should taste sea-salt, honey of dawn, feeling as in a shell in my skull the divine and eternal Mediterranean murmur! ¶There is in me an ancient Greek who rested here one day after the rosy sirens who had drawn his boat had left him mad with melody. Everything my being breathes, everything my sight encompasses, is remembered by my intimate senses: the smells, lights, echoes, noises, as in atavistic waves bring me yearning which forms my dreams, my lives and hopes. ¶But where is that marble temple, and the cave where I bit that breast soft like a fruit? Where the lithe men who gathered the round stones for the leather pouch of their slings?...

Though he apologizes to Juana de Lugones for them, these lines well catch the function of his imagination as he had come to understand it. Sight and sound are preternatural because they are remembered from another time and place. He, part-Indian and from Nicaragua, could not have known them, for that reason, and because such intensity is neither more nor less possible for any modern poet. He saw himself as David against a thousand and was more likely 'a light stone that returns to the sling'.[26] But now, the real world, which abruptly returns with the sight of commercial shipping off the coast, can hardly threaten his vision, since his poetry, at last, expresses them both. His request, in the final lines, runs:

> Mírame transparentemente, con tu marido,
> y guárdame lo que tú puedas del olvido.

Look at me transparently, with your husband, and keep for me what you can from oblivion.

# 5. Brazilian Modernism

Apart from their name and their apostolic role, the Brazilian and the Spanish American Modernists have little in common. The Brazilians' desire to be literarily 'modern' sprang not from nineteenth century Europe (above all France), but arose after the First World War under the stimulus of the Futurists and the Surrealists. Another difference is that while Modernism in the Spanish language can not too unreasonably be traced in the work of one writer (Darío), in Brazil no single figure emerges, definition and story being sooner afforded by place. For the Brazilians the expanding São Paulo of the 1920s provided a focus that the Spanish Americans, dispersed over the continent, found only limitedly in Buenos Aires. In what they wrote we get a much stronger sense of locality, of street politics even, and of the writer, like the painters and musicians of Modernism, as an artist in an immediate situation. Darío's letter to Lugones's wife, recalling shared values over immense distance, characterizes the specifically literary context of Spanish American Modernism. By contrast, São Paulo was performance, never more so than during the famous week of Modern Art there in February 1922. In this centenary year of Brazil's Independence, Villa Lobos's music, Brecheret's massive sculptures, Anita Malfatti's paintings, as well as literature by Oswald and Mário de Andrade, Guilherme de Almeida, Ronald de Carvalho, Menotti del Picchia, Manuel Bandeira, Sérgio Milliet, Ribeiro Couto and others, were presented as a communal message.

These qualities of Brazilian Modernism have encouraged critics to dwell on context: groups, tactics, manifestos, journals, what was said and done about poetry. There are several histories of the movement,[1] excellently documented in these terms, which divide it into phases or stages: after the 'heroic' fervour of the Modern Art week, the in-fighting between the *Pau-Brasil* group and their yet more nationalist rivals. And then, poets still being linked by their personal reactions to each other, the sober contribution of the *Festa* group from Rio; and finally the 'fourth stage' or generation of 1945, as exemplified by Cabral de Melo Neto, an important precursor in turn of the concrete poets of more recent decades. All this no doubt makes sense; but it has meant in practice that texts, when quoted, have tended to be illustrations of this or that event. Sometimes the consequent loss may be small, as in the case of Almeida's peroration 'Nós' (We):[2]

> NOS. Branco–verde–prêto: simplicidades–
> indolências–supersticões.
>
> O quarto-de-hóspede e a pousada – a rêde e o cigarro
> de palha – o São Benedito e as assombracões.
>
> NOS. O clã fazendeiro. Sombra forte de mangueiras pelo
> chão: recorte nítido de bananeiras pelo ar;

We. White–green–black: simplicities–indolences–superstitions. ¶The lodging house and the inn – the hammock and the cigar – the Sanbenito and the spiritualist frights. ¶We. The hacienda clan. Strong shade from mango trees on the ground: clean silhouette of banana trees in the air;

Other times, as in the case of the first important literary work of the Modernists, Mário de Andrade's *Paulicéia desvairada* (1922), the loss has been little short of disastrous.

This celebration of São Paulo, translated as *Hallucinated City*,[3] is made up of 'An extremely interesting preface', twenty one poems and a concluding oratorio entitled 'The moral Fibrature of the Ipiranga'. Because of the lively force of its insults, one of the most frequently quoted poems in the book is the 'Ode to the Bourgeois', which begins:

> Eu insulto o burguês-níquel,
> o burguês-burguês!
> A digestão bem feita de São Paulo!
> O homem-curva! o homem-nádegas!

I insult the bourgeois! The metal money bourgeois, the bourgeois-bourgeois! The well-made São Paulo digestion! The belly-man! the buttocks-man!

The message seems simple enough. True to type, the bourgeois are the dumb owners of the city, well-fed and cautious, 'guardians of tradition', not so much insensitive to art as unable to see that their idea of it excludes the excitement of modernity. Their heroes are the Parnassians, Raimundo Correia, Alberto de Oliveira, Olavo Bilac, the safe and consecrated artists of Rio de Janeiro, the political capital, who remained loyal to the idea of the Empire (which lasted under the two Pedros from 1822 to 1888) in their insistence on correct Portuguese, and who matched the ideals of the Republic with their taste for civilized clarity. These burghers thus ignore São Paulo as a New World city, with its amazing growth and turbulence. Their conservatism means that this hallucinated city has 'no poetry, no joy, no wings', a refrain which occurs at least four times in different poems in Andrade's collection. There can be no doubt that the Futurists' enthusiasm for the speed and technology of 'modern capitals' provided just the right stimulus for the Modernists after Oswald de Andrade first brought back news of Marinetti from Paris in 1912. Though he felt less fetishistic about the 'externals of modern life' (and said so in his preface) Mário de Andrade crowded his poems with telephones, Cadillacs, women more purposefully emancipated than Gutiérrez Nájera's or Darío's ever were, cinemas and electric street cars sizzling through the night ('like skyrockets clicking their heels on the tracks').

Thus far, the 'hatred and execration' of the stodgy burgher in Andrade's Ode is hardly problematic. Indeed, much early Modernist writing amounted to little more than its final expletives. But the point about the Ode, as about any one piece in *Hallucinated City*, is that it cannot be read independently of the others, any more than the 'theories' advanced from time to time in the preface can be labelled Andrade's, in disregard of the way they are presented. There is in fact no lack of clues to how much the Ode is not 'his' pronouncement, but a kind of motif, the most obvious being the Oratorio at the end. There we find a cast of singers actually embodying the alternatives of the 'São Paulo situation', the bourgeois and their opponents alike, in dramatic balance. Variously located in the Automobile Club, the City Hall, the Carlton Hotel, the bourgeois are styled 'tremulous senilities'; their tame poets are the 'conventional orientalisms', an imposing array at the windows of the Municipal Theatre. The workers and the poor stand down below as 'indifferent pallbearers', carrying the cultural corpse of old Brazil, while 'We', the 'gilt-green youths', are further off, with feet sunk in the soil of Anhangabaú Park. As a separate entity, Andrade's own 'madness' circulates among them.

The Oratorio might be thought silly, an objection anticipated in the final stage direction ('there grows a great cacophony of whistles, cat-calls and stamping of feet'). But any inadequacy would by no means be that of a manic manifesto: one thing

Andrade unquestionably succeeds in is matching enormous verve
with reflexive irony. This quality is both more pronounced and
more refined in other poems in the book and in the preface. The
detachment and elusive movements of the character 'My Madness'
are interiorized within and between poems, to produce what
Andrade half-seriously calls the effect of an arpeggiated chord.
Instead of a melodic 'I' he wants polyphony, words, phrases and
whole poems arranged to give 'the same sensation of overlay',
specifically appropriate to a situation devoid of tonic or norm.
This can be understood socially – the 'indifferent pallbearers' fail
to provide a ground bass – or culturally, Brazil's 'Latin' heritage
seeming at best evanescent. Anhangabaú Park, like his Brazil, is:

> Meu querido palimpsesto sem valor!
> Crônica em mau latim
> cobrindo uma écloga que não seja de Virgilio!...

My beloved and worthless palimpsest! Chronicle in bad Latin covering
an eclogue that is not exactly by Virgil!...

Excision or quotation from *Hallucinated City*, then, is indeed open
to abuse. In the larger context of the work, the insulting voice of
the Ode is in fact a leitmotiv, part of a Wagnerian consignment
from a whole 'Eldorado of the Unconscious'.

To get this consignment across, to smuggle it past 'what Freud
called censorship' [*Zensur*], Mário de Andrade both orchestrates
it in this way, and, further, will appear to act as a censor himself
by standing outside his poem. For example, he suddenly shuts his
enthusiasm into a saloon car, along with the energetic Modernist
Oswald de Andrade:

> Nada de asas! nada de poesia! nada de alegria!
> A bruma neva...Arlequinal!
> Mas viva o Ideal! God save the poetry!

> –Abade Liszt da minha filha monja,
> na Cadillac mansa e glauca da ilusão,
> passa o Oswald de Andrade
> mariscando gênios entre a multidão!...

No wings! no poetry! no joy! The mist snows...Harlequinate! But long
live the Ideal! God save poetry! ¶Abbé Liszt of my daughter the nun,
in the gentle sea-green Cadillac of illusion, Oswald de Andrade goes by
fishing for geniuses in the crowd.

Phrases from the most various sources (the description of Oswald was taken from a local newspaper) succeed each other, leaving 'him' both in and out of the dream. Like Eliot's in *The Waste Land* (published the same year as *Hallucinated City*), his diction ranges from the impassioned to the neutral, from classical allusion to the street slogan and the colloquial, this being as much an innovation in Portuguese[4] as it was in English. And like Eliot he hides in his poem, the better to see, the omnipresent eye in this case being glimpsed in a parenthetical phrase like 'So behold him on the throne of the All-seeing Crossed Eye' (previously São Paulo is said to be the throne). Though arguably he had less to hide, Andrade, too, had a similar ambiguity in suggesting a 'key' to his poem, fragmenting and concealing himself, and yet leaving an intricate pattern of clues to identity, mainly in allusion to classical myth. In Andrade's case the all-knowing observer, Eliot's Tiresias, is Amphion: 'a new, dark and bespectacled Amphion, I shall make the very stones rise up like a wall at the magic of my song. And within these walls we shall sequester our tribe.' The echo of Mallarmé is more inebriated than Eliot's, and the tribe needs not purer words in an impure city ('donner un sens plus pur aux mots de la tribu'), but a new Thebes to resonate in.

In any interpretation, Mário de Andrade commands respect as one of the first urban poets of Latin America, as someone who attempted (like the New York school of more recent decades) to register the discontinuous complexity of any modern urban 'story'. He differs from Eliot (and so from Mallarmé, and above all Baudelaire, with his 'immonde cité') simply in not wanting to think a 'new spirit' necessarily and quite dead: 'liberation' never means there might be somewhere *else*. If he says 'futility, civilization', it is as an ironic remark after stanzas like this:

> Central. Drama de adultério.
> A Bertini arranca os cabellos e morre
> Fugas...Tiros...Tom Mix!
> Amanhã fita alemã...de beiços...
> As meninas mordem os beiços pensando em fita alemã...
> As romas de Petronio...
> E o leito virginal...Tudo azul e branco!
> Descansar...Os anjos...Imaculado!
> As meninas sonham masculinidades...
> – Futilidade, civilização.

Main jail. Drama of adultery. Bertini tears her hair and dies. Getaways... Shots...Tom Mix! German film tomorrow...gratis...The girls bite their lips thinking about German films. . .The romes of Petronius. . .And the virgin's bed. . .All blue and white! Rest. . .Angels. . .Immaculate! The girls dream masculinities. . . – Futility, civilization.

In geography the walls of the main jail ('Central') are coincident with the possibly resonant walls of Thebes. The extravagance and dispersal of the poems is continuously matched by a movement back to this base (which, ideally, might itself be transformed). At the height of the insulting 'Ode to the bourgeois', the burghers are marched two by two back to the same prison, to 'the Main Jail of my inebriating rancour'.

In *Hallucinated City* we become aware of an agonized, inextricable involvement in urban society of just the kind that animates the novels of Machado de Assis. And it is no accident that Andrade, in his preface and in more than one poem, refers to this brilliant citizen of late nineteenth century Rio. For, as Amphion (who, besides raising the walls of Thebes, avenged his mother by killing Lycus, ruler of the town, only then to kill himself); as Watteau's 'L'Indifférent'; as Harlequin or the happy clown; or even as 'a Tupi Indian strumming a lute', he strongly resembles the Braz Cubas whose 'memoirs' constitute Machado de Assis's best work.[5] He is mesmerized by the beauty of the burgher's woman yet cannot authorize a new love for himself and her, cannot fully authorize his 'illusion' or his 'hallucination', and instead plays its dazzling possibilities against what is. He is enmeshed and knows it. The 'triangle' (of adultery) which enhanced and wasted Braz's life is alluded to again and again: 'Triangle. There are sailing ships for my shipwrecks'; 'There's no more room in this triangular belvedere', and so on. Again, the extraordinary agility with which he proposes and withdraws theories in his preface unmistakably recalls Braz's (compare: 'A little theory?' and 'I think I shall withdraw the analogy'). The main difference between them is that Andrade is not writing 'Posthumous Memoirs', but would express, however helplessly, 'this supreme pride of being *paulistamente* (in São Paulo fashion)'.

As the most articulate poet of early Modernism Mário de Andrade was, then, not the wholly blank enemy of the burgher. For all his rhetorical iconoclasm he did not altogether renounce the idea of a civilized metropolitan 'tradition', which would have its connections with Rio. His notes[6] on the last book of the Rio Parnassian Bilac, *Tarde* (1919), for example, emphasize this. Referring to it as an apogee, he speaks of the Modernists' efforts as a new phase, on the same graph. And insofar as he hinted that his energy was suicidal, harlequinate, in a bootless conflict with Lycus, he left very much open to question what he meant by his 'shocking' remark in 'The Modern Artist': 'in reality we are primitives'.

In his role as agent and friend, Oswald de Andrade made something of a response to it in his *Pau-Brasil* (Brazil Wood, 1925). Here we find the desire to be less rigorously civilized, to be more in touch with the grass roots of Brazil. Oswald even went back on his enthusiasm for such earlier mentors as Marinetti, Apollinaire and Breton because they were too 'European', and first adopted the more-national-than-thou attitude which came to characterize the poetry of the later 1920s. Of course the Modernists had shown some local atavism from the start. At one with the ordinary citizens of São Paulo they had urged that Brecheret's statue of the *bandeirantes* (the 'banner bearers' who had founded São Paulo and won so much land to the west for the Brazilian language) should be sited in Anhangabaú Park, in the centre of the town. And the manly race (*raça heril*) of the past which it commemorated was acclaimed more than once in *Hallucinated City*:

> Revivei, oh gauchos paulistas ancestremente!
> e oh cavalos de cólera sanguinea!

Revive, oh ancestrally Paulista gauchos! and oh horses of blood-red rage!

Here the civilized modernity of the Modernists is being tempered not by the self-doubt of Amphion but by a motif of fairly crude atavism. Interestingly, this is just what happened in Buenos Aires at the same period,[7] among the 'Ultraists' of the *Martín Fierro* and *Proa* groups (among whom the young Borges was prominent): though 'avant-garde', the Ultraists came to admire a writer like Ricardo Güiraldes who made a mystique of the gaucho and old creole values in *Don Segundo Sombra* (1926). And both these American developments, Brazilian and Argentinian, might illuminatingly be compared in turn with Mussolini's fascism in Italy at the same period, when the Futurist Marinetti turned to evoking the grandeur of the national past. However here it is enough to say that the *bandeirismo* (as it was called) of the Brazilian Modernists, the primitivist, historical and regional enthusiasm provoked by *Pau-Brasil*, was a complex and symptomatic event, and was intricately linked to the extreme, perhaps excessive urban consciousness of *Hallucinated City* and the early 1920s.

The Modernists' *bandeirismo* led among other things to the defiantly Brazilian journal *Verde amarelo*, which took its title from the colours of the national flag, green and yellow. Those associated with it, Menotti del Picchia, Cassiano Ricardo and others, chastized the Andrade of *Pau-Brasil* for not going far enough, for being too dependent still on writers like Breton, and on 'European primitivism' generally. (They no doubt resented the fact that Andrade published his book in Paris.) Picchia's unambiguous title *República dos Estados Unidos do Brasil* (1928), and Ricardo's *Martim Cererê* of the same year, came to celebrate a nationhood confirmed by fixed frontiers not many years previously, by relating in would-be epic fashion the native particularities of the place and the grandeur of the Discovery:

> A convite da História Universal
> que havia marcado a festa para 21 de Abril,
> o almirante Pedro Alvares Cabral
> veio com uma frota de luzidas caravelas
> num séquito naval de mastros e de velas,
> de estandartes e de cruzes,
> de sotainas, alabardas, couraças e arcabuzes
> inaugurar a futura República
> dos Estados Unidos do Brasil.
>
> (Menotti del Picchia, 'A Inauguração')

By invitation of Universal History which had marked the festival for 21 April, admiral Pedro Alvares Cabral came with a fleet of resplendent caravels in a naval procession of masts and sails, of banners and crosses, of cassocks, halberds, armour and harquebuses, to inaugurate the future Republic of the United States of Brazil.

Coming after the exploratory efforts of the Modernists, including Picchia himself at an earlier stage, this kind of public bombast recalls the worst of the 'New World' mode which José Santos Chocano developed out of Spanish American Modernism. More engaging were the Pan-American efforts of Ronald Carvalho in *Tôda a América* (1926) with its continental sweep. (Carvalho was as unusual in his attention to Spanish America as Neruda was later in his to Brazil, and it is not impossible that at this level at least the Chilean poet learned something from the Spanish translation of Carvalho's book.)[8] Even so, and despite the constant echoes of

Whitman, old problems of identity and location remained un-
resolved, with the result that the best parts of the book are mosaics
of landscapes from various areas of the continent, with thoughts
about what America's poet might one day be like:

> Teus poetas não são dessa raça de servos
> que dançam no compasso de gregos
> e latinos,
> teus poetas devem ter as mãos sujas de
> terra, de seiva e limo,
> as mãos da criação!

> Teu poeta será ágil e inocente, América!
> a alegria será a sua sabedoria,
> a liberdade será a sua sabedoria,
> e sua poesia será o vagido da tua própria
> substância, América, da tua própria
> substância lírica e numerosa.

Your poets are not of that race of slaves who dance to the rhythm of
Greeks and Latins, your poets must have their hands dirty with earth, with
sap and mud, hands of creation!... ¶Your poet will be agile and innocent,
America! Joy will be his knowledge, liberty will be his knowledge, and
his poetry will be the birth-cry of your own substance, America, of your
own lyrical and numerous substance.

For a deeper awareness of the problems of being an American
poet, even if only within Brazil, we have to turn again to the
Andrades, who formulated them in terms interestingly similar to
Neruda's, though neither of them went on to produce anything
like *Canto general*. The first premise of Oswald de Andrade's
cannibalistic manifesto in the *Revista de Antropofagia* (1928) was
that Independence had not yet been won, that economically and
culturally Brazil still depended on Europe. Addressing the rubber-
tapper from Brazil's deep south in *Clã do Jabuti* (of the previous
year), Mário agreed, saying:

> Fomos nós dois que botamos
> Pra fora Pedro II...
> Somos nós dois que devemos
> Até os olhos da cara
> Pra êsses banqueiros de Londres...

It was we two who kicked out Pedro II... It is we two who are up to our
eyes in debt to those London bankers...

In *Pau-Brasil* Oswald de Andrade had spoken of the country as a
place where 'blood runs and gold is crated up', and now turned
against the whole 'social reality, dressed up and oppressive', and

centred in the capital Rio, which allows just this capitalist *modus vivendi* to go on. He urges that it was Brazil that provided Europe with its seeds of liberation in the first place: 'The contract with Carib Brazil. *Où Villeganhon print terre*, Montaigne. Natural Man. Rousseau. From the French Revolution to Romanticism, to the Bolshevist Revolution, to the Surrealist Revolution.'[9] Further: 'We already had communism. We already had surrealist language. The age of gold.' So that Brazilians would only be being true to their heritage by wanting the 'Carib Revolution', in which the strong avenging Jabuti, the hero of Mário de Andrade's collection of 1927, and brother of Neruda's subsequent Araucanian, asserts his presence. Rather than the inoffensive paragons, the toothless heroes of Alencar and the nineteenth century bourgeoisie (representatives of a hopelessly compromised Brazilian–Indian heritage) he proposes cannibals, ingestion of the enemy body and spirit in the name of a new American golden age:

> Absorption of the sacred enemy. To transform him into totem. The human adventure. The terrestial finality. And so, only the pure elites will manage to effect carnal anthropophagy, which bears in itself the highest sense of life and avoids all the evils identified by Freud, catechismal evils. What you don't get is a sublimation of the sexual instinct. That is the thermometric scale of the anthropophagic instinct. From being carnal it becomes elective and fosters friendship. Affective, love.

Oswald de Andrade was well-read, witty and relished his own contradictions. He speaks of the Brazilian jungle-men as if they were one among themselves and with him. The Tupi of the parody of Hamlet's speech (see p. 11) who are also represented in the manifesto by a song quoted in their language, are freely identified with their native enemies. And even so, they emerge as a less likely 'alternative' than the *bandeirante* João Ramalho, first citizen of his beloved São Paulo. And furthermore, as someone preferable to 'Christian sentimentalists' like Anchieta, Alencar or Gonçalves Dias, Ramalho is made into just the patriarch Oswald de Andrade himself never wholly ceased to be, for all his 'progress' and left-wing commitment.[10] He was keenest precisely as a parodist, exposing bad faith elsewhere perhaps, but loyal, finally and after all, only to his urban(e) *paulista* style, as in his version (in *Pau-Brasil*) of Gonçalves Dias's song of exile:[11]

> Não permita Deus que eu morra
> Sem que volte pra São Paulo

> Sem que veja a Rua 15
> E o progresso de São Paulo

May God not permit that I die without returning to São Paulo, without seeing Rua 15 and the progress of São Paulo.

The last quatrain of Gonçalves Dias's poem runs:

> Não permita Deus que eu morra,
> Sem que eu volte para lá;
> Sem que desfrute os primores
> Que não encontro por cá;
> Sem qu'inda aviste as palmeiras,
> Onde canta o Sabiá.

May God not permit that I die without going back there, without enjoying the perfection that I don't find here; without glimpsing the palms where the Sabia sings.

Camp or paradoxical as it may seem and may have seemed, Oswald de Andrade's anthropophagy left its mark, on Mário, who took it much more to heart, and Raul Bopp. Contriving initially to avoid moral and social embarrassment by writing an 'inoffensive book for children', Bopp plunged deep into the Brazilian interior in *Cobra Norato*. In an atmosphere of fairy-tale suspense and in language rich with phonetic effects and indigenous words, the snake-like hero goes in search of the magic daughter of a distant queen. But even in the maturer revised version of 1931 he never emerged from the realm of jungle fantasy 'on the left bank of the Amazon'. This was also the home of the hero of Mário de Andrade's novel *Macunaíma* (1928), who is however brought back to São Paulo, the considerable humour of this 'rhapsody' (probably his best work) deriving from this cultural clash. In his poems he agonized more directly about his own identity, as he had done in *Hallucinated City*, and would do until, once again like Eliot, he returned to the Christian faith. In the two poems in *Clã do Jabuti* dedicated to Ronald de Carvalho he faces himself in São Paulo like a blank page, in a 'discovery' notably different from Picchia's:

> Abancado à escrivaninha em São Paulo
> Na minha casa da rua Lopes Chaves
> De sopetão senti um friume por dentro.
> Fiquei trêmulo, muito comovido
> Com o livro palerma olhando pra mim.

Não vê que me lembrei que lá no norte, meu Deus!
  muito longe de mim

Na escuridão ativa da noite que caiu
Um homem pálido magro de cabelo escorrendo
  nos olhos,
Depois de fazer uma pele com a borracha do dia,
Faz pouco se deitou, está dormindo.

Esse homem é brasileiro que nem eu.

Installed at my desk in São Paulo, in my house in rua Lopes Chaves,
suddenly I felt a bitter cold inside, I shook, most moved, with the stupid
book looking at me. It doesn't see that I remember that there in the
north, dear God, very far from me, ¶in the active blindness of the night
that fell, a pale thin man with hair falling across his eyes, after making a
cover from the rubber tapped during the day, went to bed a short while
ago, and is sleeping. ¶That man is Brazilian just like I am.

The phrase 'Brasileiro que nem eu' comes back like a refrain in
the other poem (quoted above) to the rubber tapper of the jungles
in the south, haunting and enclosing him. Again, in 'Improviso
do Mal da América' (1928), looking around him in São Paulo at
the skyscrapers, the immigrants and Oswald de Andrade's 'progress', sensing that there may be another country 'in the im-
penetrable jungle of my being'[12] (the Indian praying in a stone
temple, the feats of the Chim communist guerrilla), he as it were
gathers his Modernism into suffocation and a final suicide:

Mas eu não posso, não, me sentir negro nem vermelho!
De certo que essas côres também tecem minha roupa arle-
  quinal,
Mas eu não me sinto negro, mas eu não me sinto vermelho,
Me sinto só branco, relumeando caridade e acolhimento,
Purificado na revolta contra os brancos, as pátrias, as guerras,
  as posses, as preguiças e ignorâncias!
Me sinto só branco agora, sem ar neste ar-livre da América!
Me sinto só branco, só branco em minha alma crivada de
  raças!

But I cannot, no, feel black or red! Certainly these colours also weave my
harlequinate clothing, but I don't feel black, but I don't feel red, I feel
only white, exuding charity and welcome, purified in the revolt against
the whites, fatherlands, wars, property, sloth and ignorance! I feel only
white, without air in this open air of America! I feel only white, only
white in my race-riddled soul!

Few poets associated with the Modernists in the 1920s avoided
this impasse. Those that did manage to by reverting to cleanly
'universal' concerns, like the Rio group in the early 1930s (one of

them, Schmidt, said he no longer wanted anything to do with 'Brazil' or with 'geography'); by politicizing themselves more thoroughly, like Carlos Drummond de Andrade; or by shifting the weight from São Paulo to less demandingly 'modern' parts of the United States of Brazil, by making a profession of regionality. This last course was especially favoured by the poets of Bahia and the north-east: Jorge de Lima who, as we saw, adopted the black idiom of that area; Manuel Bandeira, and in his way, João Cabral de Melo Neto. The best known poem of Bandeira's collection of 1930, *Libertinagem*, is in fact an evocation of his native Recife:

RECIFE
Não a Veneza americana
Não a Mauritsstad dos armadores das Indias Ocidentais
Não o Recife dos Mascates
Nem mesmo o Recife que aprendi a amar depois –
  Recife das revoluções libertárias
Mas o Recife sem história nem literatura
Recife sem mais nada
Recife da minha infância

Recife, not the American Venice, not the Mauritsstad of the outfitters of the West Indies, not the Recife of the Hawkers nor even the Recife that I learnt to love later – Recife of the libertarian revolutions. But the Recife without history or literature, plain Recife, Recife of my childhood.

The mood is openly nostalgic, for a lost childhood, a lost town, and even a lost Brazil:

Recife...
    Rua da União...
              A casa de meu avô...
Nunca pensei que ela acabasse!
Tudo lá parecia impregnado de eternidade
Recife...
    Meu avô morto.
Recife morto, Recife bom, Recife brasileiro como
              a casa de meu avô

Recife...Rua da União...My grandfather's house...I never thought that it could end! Everything seemed impregnated with eternity. Recife...My dead grandfather. Dead Recife, good Recife, Recife Brazilian like my grandfather's house.

As if sensing the insidious attraction of just such feelings Mário de Andrade had once warned the 'modern artist' in Brazil strongly against them, saying they were inappropriate to that 'constructive' period of Brazilian poetry.[13] And he attributed such states of *cisma* (or reverie) to intellectual fatigue, exemplified in the Old World even in a work like 'Panama' by Cendrars (at any event an important poet for Bandeira). As Andrade himself evolved so he softened his critique of the mood of *Libertinagem,* which Bandeira, always an ambiguous Modernist, had worked towards from his first mournful Rio collection *A Cinza das horas* (1917), through his crepuscular interest in Musset and Lenau and the latter-day Pierrots of *Carnaval* (1919), and then the 'place' poems of *O ritmo dissoluto* (The Untied Rhythm, 1924). For 'Evocation of Recife', if nostalgic, achieves a trueness of tone, a unanimity of voice, which it is hard to find precedents for in modern Brazilian poetry.

In his poem, Bandeira first appears, after the verbless invocation, as a boy telling things as he might have told them then, assuming general recognition for remote proper names:

> A Rua da União onde eu brincava de chicote-queimado
> e partia as vidraças da casa de
> dona Aninha Viegas
> Totônio Rodrigues era muito velho e botava o pincenê
> na ponta do nariz
> Depois do jantar as famílias tomavam a calçada
> com cadeiras, mexericos, namoros, risadas
> A gente brincava no meio da rua
> Os meninos gritavam:
>
> > Coelho sai!
> > Não sai!

The Rua da União where I played crack-the-whip and smashed the windows of dona Aninha Viegas's house, Totonio Rodriques was very old and wore his pince-nez on the tip of his nose. After eating, the families would take to the street with chairs, gossip, flirtation, laughter. People leapt about in the middle of the street. The children cried: Rabbit comes out! Doesn't come out!

The choral voices affirm a regular rhythm, 'socialize' the poem's atmosphere, as Mário de Andrade put it, referring to a later stanza, where Bandeira explicitly takes the popular spoken language of Brazil as his subject. There, with treacherous courtesy, Bandeira speaks of himself and his fellow poets as 'we', while in fact separating himself off from them. He states their popular inadequacy, in the most popular of rhythms and speech:

Vinha da bôca do povo na língua errada do povo
Língua certa do povo
Porque êle é que fala gostoso o português do Brasil
　　Ao passo que nós
　　O que fazemos
　　E macaquear
　　A sintaxe lusíada

came from the mouth of the people in the incorrect tongue of the people,
certain tongue of the people, for it is they who so relish Brazilian
rtuguese. While we, what we do is copy the syntax of the Lusiads.

his chant yields to the 'boyish' arrogance and the gangling
ngth of the next line: 'Life with a portion of things that I didn't
nderstand well.' In the person of the boy in Recife, by this and
her means, Bandeira acutely conveys nostalgia for a particular
lf that is his and his old community's: a sense of 'being alone
time' and yet part of something larger. One night there is a fire
nd he is too young to go and see it: the men who 'put on their
ts' and go out, smoking, are thus both domestic and mythical.
gain, into the story of his seeing a girl naked in a straw bathhouse
ear Caxangá, his first 'illumination', private and mystic, Recife
self is intercalated, at its most tangible:

　　Cheia! As cheias! Barro boi morto árvores destroços
　　　　　　　　redomoinho sumiu
　　E nos pegões da ponte do trem de ferro os caboclos
　　　　　destemidos em jangadas de bananeiras

lood! The floods! Mud dead ox trees debris submerged in the eddies.
nd between the pillars of the railway bridge the fearless mestizos on
anana-wood rafts.

In his 'Poetica' (as a whole one of the loosest poems in *Libertin-
gem*) Bandeira rejects 'all lyricism that capitulates to all that
vants it to be outside itself'. 'Evocation of Recife' (where the
own is origins, time and language) is the most capacious example
f a lyric 'self' otherwise contented with smaller though more
characteristic' expression. He wrote of the love he bore for the
guinea pig he had as a child; in six lines and with a local newspaper as a source, of João Gostoso who danced, sang and drowned
himself. Even such minimal pieces reveal a sly prickliness which
had been associated more than once with the cactus of another

poem, perhaps first of all, and slily, by Bandeira himself, t
cactus being from the north-east and 'enormous even for tl
region of exceptional fecundity':

> Um dia um tufão furibundo abateu-o pela raiz.
> O cacto tombou atravessado na rua,
> Quebrou os beirais do casario fronteiro,
> Impediu o trânsito de bondes, automóveis, carroças
> Arrebentou os cabos elétricos e durante vinte e quatro
>         horas privou a cidade de iluminação e energia:
> – Era belo, áspero, intratavel.

One day a furious gale tore it up by the roots. The cactus fell across t
street, broke the eaves of the house opposite, stopped the movement
trams, cars, cut the electric cables and for twenty-four hours depriv
the city of light and power: It was beautiful, harsh and intractable.

In this outlandish assault on the modern city there is a kind
'knowing innocence', a naturalness that is in fact worked fo
which he drew attention to in a telling remark on Carvalho's *Tôₐ
a América*. With his continental pretensions, Carvalho, he sai
could at best do no more than echo Whitman: these echoes migl
be perhaps more harmonious, but would always be 'less naïve
less "innocent" than *Leaves of Grass*'.[14] In other words, politel
criticizing Carvalho, Bandeira was again subtly pointing out th
problems of being an 'American' poet in Brazil, and, by puttin
'innocent' in quotation marks, was alerting us to just that am
biguous quality in himself: (It is not wholly misplaced to see hin
as Andrade's hero Macunaíma speaking as a poet.) A constan
danger for him was allowing his naïvety to become sentimental,
danger he avoided less well in later collections, in fond poems t
Alencar and in certain apparently pious religious pieces. That is
when he failed to allow the boy from Recife also to be gruff and
abrasive, or to match pure regional delight with an awareness o
the modern adult and urban world. Such an awareness certainly
sustains his evocation of Recife. More cunningly yet, it becomes ir
turn the source of humour for itself in 'Vou-me embora pra
Pasárgada' ('I'm off now to Pasargada'), a most modern city from
half remembered childhood reading of the classics:[15]

> Pra me contar as histórias
> Que no tempo de eu menino
> Rosa vinha me contar
> Vou-me embora pra Pasárgada

Em Pasárgada tem tudo
E outra civilização
Tem um processo seguro
De impedir a concepção
Tem teléfono automático
Tem alcalóide à vontade
Tem prostitutas bonitas
Para a gente namorar

To tell myself the stories that at the time I was a child Rosa came to tell me, I'm off now to Pasargada. ¶In Pasargada there is everything, it's another civilization. It has a sure method of contraception, it has automatic telephones, it has alkaloid for the asking, it has pretty prostitutes for the people to love.

Beyond a certain point it is not very helpful to think of Bandeira, or of the other poets who rose to prominence after about 1930, in terms of the Modernism elaborated, revised, propagated, and in part practised by the Andrades and others in São Paulo. Those historians of the 'movement' who proceed as if it were rightly observe a common tradition linking the Modernists with modern poets. Cecilia Meireles and other members of the *Festa* group in Rio (Schmidt, Carlos Drummond de Andrade, Vinícius de Moraes) admitted precedent by consciously reacting against it. And a poet as abstract as João Cabral de Melo Neto, at least in his earlier collections, can as a north-easterner be seen to develop the regionalist manner originally and paradoxically stimulated by the *paulistas* of the 1920s. In the smaller arena of Brazilian poetry, the Modernists of that language were still more crucial and provocative than their namesakes in Spanish America, being of course also nearer to us in time. Yet Brazilian poets of more recent decades are perhaps better understood in a larger than national context; and for that reason they are discussed in a later chapter.

# 6. Precedent, self and communal self: Vallejo and Neruda

In one of his rare excursions into literary criticism, in an essay of 1927,[1] César Vallejo said that Spanish American poets were no nearer than they had ever been to creating a 'spirit of their own'. He sympathized with the aims of the Modernists and guardedly admired Darío. Nevertheless, he said, his generation still depended abjectly on Europe; or worse, continued the false and explicit kind of Americanism typified by his compatriot Chocano.[2] In some respects Vallejo's concerns were similar to those of the Brazilian Modernists, at much the same period. In fact the story of Spanish American poetry after the First World War is more diffuse than that of Brazilian and more complicated than Vallejo would admit, or could even know. For example, the work of such poets as the Chilean Vicente Huidobro, a professional 'innovator' and friend of Reverdy and the Surrealists, or at the other extreme, of the Mexican provincial Ramón López Velarde, has been fully discovered only recently, as part of a poetic tradition charted by Octavio Paz (the subject of the next chapter). In any case, at that time Vallejo was sceptical about the whole idea of Spanish American poetry. He was publishing very little poetry himself at the time, and he saw little promise in others he mentioned by name, among them Pablo Neruda. Yet he and Neruda emerged as the great figures of the interwar years, and after; and then as major poets of the twentieth century, in whom old problems of cultural identity, and so on, are quite transformed. They proved so much richer than their contemporaries that for any historical understanding of the period we must turn almost exclusively to them, tracing their common evolution from the style of the Modernists, through intense introspection, to an ideal of communal self, an 'Internationalist' awareness of mankind.

By origin, both were provincial, natives of small towns on the far side of the Andes. César Vallejo was born in 1892, in Santiago de Chuco in northern Peru; Neftalí Ricardo Reyes (Neruda was a pen-name) in 1904, in Parral in central Chile (he grew up in Temuco further to the south). They went to the capitals of their respective countries (Lima, Santiago) in late adolescence and the experience was important to the first collections they published. They both then left America, a departure which had a crucial effect on their self-awareness. The Communist ideology they both came to defend was importantly linked to close knowledge of the Civil War in Spain, which provoked an important collection of poems from each of them. Within this pattern of development they differed considerably; comparing them at each stage seems a good way of approaching them both.

I

Vallejo's first book *Los Heraldos negros* (The Black Heralds, 1919) lacks conspicuous unity, being divided into six sections which have ostensibly little to do with each other. Perhaps the most arresting is that entitled 'Nostalgias imperiales' (Imperial Nostalgias) because in it we can see Vallejo moving from an explicitly Modernist manner to one which might be called embryonically his. Like Darío he is nostalgic in the first instance for the grandeur of America's past. Seeing an old Andean woman at her spinning, her disdainful mouth like 'the relief on a pre-Incaic block', he detects in her an 'imperial tiredness' and is reminded of the splendour proper to the 'sensual legendary Inca' of *Profane Prose*. On occasion Vallejo does in fact catch just that sense of aristocratic intoxication which marks Darío's collection: the comparison has often been made between his early poems and the opening lines of 'Era un aire suave' (a brilliant example of the Modernists' technical ability):

> Era un aire suave, de pausados giros:
> el hada Harmonía ritmaba sus vuelos,
> e iban frases vagas y tenues suspiros
> entre los sollozos de los violoncelos.

It was a gentle air, of paused turns: the fairy Harmony was rhyming her flights, and vague phrases went by and tenuous sighs among the sobs of the cellos.

This is palpably close to Vallejo's 'Nochebuena', and to 'Retablo' (originally entitled 'Simbolista') which refers explicitly to Darío, with his 'lyre in mourning':

> Con paso innumerable sale la dulce Musa,
> y a ella van mis ojos, cual polluelos al grano.

> La acosan tules de éter y azabaches dormidos,
> en tanto sueña el mirlo de la vida en su mano.

With an innumerable step the sweet muse comes out, and my eyes go towards her, like chickens to the seed. Tulles of ether and sleeping jets surround her, while the blackbird of life dreams in her hand.

Yet Vallejo's verse has 'homely' chickens in it, and indicate how he blends the lost 'high' cultures of the past into present Andean life and landscape. But at this stage these do not appear as an intrusive extra-literary reality: they are shaped by French writers whom he had read[3] and who had been important to certain Modernists if not Darío. Vallejo catches especially that Biblical sentimentality which emanated from Ernest Renan[4], and which affected the Uruguayan poet Julio Herrera y Reissig. His native countryside, its old church and way of life little disturbed since colonial days, acquires the features of the Holy Land: the fields around Mansiche are a 'biblical opuscule'; an Indian girl in the corn is Ruth. To this 'Hebraic unction' Vallejo, also in Modernist fashion, adds a classical one. A cow bell evokes the sound of a Virgilian hymn; a labourer passes by like an 'Incaic Achilles'. And so on.

Vallejo's recognition of Darío as 'cosmic', as 'the archpriest of the celestial Americas', though admiring, indicates the distance which in fact separates them. A *mestizo* like Darío (both his parents were the children of Spanish priests by local women), in the last instance he is less prepared to gloss over the fact literarily: he would later refer savagely to himself as 'your unforgettable *cholo*'.[5] In 'Oracle', for which he uses the Quechua word 'Huaco', he announces the nervousness and corrosiveness of his feelings within the legend. The *coraquenque* (the bird sacred to the royal Incas), the *coricancha* (the golden temple at Cuzco), and the 'old *yaraví*' of the Andes that adorns the sound of his poetry, are destroyed, as before, by a 'Latin harquebus'; but, more important, their glamour is radically undermined. Details of his 'ferment' (puma, phosphate) anticipate later poems.

> Yo soy el coraquenque ciego
> que mira por la lente de una llaga,
>
> . . .
>
> Soy el pichón de cóndor desplumado
> por latino arcabuz;
>
> . . .

Yo soy la gracia incaica que se roe
en áureos coricanchas bautizados
de fosfatos de error y de cicuta.
A veces en mis piedras se encabritan
los nervios rotos de un extinto puma.

I am the blind *coraquenque* who looks through the lens of a wound . . .
I am the young condor unfeathered by the Latin harquebus. . .! I am
that Inca grace gnawed at in golden coricanchas that are baptized with
phosphates of error and with hemlock. At times in my stones the broken
muscles of an extinct puma twitch.

The poem in 'Imperial Nostalgias' which reveals this mood most
keenly, and is furthest from the Hebraic or Classical Indian idylls
of the Modernists, is 'Hojas de ébano' (Leaves of Ebony). Here
Vallejo faces death not as a source of nostalgia, but as unease and
disintegration. He is there in the poem from the first line, impure
and intrusive like his cigarette: 'My cigarette glows; its light is
cleansed in powders of alert'. We gradually become aware of the
dark house in a mountain village, and of a recent death. The old
woman who has gone was close to him, an intimate childhood joy.
What he calls the 'grandmother bitterness' of the keening of her
death defeats his 'legendary muse', as it had once been defeated by
the Conquest. At the end, his inner ferment is dramatically opposed
to the starkness of the foursome vigil of the '*tahuashando* on the
path/with their ponchos of frost, hatless'.

The suggestion has been made that the death of Vallejo's
mother led him to recast this poem before publishing it in *The
Black Heralds*;[6] and it is appropriate that we should learn most
about his intimacy in another section of that book which presents
itself as familial: 'Canciones de hogar' (Home Songs). Here the
figures of his parents, his father, seventy-eight years old and 'an
evening', his mother, become 'so much love' with age, are the
term of his own distance. Down in Lima with its 'mortiferous'
rain he feels exiled from that 'eternal day' of childhood, 'a day
ingenuous, infant, choral, orational'. Memories of his brother
Miguel who died still a child put him back into a game of hide
and seek from which Miguel never emerged, and urge on him
even the language they spoke in common:

Y tu gemelo corazón de esas tardes
extintas se ha aburrido de no encontrarte. Y ya
cae sombra en el alma.

Oye, hermano, no tardes
en salir. Bueno? Puede inquietarse mamá.

And your twin heart of those extinct evenings got tired of not finding you.
And now shadow falls into the soul. ¶Hey, brother, don't be too long
coming out. All right? Mummy might get worried.

This apparently innocuous regression to child-like care erupts in
other poems into open defiance of God, erstwhile patron of a
harmonious world. Here his reading of the Spanish Romantics
(on whom he wrote a thesis in 1915), and of their predecessors,
the villains of Counter-Reformation theological drama, add grand
power to his protest, his 'thunder' as he put it.[7] From being a
possible source of reconciliation, Judeo-Christian faith becomes a
reason for pained and insistent blasphemy. Partly under the influence of the atheist reformer Manuel González Prada (to whom
one of these poems, 'Los dados eternos,' is dedicated), this leads
in turn to the intimation that his own needless sufferings are the
Black Heralds of a larger fate.

Disconsolate in Lima, Vallejo turned this way and that in
search of a spiritually orphaned self, and if the various sections
of *The Black Heralds* have a common preoccupation it would be
this. Orphaned that is, because, the youngest of eleven children
(he claimed twelve) he misses his family; because he could no
longer believe in Our Father; and because his 'imperial nostalgia'
grew too acute to be borne. Drawing all these things together,
he also lamented present insufficiency as the exile of maturity, in a
few unhappy love poems in the section 'De la tierra' (Of the Land)
and elsewhere. Making his sexuality the unavoidable enemy of
known happiness he echoes the medieval theologian Thomas
Aquinas in wishing to be the man who like God 'loves and engenders without sensual pleasure'. His language changed with
his mood and those he addressed; but we are often aware of him
breaching a given decorum: Modernist literariness, the Romantic
outcry, the conventional love poem. He breaks Hispanic taboos
left intact by Darío by inferring his racial origins (Darío was
always silent on this subject), and by exposing the intimacy of the
household. And in the family poems of the final section, for
example when he addresses Miguel, he speaks with a voice of his
own, and as no one had spoken before in Spanish.

From the very start Pablo Neruda was much more prolific and
publicly more successful than Vallejo (whose first book had a

quite mixed reception). What are merely sections in *The Black Heralds* correspond to whole collections with Neruda: by the time he was twenty-three he had written six volumes and had been sent abroad as a diplomat on the strength of one of them. Perhaps as a consequence his successive styles seem more easily won. In *Crepusculario* (1923), his first important collection, we again find a contrast between a lost childhood world and a present that the poet, removed to the capital, finds disagreeable. But the two times and places in question are less part of an intimate self-implicating process. By the same token the Modernist poems in this volume are far more obviously that, and are more separable as such: the section 'Pelleas y Melisanda' for example. Or the poem 'Tengo miedo' (I am Afraid), where he says: 'My heart has the sob of a princess/forgotten in the depths of a deserted palace.' To this extent his Modernism may be thought less an initiation than the illusion of a provincial, as it was for poets in Spain in the first decades of this century. For Neruda, as for Spaniards like Juan Ramón Jiménez, Darío is hardly a 'cosmic' presence, hardly a way of intuiting an imperium, a large America that was real even if now inaccessible. There is no Inca spinning woman to provide an ancestral and familial thread. Unlike the *coricancha*, Neruda's deserted palace is strictly nowhere, and his unease is unplaced.

Neruda's crepuscular nostalgia leaves him thoughtful enough, but on a margin. In a landscape poem like 'El pueblo' (The Village) there is a striking coincidence between him and Jiménez, who so purposefully immersed himself in the provincial Spanish countryside. In idyllic surroundings the noise of urban transport can just be heard and a grey sadness emanates from the long streets. The poet is barely held in the atmosphere of his poem, a precipitate in liquid; and the shadow of the hill covers him like 'a fresh rural Indian blanket': an American note perhaps, but with none of the demands and complications felt by Vallejo. In his room in Maruri Street in Santiago, where much of *Crepusculario* was composed, Neruda's principal occupation was watching the sun set. This sought and repeated experience had its own vague nostalgia, its *saudade*, its lonely melancholy: a luxury Vallejo never allowed himself. So that when Neruda does put his physical self, his person, into one of his sunset poems, it is less awkwardly part of 'him', and does not preclude an almost effortless pantheism and release into a greater whole:

Yo no sé por qué estoy aquí, ni cuándo vine
ni por qué la luz roja del Sol lo llena todo;
me basta con sentir frente a mi cuerpo triste
la inmensidad de un cielo de luz teñido de oro,

la inmensa rojedad de Sol que ya no existe,
el inmenso cadáver de una tierra ya muerta,
y frente a las astrales luminarias que tiñen el cielo,
la inmensidad de mi alma bajo la tarde inmensa.

I don't know why I am here, or when I came or why the red light of the
Sun fills everything; it is enough for me to feel before my sad body the
immensity of a sky of light dyed with gold, ¶the immense redness of a
Sun that no longer exists, the immense corpse of an earth already dead,
and before the astral luminaries that dye the sky, the immensity of my
soul under the immense evening.

His 'I don't know' is markedly less urgent than Vallejo's in the
title poem of *The Black Heralds* ('There are knocks in life, so
hard. . . I don't know!'). Correspondingly, his strictures on the
God who can no longer sustain faith and his sense of familial loss
are far less tense and agonized.[8] 'Bread', that obsessive emblem of
*The Black Heralds*, the good heart of family and faith, is gen-
eralized into the smell of the Pater Noster in a lowly church:
'Good smelling black bread that back in white childhood surrendered its secret to every fragrant soul who wanted to listen . . .'
And when this 'our father' is lost into the night his escape provokes something not unmixed with amused detachment: this
figure is made to run naked over the countryside and plunge into
the sea.

Yet more eloquent testimony of the different emphases and
loyalties of the early Neruda comes in the 'family' poem 'Today,
Which is my Sister's Birthday'. Writing to his sister back at home
and far from Santiago, Neruda, like Vallejo to Miguel, appeals to
childhood intimacy, separate from the adult world of parents.
But showing signs of his great capacity (quite alien to Vallejo) to
handle personae within the formal exchange of oratory or, as here,
the letter, Neruda does this precisely to *dis*own his pain as
'poetic':

Pero para qué es esto de pensamientos tristes!
A ti menos que a nadie debe afligir mi voz!
Después de todo nada de esto que digo existe.
No vayas a contárselo a mi madre, por Dios!

Uno no sabe cómo va hilvanando mentiras,
y uno dice por ellas, y ellas hablan por uno.
Piensa que tengo el alma toda llena de risas,
y no te engañarás, Hermana, te lo juro.

But what is all this business of sad thoughts for! My voice should afflict you less than anyone! After all nothing of what I am saying exists. Don't tell Mummy, for Heaven's sake! ¶One doesn't know how one goes contriving lies, and you speak through them, and they talk for you. Think that my soul is full of laughter, and you'll not be wrong, sister, I swear to you.

Coming after *Crepusculario* and the poems of *El hondero entusiasta* (The Enthusiastic Slinger, not published till 1933), Neruda's next collection *Veinte poemas de amor y una canción desesperada* (1924; Twenty Love Poems and a Song of Despair)[9] strongly asserted a new persona of the poet. He had been the passive and consumed object: 'Let me be oil in your lamp;' he had said, echoing the extreme 'femininity' of Spanish mystics like St John of the Cross. And despite the masculine posture indicated by the title of *The Enthusiastic Slinger*, he had in fact often found himself receiving his lover 'as the furrow does the seed'. In the *Twenty Poems* this crepuscular passivity and this sexual uncertainty are replaced by quite unequivocal masculinity. Neruda, the male, commits himself to sexual love as a form of self-discovery and illumination, something far more powerful than his poetry had dealt with before. The scale of the adventure is announced in the opening poem, where whole worlds are compressed into four stanzas of alexandrines:

Cuerpo de mujer, blancas colinas, muslos blancos,
te pareces al mundo en tu actitud de entrega.
Mi cuerpo de labriego salvaje te socava
y hace saltar el hijo del fondo de la tierra.

Fui solo como un túnel. De mí huían los pájaros.
y en mí la noche entraba su invasión poderosa.
Para sobrevivirme te forjé como un arma,
como una flecha en mi arco, como una piedra en
mi honda.

Body of a woman, white hills, white thighs, you look like the world in your posture of surrender. My wild peasant's body digs in you and makes the child spring from the depth of the earth. ¶I was alone like a tunnel. The birds fled me, and night entered its powerful invasion in me. To survive myself I forged you like a weapon, like an arrow in my bow, a stone in my sling.

The first quatrain situates the woman as the body and that body as a landscape. He, her partner, penetrates this proffered world to make it yield fruit. His identity derives from this primal act, just as in myth and etymology culture derives from man's first tilling of the earth (from the Latin *colere*), the incision of the iron into the breast which up till then had given milk in purely maternal and pastoral fashion ('white hills, white thighs'). From the second quatrain we learn that this act had been necessary to overcome loneliness and darkness, to survive a previous self. And here we find a further echo of that transition from the pastoral to the georgic, from the golden to the iron age, discussed more fully in chapter 3. As iron and stone from the earth, mined and shaped by man for his use, the woman becomes herself the means of protection. Darío had sung 'the celestial flesh of woman', the panerotic and sacrilegious antidote to death and despair. For Neruda she is significantly terrestrial, and always in the same world or cycle as he. In allusions that are firmly rooted in a basic situation (the sexual act of 'I' and 'you') Neruda gives us a concise history of his own and man's loss of pastoral innocence; and then of his dilemma in what he has done. For the poem turns as on a hinge into its second half. The vengeance wrought on him is that he loves her ('But the hour of vengeance falls and I love you'), loves her still for her body of 'firm and eager milk'. She it is who has the 'grace' in which he may persist, while condemned to thirst, and uncertain road on the earth and 'infinite pain'.

The poem contains the 'story' of the volume: the utter excitement of love and the body of a woman: its promise to and final bewilderment of the male who is limitless, incomplete and pained. The early Vallejo, in *The Black Heralds* and certain poems in his next book *Trilce* (1922), records a similar dilemma. But he differed in not establishing so robust a male persona as Neruda. As we shall see, his deep attachment to his mother held him closer so that sexual experience, the tilling of the earth, led to contradictions in him too violent and erratic to be contained in a biographical and sensual myth such as that of the *Twenty Poems*. When Vallejo thinks of women he has loved they are disturbingly specific and often named (Rita, Otilia) and together with his mother do not constitute a sex against which his own can be measured as an identity. This is not said to suggest that he was either maturer or less mature than Neruda on some psychological scale. In his poems sexuality was inextricable from theology (hence that echo of Aquinas), as it was later to be from politics, and could far less easily become the medium of a poetic persona such as Neruda's. For the accomplishment of Neruda's *Twenty Poems* (which had huge editorial success) is chiefly the poet's handling of himself, his steering of himself through pain and 'shipwreck', however severe. Rather than explore some fraught and untransferable intimacy of the kind which makes Vallejo's love poems idiosyncratic and difficult, he generalizes his experience for the benefit of an audience.

How far Neruda went in this direction is made splendidly clear by the fact that the *Twenty Poems* are to and about a lover who was initially two women, not one. The body of the opening poem belongs to an erotic companion in Santiago, who also inspired poems 2, 7, 11, 13–15, 17–18. She is physical and terrestrial to the point of being a mappamundi, a white atlas marked by his crosses of fire; her presence 'unwinds' the twilight, overwhelms nostalgia, only to be again too vast to be fully known, and in her very immediacy she becomes alien and distant. She thus comes to complement, neatly, almost schematically, the other, the earthy girl from the South, whose very absence ensures her ineludible presence, the memory of her being like ivy. However, the superb interaction between the poems, and the occasional transference, mean that the two can hardly be distinguished as people. The only constant is the poet 'in love'. Though love tears him apart and ultimately offers him no more guarantee than it offered Vallejo, Neruda stays to record the fact, in verses whose poignancy derives in part from just this survival:

> Ya no la quiero, es cierto, pero tal vez la quiero.
> Es tan corto el amor, y es tan largo el olvido.
>
> Porque en noches como ésta la tuve entre mis
>     brazos,
> mi alma no se contenta con haberla perdido.
>
> Aunque éste sea el último dolor que ella me causa,
> y éstos sean los últimos versos que yo le escribo.

I no longer love her, it's true, but perhaps I love her. Love is so short, and forgetting is so long. ¶Because on nights like this I held her in my arms, my soul will not accept having lost her. ¶Although this may be the last pain she causes me, and these be the last verses I write to her.

The final 'Song of Despair' appended to the *Twenty Poems*

confirms this quality. Neruda shows that he can control the violence and tenderness of his feelings however extreme. He has been in an experience, felt his way around in it with extraordinary and powerful sensuality, but has guarded that part of his self which Vallejo exposes with his tortured 'I don't know'. The 'crucifixion' of love-making is in Neruda an image he allows us to pass on from. In Vallejo it threatens the articulation of a poem. In the various styles and attitudes of Neruda's first volumes we see the poet locating and identifying himself, chiefly in terms of recurrent images (often sexual), and in the management of personae. In *The Black Heralds* we see Vallejo implicated without reserve in his formative experience, and sense already some raw and ultimate self 'in every poem'.

2

The differences that we have noticed so far between Vallejo and Neruda become more pronounced in the poetry they went on to publish. In the history of their development, *Trilce* conveyed the crisis of poetic identity for Vallejo that *Residencia en la tierra* did for Neruda. In both cases the exercise was unprecedented in the history of poetry in Spanish. In these books they pressed their poetry to the limits of articulation, as they themselves did neither before nor afterwards. Both poets struggle not just with the prosody but with the very syntax of the language. So that recognizing where they respectively found the strength to go on being poets teaches us a good deal about their work as a whole.

The seventy-seven poems of *Trilce* are among the most intractable in Spanish: certain of them have left critics perplexed and have defied translation into other languages. The difficulty begins with the title, a neologism of Vallejo's. It has been interpreted as a deliberately awkward conjunction of *triste* and *dulce* (sad and sweet); as a noun indicating the importance of the number *tres* and the concept of trinity in some of the poems; as a word with no meaning at all. Its significance would at best seem to lie precisely in an opaqueness that is somehow suggestive, if grudgingly. In this it would typify the tight-lipped communicativeness of the collection as a whole. A quality of many poems in *Trilce* is the sense they give of being forced out, maltreated, stepped on quickly, even contemptuously. Vallejo is capable of insising on the partiality and inadequacy of language to the point of reducing it to grating sound: '999 calories./Rumbbb. . .Trrraprrr chaz'. Words are spelt backwards, wilfully dismembered over a line break ('un poquito no má/s, 'a little bit no mor/e) in answer to the same pressure that distorts his punctuation and his typography. If he says 'namE' or 'exIles' (nombrE, destieRRA) it is to make the opposite of a calligramme (the literally beautiful word patterns of Apollinaire or the Mexican Juan José Tablada): an ugly or harsh picture of an unsatisfied and unsatisfying thought. His diction is correspondingly rough. At one point he says this must be so, contrasting himself with the gentle French symbolist Albert Samain: 'Samain would say the air is quiet and of a contained sadness./Vallejo says today Death is joining every border to every thread of lost hair', and so on. Poetic clichés, undefended statements however innocuous, are pounced on and tortured, contradicted with rapid obliqueness. By the same token, random phrases of everyday speech or fragments of set phrases are used almost sarcastically to fill gaps in an argument or a train of thought. Parts of speech are thus robbed of their normal grammatical support. It is as if when two or three words are gathered in Vallejo's name they must answer for themselves, not etymologically or within their own sensuality, but epistemologically, bearing the poet's scrutinizing intelligence.

> Cual mi explicación.
> Esto me lacera de tempranía.
>
> Esa manera de caminar por los trapecios.
>
> Esos corajosos brutos como postizos.
>
> Esa goma que pega el azogue al adentro.
>
> Esas posaderas sentadas para arriba.
>
> Ese no puede ser sido.
>
> Absurdo.
>
> Demencia.
>
> Pero he venido de Trujillo a Lima.
> Pero gano un sueldo de cinco soles.

Like my explanation. This lacerates me with earliness. ¶That way of walking along trapezes. ¶Those angry brutes like switches of hair. ¶That gum which sticks the quicksilver to the inside. ¶Those butts seated upwards. ¶That cannot be, been. ¶Absurd. ¶Dementia. ¶But I've come from Trujillo to Lima. But I'm getting a wage of five *soles*.

Words and phrases that survive in this way become as it were minimal but tried weapons to shield him from an aggressive silence around him, by now of cosmic proportions. This is most obviously true when it is a question of the first person singular, the 'I' pronoun that he intrudes into and extracts from his poems. (He was wariest of all of what he called 'the still-born gift of the immense pronoun that the animal reared under its tail'.) Often enough, as in *Trilce* LVI, he will start off speaking as himself, ironically asserting the existence of that self by the very repetitive deadness of the situation it is in:

> Todos los días amanezco a ciegas
> a trabajar para vivir: y tomo el desayuno,
> sin probar ni gota de él, todas las mañanas.
>
> Sin saber si he logrado, o más nunca,
> algo que brinca del sabor
> o es sólo corazón y que ya vuelto, lamentará
> hasta dónde esto es lo menos.

Every day I rise blindly to work to live: and I have breakfast not tasting a drop of it, every morning. ¶Not knowing if I have made it, or ever shall, something that leaps out from the taste or is only heart, something come back that will lament until this is the least thing here.

As that 'normal' situation disintegrates so does he, leaving us with the verb-less and impersonal cry: 'Match after match in the dark,/tear after tear in a cloud of dust.' Other times, because of the forms of Spanish verbs, it is actually impossible to know whether it is he speaking or not. The word 'era', repeated as a refrain in *Trilce* III, could as well mean 'I was' as 'he, she or it was'. Similarly, because Spanish (like French) does not formally distinguish between animate and inanimate pronouns (*él, ella*) we sometimes cannot know how much he is part of them. As a consequence, *Trilce* can be unusually hard to translate into a language like English, which demands that in such cases we choose between formal alternatives. But this does not mean that all its difficulties are arbitrary: the volume has strictures and logic of its own.

For example, *Trilce* reveals an intricate, at times near cabbalistic concern with numbers, as indicated perhaps already by the title, and by the total number of poems (77). Indeed, in a predominantly mathematical poem, XLVIII, Vallejo observes that 'the whole of life' may end up being figures. This kind of concern permeates feelings which survive from *The Black Heralds*, and feelings which first appear in *Trilce*: his sense of exile in Lima; his relationship with his family, especially after his mother's death; his sexuality; the failure of his love affair with a girl called Otilia, at the root of a heavily disguised sequence of poems within the book;[10] his experience of prison. Only now so little is extraneous, or anecdotal that we should have difficulty classifying the poems as they were classified in the first volume. Everything, including his feelings about poetry itself, is referred directly to the same central consciousness, even if this often remains virtual, implied by the patterns it creates. As a highly concentrated, apparently impersonal volume, *Trilce* was undoubtedly affected by the three and a half months which the poet spent in a jail in Trujillo shortly after *The Black Heralds* appeared. A voice in a later book says 'The gravest moment of my life was my imprisonment in a Peruvian jail', a moment when the bare solitude of the cell reduced feelings to their possible essentials.

Because they have a link with *The Black Heralds*, and because they are more accessible than others, *Trilce* is perhaps best approached in detail by way of those poems which betray their 'family' origins. Number III is a famous example. It is getting dark and he is waiting with his brothers and sisters (among them Miguel) for his parents to return to the house. We learn this from the things they say, as we did in the earlier poem to Miguel:

> Las personas mayores
> ¿a qué hora volverán?
> Da las seis el ciego Santiago,
> y ya está muy oscuro.
>
> Madre dijo que no demoraría.

Our parents, what time will they be back? Blind Santiago is ringing six, and it's already very dark. ¶Mother said she wouldn't be long.

So as not to be scared they encourage each other by talking about the games they played during the day and will play tomorrow. Their courage is that of children in a drama that we sense is increasingly larger than they are, and we break through to that bigger and yet more painful world in a remarkable twist in the last line of the penultimate stanza:

> Aguardemos así, obedientes y sin más
> remedio, la vuelta, el desagravio
> de los mayores siempre delanteros

> dejándonos en casa a los pequeños,
> como si también nosotros
>               no pudiésemos partir.

Let's wait like this, obedient and with no other choice, for the return, the making amends of our parents always up front, always leaving us little ones at home, as if we could not go away too.

The fact they all would have to leave one day anyway gives the childish assertion a poignancy rapidly expanded in the closing lines. The darkness is still that of the original scene, but also that of an oppressive present, which precipitates the unwilling and emphatic assertion of self in the final pronoun, yo:

> Aguedita, Nativa, Miguel?
> Llamo, busco al tanteo en la oscuridad.
> No me vayan a haber dejado solo,
> y el único recluso sea yo.

Aguedita, Nativa, Miguel? I call, I feel my way in the dark. They can't have left me alone, the only prisoner here can't be me.

Here we see Vallejo reversing the progression of LVI, stumbling as it were on himself by recapitulating origins he shows to be unsure and inadequate. If being alone and single is in fact a condition he is coming to terms with in *Trilce*, the first cause of his distrust of the personal pronoun and of the numerical concern of the book, then it is a condition he very rarely exults in. In this respect XXXVI is an unusual poem. His effort may be doomed from the start, but at least the will is strong, and almost capable of breaking the last corner of the 'prison':

> Pugnamos ensartarnos por un ojo de aguja,
> enfrentados, a las ganadas.
> Amoniácase casi el cuarto ángulo del círculo.

We are matched with ourselves, thread to the eye of a needle, face on, out to win. The fourth angle of the circle almost revives.

The struggle, with its unmistakable sexual flavour, suggests an existence which his very 'perennial imperfection' prolongs (or 'yets' as he puts it). The poet becomes confident enough even to address others as *vosotros*, the rarest of gestures in *Trilce*, urging them to refuse the double security of Harmony:

> Rehusad, y vosotros, a posar las plantas
> en la seguridad dupla de la Armonía.
> Rehusad la simetría a buen seguro.

> Intervenid en el conflicto
> de puntas que se disputan
> en la más torionda de las justas
> el salto per el ojo de la aguja!

Refuse, you too, to place your soles on the double security of Harmony. Refuse trusty symmetry. Intervene in the clash of points in conflict in the most ruttish of jousts, the leap through the eye of the needle!

He then becomes aware of his little finger, as 'superfluous', like some stark phallic integer, reminiscent of the 'monodigital fate', and the 'monarch' of other poems, and registers his surprise that it is part of him. But here at least he owns the identity:

> Y me inspira rabia y me azarea
> y no hay cómo salir de él, sino haciendo
> la cuenta de que hoy es jueves.
>
> ¡Ceded al nuevo impar
>                       potente de orfandad!

And it enrages and perplexes me and there's no way out of it, except by reckoning that today is Thursday. ¶Make way for the new masculine number, mighty in orphanhood.

Self-possessed confidence of this kind in *Trilce* much more characteristically results in exile ('this pleasure which exiles us'), in a further orphanhood that is again lonely, in the awareness of being uncomfortably one in a series of numbers. His difference from Neruda is thus subtle but crucial. His concern is less that love should prove inadequate *for* a person like that of the *Twenty Poems* (and, as we shall see, the *Residences*) than it is the very incorporation of the phallic self, existentially, into one's being in the first place. *Trilce* IX amounts to an exasperated statement, amused and violent by turns, of Vallejo's primary effort:

> Vusco volvvver de golpe el golpe.
> Sus dos hojas anchas, su válvula
> que se abre en suculenta recepción
> de multiplicando a multiplicador,
> su condición excelente para el placer
> todo avía verdad.

Vvaliant I strivve to back the blow. Her broad double leaves, her valve which opens in succulent admission from multiplicand to multiplier, her condition excellent with pleasure, the whole guaranteed truth.

The experience means that at such moments he 'does not live absence, not even to the touch'. The 'fall' comes not because presence is the necessary enemy and corollary of this absence (as it is when Neruda opposes eroticism with nostalgia) but because of an egoism which Vallejo suggests, in the ironic final lines, may have to be owned:

> Fallo volver de golpe el golpe.
> No ensillaremos jamás el toroso. Vaveo
> de egoísmo y de aquel ludir mortal
> de sábana,
> desque la mujer esta
>          ¡cuánto pesa de general!
>
> Y hembra es el alma de la ausente.
> Y hembra es el alma mía.

I fail to back the blow. Saddle the bullhip we never shall. I foam from egoism and that mortal chafing on the sheet, for this woman, how she weighs! ¶And female is the soul of the absent one. And female is my soul.

What to do then with this number, single and 'uneven' (*impar* also means masculine in Spanish prosody)? Complete harmony with another is no good because it merely duplicates egoism, and for that reason must be refused as 'trusty symmetry'. Two-ness is in fact the mark of preterite love in certain nostalgic poems like xv. In the last stanza he jumps to life only to realize that it's all over now:

> En esta noche pluviosa,
> ya lejos de ambos dos, salto de pronto...
> Son dos puertas abriéndose cerrándose,
> dos puertas que al viento van y vienen
> sombra          a          sombra.

On this rainy night, now far from both of us, I start up... It's two doors opening, closing, two doors that come and go in the wind, shadow to shadow.

While there is no sure way out of this dilemma, certain poems do at least not preclude all hope. Of these, number v is perhaps the most closely worked, the most rigorously arithmetical. He evokes the dicotyledon (a botanical term), the pair which should not 'transcend' outwards or 'slip into the great collapse'. It is better than the egoistic '1', which 'will resound to infinity', and better than a quietistic (or onanistic?) '0', which 'will be so silent as to awaken 1 and stand it up'. But again the dicotyledon is good not because of some dual self-sufficiency, but because from it 'petrels overture', with 'propensities of trinity'. With this last phrase

Vallejo may be said to theologize his sexuality openly; but in truth he gives us no more than a hint. The dogma of love, with its numerical logic, is left for the reader to discover if he can. We get more clues in XVIII where he sits between the four walls of his cell. To be free he needs his 'loving woman with her innumerable keys'. 'Against them [the four walls] we should be with you, the two of us, more two than ever.' The grammar is strange and worth noting: the more normal 'I should be with you' is avoided as if damagingly self-assertive, preclusive of just the 'I' he goes on to allude to:

> Ah las paredes de la celda.
> De ellas me duele entretanto, más
> las dos largas que tienen esta noche
> algo de madres que ya muertas
> llevan por bromurados declives,
> a un niño de la mano cada una.

Ah the walls of the cell. I'm pained by them meanwhile, most by the two longest which tonight have something of mothers who already dead lead along bromide slopes a child by the hand, each one.

Then alone once more he reaches out for a 'tertiary arm'

> que ha de *pupilar*, entre mi donde y mi cuando,
> esta mayoría inválida de hombre.

which shall pupil, between my where and when, this invalid manhood.

The inference of this and other poems in *Trilce* is that man remains 'invalid' without the love and hope he may expect to have as a child. The first will escape him because of his sexuality (Vallejo presses to their limits the innocence and 'candour' of children's love games in XI). The second seems to be removed from him deliberately by forces superior to himself. 'Christian I wait, I always hope', he says sarcastically,

> Y Dios sobresaltado, nos oprime
> el pulso, grave, mudo,
> y como padre a su pequeña,
>               apenas,
> pero apenas, entreabre los sangrientos algodones
> y entre sus dedos toma a la esperanza.

And God astonished, presses our pulse, grave, mute, and like a father with his fingers picks out hope.
with his little girl, scarcely, but scarcely, parts the bloodied cotton and

Vallejo's estimate, in these terms, of the likelihood of his own coming of age varies considerably. He may feel a rush of confidence, even when imprisoned and threatened with further prosecution, as in XXII (again by *four* judges, 'four fat ones'). Ill-treatment (*burlas*) cancels sooner than it encourages pity for one's self, for having faith, like Jean Jacques Rousseau, in man's natural goodness:

> Don Juan Jacobo está en hacerio,
> y las burlas le tiran de su soledad,
> como a un tonto. Bien hecho.

M. Jean Jacques is the object of attention, and ridicule throws him like a fool from his solitude. Well done.

His optimism, his insatiable desire for 'level and love', is then shown to depend on a presence that is urgently addressed but undefined: 'Here I am, you whom I depend on, I'm on the line. Here I am!' This dramatic appeal has just the hectic nuance that marked the 'confident' close of XXXVI: 'Make way for the new masculine number, mighty in orphanhood.' In *Trilce* optimism of this order is felt to be daring, an exposure, a hazard which Vallejo would have the reader witness, and even be responsible towards, in so far as his 'you' does not preclude us.

Far more frequent in *Trilce* are those poems which show the hazard as doomed, which elicit a dogged patience ('Of wood is my patience, silent vegetable'). Less rarely than exultation we feel a lank throb at the prospect of 'major' heights:

> Craterizados los puntos más altos, los puntos
> del amor de ser mayúsculo, bebo, ayuno, ab-
> sorbo heroína para la pena, para el latido
> lacio y contra toda corrección.
>
> ¿Puedo decir que nos han traicionado? No.
> ¿Que todos fueron buenos? Tampoco. Pero
> allí está una buena voluntad, sin duda,
> y sobre todo, el ser así.
>
> Y qué quien se ame mucho! Yo me busco
> en mi propio designio que debió ser obra
> mía, en vano: nada alcanzó a ser libre.
>
> Y sin embargo, quién me empuja.
> A que no me atrevo a cerrar la quinta ventana.
> Y el papel de amarse y persistir, junto a las
> horas y a lo indebido.
>
> Y el éste y el aquél.

The highest points are craterized, the points of the love of being the first letter, I drink, I fast, I shoot heroin into the grief, straight into the lank throb and against all correction. ¶Can I say they have betrayed us? No. That they were all good? No again. But a willingness exists there, without doubt, and above all, that's how it is. ¶And what if you love yourself very much! I search for me in my own design which ought to have been my own work, in vain: it gained nothing by being free. ¶All the same, who is pushing me. To the point I don't dare close the fifth window. And the act of loving the self and persisting, up against the hours and the wrongness. ¶And the this man and the that man.

The raw desperation of the first stanza, which threatens to curtail the poem, is caught in an internal dialogue, which derives its force from its very appearance of patient calm. The great efforts, aspirations, exposures and anger of other poems are here subjected to the austerity of one whose role is also to 'persist', and who would find a language to do that in. In other words, this is a holding action and his neutral diction demonstrates why he should have 'gained nothing by being free'. The longer the poem is heard, the more that irony vibrates. Imprisonment, Rousseau in his solitude, the child in the womb, cannot be the only form of self-love.

*Trilce* has no single key; it is an inexhaustible book, just off some implied infinite centre.[11] Linguistically it takes the consequences of its own daring. Critics have certainly borne this in mind when discussing the two poems which announce and end the volume, the first and the seventy-seventh. The first is charged with patient doubt about his insular heart ('Who is it so shrill and who keeps/the remaining islands from their last will'). In the last he makes poetry the water which issues from storm and fire. These he has braved and his persistence earns him the right to a final appeal and the remote promise of communication (through that 'fifth window' of the senses), of a self peninsular if not continental: 'Sing, rain, on the coast still without sea!'

Neruda's poetry went through a crisis of expression in *Residence on Earth*, which like *Trilce* is a book of extreme doubt and ultimate affirmation. When writing it he was residing on a part of the earth far removed from Chile, in his capacity as a diplomat in the Far East. The oppressive climate, the damp rooms of the cities he lived in (Rangoon, Colombo, Djakarta), and his sense of utter isolation there, inform his poems much as Vallejo's sense of exile in Lima and of imprisonment informed *Trilce*. And he was prompted to hazardous self-exploration, to impatience with the diction and assumptions of his earlier poetry.

This process had in fact begun before Neruda left Chile, in the volume *Tentativa del hombre infinito* (Assay of the Infinite Man, 1926). In this 'attempt' he abandoned formal restraint: the well-turned quatrains, the neat assonance of the past, all punctuation even. Lines of varying length succeed each other with something of the uninhibitedness of the surrealists' automatic writing. With his psyche at a high level of exposure (Neruda referred to the *Assay* as one of his most honest and least successful volumes), our attention is drawn to such constants as do remain.

> estoy de pie en la luz como el medio día en la
> tierra.
> quiero contarlo todo con ternura
> centinela de  las malas estaciones ahí estás tú
> pescador intranquilo déjame adornarte por
> ejemplo
> un cinturón de frutas dulce la melancolía
> espérame donde voy ah el atardecer
> la comida las barcarolas del océano oh espérame
> adelantándome como un grito atrasándote como
> una huella oh espérate
> sentado en esa última sombra o todavía después
> todavía

I am standing in the light like the midday on the earth. I want to tell it all with tenderness, sentinel of the bad seasons there you are, let me, uncalm fisherman, adorn you for example, a belt of fruit sweet melancholy, wait for me wherever I go, oh the evening the food the barcarolles of the ocean oh wait for me going forward like a shout, you lingering like a footprint oh wait, sitting on this last shade or still after still

Neruda certainly rearranges 'normal' syntax here, and juxtaposes words strangely. But he does not much restrict the sensuality of words as material images ('uncalm fisherman', 'belt of fruit'); nor does he preclude a 'straight' admission of tenderness. For, above all, he leaves his 'I' still unscathed: the would-be infinite man remains quite finite and intact, in gesture and expectation.

In the poems of his first *Residence*, which belong to the period 1925–31, Neruda went on to achieve what he has called 'the dominion of personality'. His choice of terms is wholly apt: personality, the inclusive general form of personae previously adopted (such geo-political and psychological vocabulary being quite alien to Vallejo's idea of self). The obscurities of this personal expression in this volume and in the second *Residence* (which followed it and covers the years 1931–5) have provoked a good deal of commentary, beginning with Amado Alonso's fundamental study of 1940 (*Poesía y estilo de Pablo Neruda*), a thorough and detailed work. But as Emir Rodríguez Monegal has pointed out,[12] Alonso effectively ignores what is perhaps the first and original quality of Neruda's new poetry, treating it as hermetic, in wanting to find in the *Residences* a modern version of Góngora's *Solitudes*: deep and self-insulating patterns of images and a grammar that has some ultimate internal responsibility to itself. Such an approach can make the poems even more difficult than they are. For certain of them cannot be understood except as a series of impressions and of mood associations that is 'uniform' perhaps, but by no means necessarily consequential. Unless we recognize and accept the way Neruda has of moving and standing still in language he is hard to hear. He has a rein of his speech, to be sure; but it is often loose (in any case rarely as taut as Vallejo's).

This is true *par excellence* of the opening poem of the first Residence, 'Galope muerto' (Dead Gallop). In the evolution of Neruda's work its importance is hard to exaggerate. It is quite exceptional in suppressing that personal presence which normally matters to Neruda in one form or another. He plunges in search of some ulterior reality, more intent on it than on himself, or on himself registering it. It is a daring moment which he might well not have emerged from, or have emerged silent. The much-quoted first stanza runs:

> Como cenizas, como mares poblándose,
> en la sumergida lentitud, en lo informe,
> o como se oyen desde el alto de los caminos
> cruzar las campanadas en cruz,
> teniendo ese sonido ya aparte del metal,
> confuso, pesando, haciéndose polvo
> en el mismo molino de las formas demasiado lejos,
> o recordadas o no vistas,
> y el perfume de las ciruelas que rodando a tierra
> se pudren en el tiempo, infinitamente verdes.

Like ashes, like seas peopling themselves, in the submerged slowness, in shapelessness, or as the crossed bells are heard crossing from the height of the roads, having that sound now separate from the metal, confused, weighing, being made dust in the very mill of shapes too distant, either recalled or not seen, and the scent of the plums that rolling on the ground rot in time, infinitely green.

We look in vain for logic or a guide: the 'sentence' is a comparison that omits the term compared, and, like the whole poem, is devoid of a main verb. And not only is the term of comparison omitted, it is not even implied. Our only possibility, our only form in this submerged formless world, are those of the sensations themselves. And these disturb us violently from the start: dead ash is juxtaposed with the nascent life of the sea; the dry and the wet find connexion only in some pre-human chemistry. From depth we move to some high sound, that is in turn divorced from solid origin. The confusion is weighty, only to fragment in dust and to be taken just out of focus. And when our reliance on sound, touch and sight has been thus unsettled, our smell tells us of a further distressing intimacy between putrefaction and green life, decomposition and generation.

Because there are no co-ordinates ('Whence, which way, on what bank?' as he asks in the second stanza), the cycles of life accelerate absurdly 'so rapid, so alive, motionless however, like the pulley mad in itself'. To exist in this vast and oceanic disorder, to reach what his 'pale heart' cannot encompass, the best he can do is 'slow down' and perceive in some apparently motionless centre, so that his poems, including this one, themselves resemble a dead gallop.

The perilous obscurities of this poem, once expressed, underlay what he wrote from then on. But he did not again leave himself so exposed in the dream or nightmare reality of what Alfredo Lozada[13] has called his 'agonic monism', in which all matter ceaselessly disintegrates. More characteristic of the *Residences* is a poem like 'Caballo de los sueños' (Dream Horse), where, as he says in the first line, he observes his discoveries.

> Innecesario, viéndome en los espejos,
> con un gusto a semanas, a biógrafos, a papeles,
> arranco de mi corazón al capitán del infierno,
> establezco cláusulas indefinidamente tristes.

Unnecessary, seeing myself in mirrors, with a taste of weeks, biographers, papers, I tear from my heart the captain of hell, I establish clauses indefinitely sad.

The language of his sadness may still be indefinite, but he is there all right establishing it and dragging hell out of his heart. We now may accompany *him* at least as he moves slowly from 'one point to another', absorbing illusions and even conversing. This allows him to balance that submerged violence which constantly threatens to erupt in his poems with just that willed slowness and deliberation, which acquire their own (very Nerudian) irony.

> Hay un país extenso en el cielo
> con las supersticiosas alfombras del arco-iris
> y con vegetaciones vesperales:
> hacia allí me dirijo, no sin cierta fatiga,
> pisando una tierra removida de sepulcros un tanto frascos,
> yo sueño entre esas plantas de legumbre confusa.

There is an extensive land in the sky with the superstitious carpets of the rainbow and with vesperal vegetation: I steer myself towards it, not without a certain fatigue, treading an earth disturbed by somewhat fresh graves, I dream among those plants of confused growth.

His reluctant progress through such an unsure state of things is marked by polysyllabic alliterative phrases like 'vegetaciones vesperales' (alliteration has traditionally been considered ugly and heavy in Spanish poetics), and by finicky qualifiers like 'no sin' and 'un tanto'.

The fresh graves he passes over, which might well contain those rotting green plums of 'Dead gallop', also recall the sprouting corpse of Eliot's *The Waste Land*, which Neruda read when he was in the Far East. Like Eliot he is obsessed by the feeling of life being out of touch with itself, of an appalling unawareness around him of its natural truths. And as his own antidote he occasionally suggests his own rituals, at least allows them to exist, within a certain ironic monotony: 'I love the wasted honey of respect,/the sweet catechism between whose leaves sleep aged, faded violets.' And with a self-love very different from Vallejo's in its helpless easiness he says (in 'Sonata and destructions'): 'I adore my own lost being, my imperfect substance,/my silver set and my eternal loss.' But quite unlike Eliot (and more in line with D. H. Lawrence, whom he also read at this period) he is not nostalgic for a golden bough, for a more proper cultural order. His awe now before life's primary processes and the horrible intimacy of decomposition with growth is too strong for that. Hence we find his irony waxing to open sarcasm in a poem like 'Gentleman Alone':

> Los jóvenes homosexuales y las muchachas amorosas,
> y las largas viudas que sufren el delirante insomnio,
> y las jóvenes señoras preñadas hace treinta horas,
> y los roncos gatos que cruzan mi jardín en tinieblas,
> como un collar de palpitantes ostras sexuales
> rodean mi residencia solitaria,

The homosexual young men and the amorous girls and the long widows who suffer from delirious insomnia, and the young wives thirty hours pregnant, and the raucous cats that cross my garden in the dark, like a necklace of throbbing sexual oysters encircle my solitary residence.

This kind of weary contempt no doubt recalls Eliot's, and indeed later in the poem we find close echoes of the sordid sexual activity of 'Mrs Porter in the spring' and of the 'small house agent's clerk' in the Fire Sermon in *The Waste Land*:

> El radiante verano conduce a los enamorados
> en uniformes regimientos melancólicos,
> hechos de gordas y flacas y alegres y tristes parejas:

The radiant summer leads the lovers in uniform melancholy regiments, made up of fat and thin and happy and sad couples.

And:

> El pequeño empleado, después de mucho,
> después del tedio semanal, y las novelas leídas de noche en
>     cama,
> ha definitivamente seducido a su vecina,

The small clerk, after some time, after the weekly tedium, and the novels read in bed at night, has definitively seduced his female neighbour.

But Neruda does not extend his distaste for this state of affairs around him into the snobbery of Eliot (whose clerk is 'one of the low on whom assurance sits/as a silk hat on a Bradford millionaire'); or, for that matter, into voyeurism (as Tiresias, Eliot watches the woman who says 'By Richmond I raised my knees/ supine on the floor of a narrow canoe').

Though he generalizes the inadequate beings we encounter in *The Waste Land*, Neruda in the end remains much more among them, 'surely and eternally surrounded by this great breathing and entangled forest', with its 'great flowers like mouths and teeth', and 'its black roots in the shape of fingernails and shoes'. He demands to be still in touch with matter, however sordid; to disown it would mean a disembodiment that his poetry could not survive. This had been the message of the early 'Unidad' (Unity), where he shows himself 'surrounded by geography', and it becomes explicit in the 'Three Material Songs' of the second *Residence*. In the first song, 'Entrada a la madera' (Entry Into Wood, – *madera* derives from the word *materia*), he again submerges himself into the depths of things. But once 'inside', and anticipating if only briefly later developments in his poetry, notably in the *Elemental Odes* of the 1950s, he hints at a way out through the natural structures of things. The language he says this in has unmistakable overtones of the Christianity to which Eliot became a convert, but which Neruda, like Vallejo, found himself unable ever fully to re-embrace.

> Dulce materia, oh rosa de alas secas,
> en mi hundimiento tus pétalos subo
> con pies pesados de roja fatiga,
> y en tu catedral dura me arrodillo
> golpeándome los labios con un ángel.

Sweet matter, oh rose of dry wings, in my sunken collapse I climb up your petals with feet heavy with red fatigue, and in your hard cathedral I kneel beating my lips with an angel.

In the other two songs, to celery and to wine, these things, less religious than ordinary and secular in their associations, offer a possible guarantee against ceaseless disintegration which was to prove more consonant with the political beliefs he later adopted.

Perhaps the most powerful moment of Neruda's *Residences* is the long poem entitled 'Las furias y las penas' (The Furies and the Pains), which constitutes the second section of his third and last *Residence*. This is really the last poem of the *Residences* as we have encountered them so far, before the big change in his poetry and the political commitment of sections 3 to 5 of the third *Residence* (which belong to the years 1935 to 1945). Neruda is a lover in the poem, as he was in the *Twenty Poems* of his late adolesence. But like the woman, the *tu* addressed and invoked, he has obsessions which go deeper than that story. For, an older man in Madrid with an unsuccessful marriage behind him, he is not returning to 'love' with renewed illusion, as a way of forgetting the 'song of despair'. He and she embody instincts so intense and compelling that their tenderness can hardly be distinguished from violence, love from hatred and destruction. As in certain poems in *Canto general* mentioned in an earlier chapter, they inhabit an ocean, a damp shade, in which their physical shapes (teeth, nails, mouths) assume a kind of dreadful autonomy, beyond or before moral, or even human understanding. Their sense of their matter, their bodies, radiates mercilessly through clothes and all social form. Indeed, they are announced as beasts, lurking and insatiable

En el fondo del pecho estamos juntos,
en el cañaveral del pecho recorremos
un verano de tigres,
al acecho de un metro de piel fría,
al acecho de un ramo de inaccesible cutis,
con la boca olfateando sudor y venas verdes
nos encontramos en la húmeda sombra que deja
    caer besos.

In the depth of the heart we are together, in the canefield of the heart we go through a summer of tigers, on the lookout for a yard of cold flesh, for a branch of inaccessible skin, sniffing sweat and green veins with our mouths we meet in the damp shade which drips kisses.

She is his enemy (*enemiga*) but far too erotic a one for any conceivable courtly convention: 'But there are your eyes smelling of hunting, of a green ray that riddles chests.' She is possessed by 'fury' to the point of blindness and is left rolling on the floor, handled and bitten, while 'the old smell of semen like an ivy/of ashen flour slips from your mouth'. True to his material instinct he will not distinguish his fury from hers, making zeal of jealousy, but has only a helpless deliberate zeal appropriate to the first realization of the *Residences*:

Yo era un hombre transportado al acaso
con una mujer hallada vagamente,
nos desnudamos
como para morir o nadar o envejecer
y nos metimos uno dentro del otro,
ella rodeándome como un agujero,
yo quebrantándola como quien
golpea una campana,
pues ella era el sonido que me hería
y la cúpula dura decidida a temblar.

I was a man transported by chance with a woman vaguely found, we undressed as to die or swim or grow old and we put ourselves each in the other, she surrounding me like a hole, I breaking her like someone striking a bell, for she was the sound that wounded me and the hard cupola determined to tremble.

As submerged as ever he is in the *Residences*, and as hard on the frontiers of sensation, Neruda here gathers the power of the book into a final rush of acts, perceiving them vigilant and 'motionless, like the pulley mad in itself'. Committed to his matter, his body, and refusing now in this irreducible persona to observe himself or others with irony, still less with sarcasm, he finds his own capacity to persist in the paradox of the closing stanza:

> Es una sola hora larga como una vena,
> y entre el ácido y la paciencia del tiempo arrugado
>     transcurrimos,
> apartando las sílabas del miedo y la ternura,
> interminablemente exterminados.

It is a single hour long as a vein, and between the acid and patience of wrinkled time we go by, separating the syllables of fear and tenderness, interminably exterminated.

With its paradoxical final line, where the adverb itself appears interminable, this poem offers after, and despite, everything, the same hint of continuation as the last poem of Vallejo's *Trilce*.

## 3

After the crises explored poetically in *Trilce* and the *Residences*, Vallejo and Neruda shifted the emphasis of their concern and came to understand self in less obsessively individual terms. They were prompted to this by the political atmosphere in Europe in the interwar period and, decisively, by the military assault on the Spanish Second Republic which began in 1936. With Vallejo the change was a long one. Having left Peru (for ever) in July 1923, less than a year after *Trilce* appeared, during his days of penury in Paris he involved himself increasingly in Marxist thought. He reported committedly on the Soviet Union after a visit there (Russia in 1931). This and other works, like his socialist realist novel *Tungsten*, suggest a much simpler literary adherence to communism than do his poems, which remained unpublished until after his death in 1937. The manuscripts of his last collections, *Poemas humanos* (Human Poems) and *España, aparta de mí este cáliz* (Spain, Take Away This Cup From Me), indicate a great intensifying of poetic activity towards the end, a driving effort to match his poetic self, also, to a politicized situation. This was the same situation that changed Neruda. After arriving in Madrid in 1931 he got to know poets there with Republican

sympathies, especially Lorca, and Rafael Alberti, whom he called
the brother who taught him to be the best kind of Spaniard. The
Civil War itself elicited firm adhesion from both Vallejo and
Neruda, as it did from countless other poets, among them Alberti
and the Cuban Nicolás Guillén. Neruda's counterpart to Vallejo's
*Spain* was entitled *España en el corazón* (Spain in the Heart). The
war also brought them together briefly, in their work for anti-
fascist organizations, an encounter which Neruda alluded to in
the tribute he paid to Vallejo on his return to Chile in 1938.[14]

Even in this third phase (Vallejo's last), and despite their
ideological closeness, the poetry of Vallejo and Neruda continued
to differ and just as instructively. They faced similar, perhaps the
same problems as the poet they each had become.

Vallejo's *Human Poems* is a large collection and covers the
whole of his time in Europe (from 1923 to 1937). The ninety-
four poems in it vary in such a way as to tempt us to see an evolution, from *Trilce*, to *Spain*, that sheaf of fifteen poems with which
it is intimately connected at the other end. For her part Vallejo's
widow Georgette has distinguished a sequence of 'poems in
prose' assigning to them an earlier date and claiming that Vallejo
intended to publish them separately.[15] They are perhaps the least
remarkable of the 'human poems'. They are the work of an ex-
patriate coming to terms with that condition. The further exile
leads him to demystify his past. In Paris, 'a very large and distant
place', inner contradictions less easily uphold a universe, notably
in the poem sarcastically entitled 'I'm going to talk about hope'.
From here on explicit references to his past fade out. He says he
can best make himself understood on a *quena* (the Andean flute),
not expecting us to believe him, and remarks that the condors of
an early poem like 'Huaco' simply bore him. 'Your unforgettable
*cholo*' from Peru, as he dubs himself, becomes as such quite for-
gettable, though, as some critics have suggested, only because he
goes to the ultimate depths of that condition: the figure wholly
becomes a consciousness. His human poems increasingly infer
solidarity, in less local terms that are nonetheless his. The private
mythologies and hermetic number systems of *The Black Heralds*
and *Trilce* disappear or are modified to involve others as well as
him.

For example, the following poem at first sight involves just that
emotional contradiction characteristic of *Trilce*. The poet moves

brusquely towards and away from confidence in himself, wanting
and then not wanting the red badge of courage of his own body.

> Quiere y no quiere su color mi pecho,
> por cuyas bruscas vías voy, lloro con palo,
> trato de ser feliz, lloro en mi mano,
> recuerdo, escribo
> y remacho una lágrima en mi pómulo.

My heart will and won't have its hue, through those brusque tracts I go,
weep with a splint, try to be happy, weep in my hand, remember, write
and clinch a tear on my cheek-bone.

But his very capacity to remember and 'clinch a tear' leads to
impatience with it, and in the next stanza his limitation becomes
more generally that of man, a mortal wingless species torn between evil and good, who 'won't be crouched in his soul, horn-
throbs in his temple,/bimane, most brutish, the great philosopher'.
Awareness of having such a Darwinian condition may not answer
the problem, but it does spread it; so that the violent outburst at
the end now appears just that, tear-away even rash in all its huge
lyrical power:

> Y no! No! No! Qué ardid, ni paramento!
> Congoja, sí, con sí firme y frenético,
> coriáceo, rapaz, quiere y no quiere, cielo y
>     pájaro;
> congoja, sí, con toda la braqueta.
> Contienda entre dos llantos, roba de una sola
>     ventura,
> via indolora en que padezco en chanclos
> de la velocidad de andar a ciegas.

And no! No! No! Still less tricks or trappings! Grief, yes, with a yes firm
and frantic, leathery, rapacious, will and won't, bird and sky; grief, yes,
with the whole of one's fly. A match between two sobs, theft of a single
bliss, unpained *via* on which I endure in galoshes the velocity of walking
blind.

As if to prevent this blind speed from accelerating out of control, now that it is out of the tense hermeticism of *Trilce*, Vallejo
sometimes provides it with the kind of formal restraint he had
not used since *The Black Heralds*. Throughout *Human Poems*
he shows a marked preference for the classical hendecasyllable,
and will use a sonnet or near sonnet form. This produces a new
and remarkable effect in the (eerily accurate) prophecy of his

death in 'Piedra negra sobre una piedra blanca' (Black stone on a
white stone), where he introduces himself by name. But the formal
structure, a sonnet with 11-syllable lines and a rigorous assonance
pattern, serves to 'frame' him, both reducing and enhancing the
self-pity:

> Me moriré en París con aguacero,
> un día del cual tengo ya el recuerdo.
> Me moriré en París – y no me corro –
> talvez un jueves, como es hoy, de otoño.
>
> Jueves será, porque hoy, jueves, que proso
> estos versos, los húmeros me he puesto
> a la mala y, jamás como hoy, me he vuelto,
> con todo mi camino, a verme solo.
>
> César Vallejo ha muerto, le pegaban
> todos sin que él les haga nada;
> le daban duro con un palo y duro
>
> también con una soga; son testigos
> los días jueves y los huesos húmeros,
> la soledad, la lluvia, los caminos. . .

I shall die in Paris in heavy rain, the day is entered in my brain, I shall
die in Paris – and that's a promise – maybe some Thursday, like this one,
in autumn. ¶Thursday for sure, this Thursday when I churn these verses,
I've placed my arms with bad grace and never as today have I turned
with my whole load, to see myself alone. ¶César Vallejo is dead, they
nailed him down, everyone did, though he did nothing they hit him heavy
with sticks and heavy ¶with a rope: for witnesses are the Thursdays, these
armbones, the aloneness, the rain, the road. . .

Again, in 'Paris, October 1936', sonnet of 11- and 7-syllable lines
and even a rhyme scheme which is perfect save for the wilful
stanza division, he achieves a similar effect, becoming a ghost of
intense immediacy ('surrounded by people, solo, insulate,/my
human semblance rotates/and loosens its shades one by one').

    Implicit in these poems is the problem of locating himself in a
bigger, less personal context. It is not that he disowns his feelings
but that he would make them compatible with his experience of
others, would reconcile what in another poem he calls the 'yo
profundo' ('deep I') with the 'no yo' ('non-I').

> Un hombre pasa con un pan al hombro.
> ¿Voy a escribir, después, sobre mi doble?
> . . .

Un cojo pasa dando el brazo a un niño
Voy, después, a leer a André Bretón?

Otro tiembla de frío, tose, escupe sangre
Cabrá aludir jamás al Yo profundo?

Otro busca en el fango huesos, cáscaras
Cómo escribir, después, del infinito?

. . .

Un paria duerme con el pie a la espalda
Hablar, después, a nadie de Picasso?

. . .

Alguien pasa contando con sus dedos
Cómo hablar del no-yo sin dar un grito?

A man goes by with a loaf of bread on his shoulder. Am I going to write, after that, about my double?... ¶A lame man goes by giving his arm to a child. Am I, after that, going to read André Bretón? ¶Another shakes with cold, coughs, spits blood. Is it ever appropriate to allude to the deep I? ¶Another looks for bones and rinds in the mud. How to write, after that, about the infinite?... ¶A pariah sleeps with his foot to his back. Talk, after that, to anyone about Picasso?... ¶Someone goes by counting on his fingers. How to speak of the non-I and not cry out?

Compared with Neruda's of course, his poetry had little to do with the literary and artistic mode invoked by the mention of the Surrealist Breton and by other names and terms in the poem (Picasso; psychoanalysis). Even so he is clearly saying that his focus if not his poetic needs adjustment.[16]

The hungry and the sick who pass through these couplets become, accordingly, the subjects of further poems. In 'La rueda del hambriento' (The Hungry Man's Rack) it is in fact the undeniable and overwhelming power of hunger, a savage inhuman force, which pulls him out of himself:

Por entre mis propios dientes salgo humeando,
dando voces, pujando,
bajándome los pantalones . . .
Váca mi estómago, váca mi yeyuno,
la miseria me saca por entre mis propios dientes,
cogido con un palito por el puño de la camisa.

Out through my own teeth I go fuming, shouting, pushing, dropping my pants... My stomach vacates, my jejunum vacates, lack pulls me out through my own teeth, caught with a toothpick by my shirt-cuff.

Wrenched out of 'personal' existence, he turns to ask for the smallest comfort, a stone even instead of biblical bread, the humblest and vilest stone. The request is incantatory and remote, as if conscious of its failure, and leaves him again as a 'strange shape'. But this shape haunts us like a minimal humanity, disturbing, and even vaguely threatening: 'but give me/in Spanish/ something, finally to drink, to eat, to live, to rest,/ and then I'll go away'. The phrase 'in Spanish' effectively shows the speaker to be alienated even within his language: from somewhere beyond or inferior to it (Vallejo's lost Indian world?) we have the sensation that it *ought* to work as entreaty. As someone at the limits of human endurance who will not simply 'go away', this beggar thus anticipates the cohorts of beggars whose pain is a weapon for the 'other' (Republican) Spain in a later poem (see below). Vallejo appears again as a hungry man in 'Los desgraciados' (The Unfortunate), an internal dialogue which however implies and then evokes the 'objective' category of victim. Waking early in the morning in some miserable boarding house he says:

> Necesitas comer, pero, me digo,
> no tengas pena, que no es de pobres
> la pena, el sollozar junto a su tumba;
> remiéndate, recuerda,
> confía en tu hilo blanco, fuma, pasa lista
> a tu cadena y guárdala detrás de tu retrato.
> Ya va a venir el día, ponte el alma.

You need to eat, but I say to myself don't feel sorry, for sorrow is inappropriate to the poor, so is weeping by their tomb; patch yourself up, remember, trust in your white thread, smoke, check your chain and put it behind your photograph. The day is about to come, put your soul on.

He finds once again dangerous contradictions in himself (heat and the cold of hunger, for example), but that recurrent one between the soul and the body is resolved momentarily at least in the notion of social exploitation: 'in any case, refrain from being poor with the rich,/poke/your cold, because my warmth is one with it, beloved victim./The day is about to come, put on your body.' In 'Parado en una piedra. . .' (Stopped on a stone) the sight of thousands of unemployed during the Depression led him further to address them as comrades. They, in a contradiction akin to his own, were condemned to 'sweat inwardly' in their forced idleness. Their plight is heard and felt 'in the plural, humanly'.

The struggles and torments of *Trilce* are then translated, in

part through personal experience and with no loss of energy, into
those of men generally, the basic and extreme sufferings of
poverty, indignity and deprivation. But this does not result in the
easy adoption of a political stance, or sympathy with one category
of men at the expense of another. He never put aside the knowledge that the slightest shift in his attitude and impulse towards
his fellow men finally implicated him too, as one of them. Even
in his solidarity with the victims of the Depression he remains
preoccupied with what man is in the first place, existentially, and
what he can do to help himself. And while attributing misery to
the social and economic interests he criticized so implacably in
his prose[17] he sees it still as a consequence of man's primary condition (his address to the 'comrade' workers as a class is startling
and unique in *Human Poems*). The human soul suffers first of
all 'from being its body', as the title of one poem has it. Man is a
miserable ape, 'Darwin's little lad', striving against near-impos-
sible odds. Vallejo speaks of him repeatedly in the biological
language of evolutionary science as a species that resembles others
all too closely anatomically. He is filled with sudden 'political'
love for his 'brother humans', only to be drawn back perilously
close to biological pessimism and admission of Original Sin. As
we see, the problems he reserved for his poetry did not cease to be
theological: if anything, his pained echoes and resigned references
to the Scriptures become more frequent than in earlier collections.
So that when he makes an act of faith in man it is expressly that
and goes some way from dialectical materialism.

If there is a positive hero in *Human Poems* it is the Bolshevik.
This eminently secular creature is however greeted in an Annun-
ciation ('Salutación angélica') that is pointedly reminiscent of the
announcement of Christ's birth in the Bible. The Bolshevik is
above nationality, the embodiment of a better humanity and
'another life':

> Mas sólo tú demuestras, descendiendo
> o subiendo del pecho, bolchevique,
> tus trazos confundibles,
> tu gesto marital,
> tu cara de padre,
> tus piernas de amado,
> tu cutis por teléfono,
> tu alma perpendicular
> a la mía,

> tus codos de justo
> y un pasaporte en blanco en tu sonrisa.

But only you show, falling or rising from the heart, Bolshevik, your con-
fusable features, your marital gesture, your father face, your lover legs,
your telephoned skin, your soul perpendicular to mine, your just man's
elbows and a blank passport in your smile.

Vallejo exalts the Bolshevik's doctrinal warmth, his liberation
through technology and love, against his own old mixed nature,
suggesting even that this admiring poem of his may be vanity and
a way of attracting attention. He attributes to his hero not only
the right to act on behalf of other men, but a knowledge of their
imperfections which he, Vallejo, may possibly not now go beyond:

> Y digo, bolchevique, tomando esta flaqueza
> en su feroz linaje de exhalación terrestre;
> hijo natural del bien y del mal
> y viviendo talvez por vanidad, para que digan,
> me dan tus simultáneas estaturas mucha pena,
> puesto que tú no ignoras en quién se me hace
>     tarde diariamente,
> en quién estoy callado y medio tuerto.

And I say, Bolshevik, taking this weakness in its fierce lineage of terrestrial
exhaltation : natural child of good and evil and living perhaps for vanity,
so they notice, your simultaneous statures give me much pain, since you
are not unaware in whom it gets late for me daily, in whom I am silent
and half-one-eyed.

It is only a short step from here to Vallejo's longest and most
ambitious poem, the 'Himno a los voluntarios de la República'
(Hymn to the volunteers of the Republic), which opens *Spain*.
The volunteers, the militia with their bones 'so worthy of faith',
move him as the Bolshevik did, here to the point of perplexity:

> no sé verdaderamente
> qué hacer, dónde ponerme; corro, escribo
>     aplaudo,
> lloro, atisbo, destrozo, apagan, digo
> a mi pecho que acabe, al bien, que venga,
> y quiero desgraciarme;

I really don't know what to do, where to put myself; I run, write, applaud,
weep, spy, destroy, they put it out, I say to my chest it should end, to
good it should come : and I want to ruin myself.

Faced with heroes of such positive courage he cannot adjust himself to his own 'size'; what he calls his 'smallness in the dress of

greatness' he would break against the volunteers' 'double-edged speed'. Then for the first time in his poetry he introduces a sense of history, if only obliquely and briefly. The volunteers' cause is justified by the electoral mandate of the Republic, especially during the 'biennium of murky supplicant semesters' (1934–6), as it is strengthened by the latent if contradictory strengths of the Spanish tradition: the stoic Quevedo for example is pictured as 'the instant godfather of dynamiters'. As if intimately admitting the possibility of the tradition in himself he goes on now holding his ground and addresses the liberator, the peasant and 'the agricultural, civil and martial builders of a world of sudden gold'. This is a world beyond the revolution where man's endemic imperfection may be overcome. In language once again close to biblical prophecy he sees the fulfilment of mankind: even the ants and elephants, which he and other humans had been reduced to, themselves become human:

> Entrelazándose hablarán los mudos, los tullidos
>     andarán!
> Verán, ya de regreso, los ciegos
> y palpitando escucharán los sordos!
> Sabrán los ignorantes, ignorarán los sabios!
> Serán dados los besos que no pudísteis dar!
> Sólo la muerte morirá! La hormiga
> traerá pedacitos de pan al elefante encadenado
> a su brutal delicadeza;

The dumb will speak intertwined, the maimed will walk! The blind, returning now, will see and quivering the deaf will hear! The ignorant will be wise, the wise ignorant! The kisses you could not give will now be given! Only death will die! The ant will bring crumbs of bread to the elephant enchained in its brutal delicacy.

The following lines affirm this as a new scripture, a strictly human Pater Noster: 'Worker, our saviour and redeemer, forgive us, brother, our debts!' Still without distinguishing the 'enemy' politically he justifies the volunteers' need to kill for life, 'for the good'. 'Do it for the freedom of all', he says, 'of the exploited and the exploiter.' Vallejo proceeds then, even at such an intense and climactic moment as this, not by denouncing evil in the other (which always includes him), but by invoking the good which his act of faith demands should accompany those he addresses:

> Marcha hoy de vuestra parte el bien ardiendo,
> os siguen con cariño los reptiles de pestaña inmanente

> y, a dos pasos, a uno,
> la dirección del agua que corre a ver su límite antes que arda.

Today good marches in flames on your behalf, reptiles with immanent eyelashes follow you with affection and, two steps, one step behind, the direction of the water coursing to see its limit before it burns.

Yet at the very height of this assertion, this trusting extension of himself, he hints that the impossible may not happen. The last of the fifteen poems in *Spain* poses the question : what will happen 'if Spain falls'? The cup that he would not drink at the extremity of his own life (like Christ at Gethsemane) is the vision of defeat, of the return to a situation in which '2' again seems 'old in an exercise book' and we descend the steps of the alphabet to the letter 'at which grief was born'. His small surviving hope is that in this inadmissible case the children of the world will go out to look for their 'mother', will not give up embarking on a journey to majority or adulthood which for him was so painful and contradictory. Without a messiah (who has 'come and gone'), orphaned, man must proceed with the 'frank rectitude of a bitter lame man', as he says in one of the *Human Poems*. That is, until the day 'he' returns, he would proceed with the unquenched hope that 'the animal that I am will walk among judges' and that

> nuestro bravo meñique será grande,
> digno, infinito dedo entre los dedos.

Our bold little finger will be big, worthy, and infinite finger among the fingers.

Then the youngest child (as Vallejo biographically was) will assume his place among his only possible judges, his fellows. The 'size', the number 1, the ego, the little finger, which induce sickening paranoia in *Trilce*, and in a human poem like 'The accent hangs' (where the judges spy on him and render more explicit that phallic overtone we noted earlier), the size which caused such perplexity in the 'Hymn', will thus become just, infinite yet comradely. If Vallejo wrote a final poem it is the one which sums all this up. 'Masa' (Mass) is a statement whose simplicity in the context of his work makes it vigorous and irrefutable. Only when men inhabit themselves and without exception wish to live can they overcome their greatest absurdity, death.

> Al fin de la batalla,
> y muerto el combatiente, vino hacia él un hombre

y le dijo: «¡No mueras; te amo tanto!»
Pero el cadáver ¡ay! siguió muriendo.

Se le acercaron dos y repitiéronle:
«¡No nos dejes! ¡Valor! ¡Vuelve a la vida!»
Pero el cadáver ¡ay! siguió muriendo.

Acudieron a él veinte, cien, mil, quinientos mil,
clamando: «¡Tanto amor, y no poder nada contra
   la muerte!»
Pero el cadáver ¡ay! siguió muriendo.

Le rodearon millones de individuos,
con un ruego común: «¡Quédate hermano!»
Pero el cadáver ¡ay! siguió muriendo.

Entonces todos los hombres de la tierra
le rodearon; les vio el cadáver triste, emocionado:
incorporóse lentamente,
abrazó al primer hombre; echóse a andar...

At the end of the battle, with the combatant dead, a man came up and
told him: 'Don't die, I love you so much!' But the corpse, alas! went
on dying. ¶Two others came up and said to him again: 'Don't leave
us! Courage! Come back to life!' But the corpse, alas! went on dying.
¶Twenty, a hundred, a thousand, five hundred thousand ran up to him,
crying out: 'So much love and no way of countering death!' But the
corpse, alas! went on dying. ¶Millions of individuals stood round him,
with a common plea: 'Stay here brother!' But the corpse alas! went on
dying. ¶Then all the men on earth stood round him; the sad corpse saw
them, with emotion; he got up slowly, embraced the first man; began to
walk...

The pace of the development which culminated in this poem had
accelerated towards the end of Vallejo's life. Most of the *Human
Poems* and all of *Spain* were written in his last year. While the
urgent concerns of the 1930s in the Spanish Civil War can hardly
be said to have affected Neruda less deeply, the change was prolonged and fully effected only with his becoming a communist in
1944. And it was expressed fully only in the poetry which accompanied and followed that event: the poems of the last (5th) section
of the *Third Residence* (which praise the Red Army for their
feats in the World War); *Las uvas y el viento* (The Grapes and the
Wind, 1954), an account of his departure from the Chile of
González Videla and his journeys through Europe, especially
communist Europe; the four books of *Elemental Odes* (1954–9),[18]
in which he elaborates the basic thoughts of the 'Three Material
Songs' into an aesthetic; and above all the great *Canto general*,

which we discussed at some length in chapter 3. Because they register the beginnings of the change it is worth looking at the third, transitional section of the *Third Residence*, 'Reunión bajo nuevas banderas' (Meeting Under New Flags), and *Spain in the heart*, which constitutes the fourth section of that book.

Though the Civil War entered Neruda's poetry more abruptly than it did Vallejo's, he prepares us for a change in his 'Meeting', and in statements about the nature and function of poetry published shortly before hostilities began. Referring to his 'residences' up to that point, he reports in 'Meeting' how he sounded the murkiest depths: 'I sank my heart in all this, I heard all/the baneful salt: at night/I went to plant my roots: I registered the bitterness of the earth.' And evoking the destructive intensity of 'The furies and the pains', he says he then walked as a wolf. All this must now yield to a human imperative, must give way to human passage. The earth, however dark and bitter, has produced a wild cereal that is like a 'day palpitating with human dreams'. He recognizes and affirms his humanity in his very imperfections and impurity and will no longer be dismayed by bestial instinct or sense of innate destruction and decay. The poem is thus consistent with his manifestos of the period. If the poet makes himself his *persona preferida*, his preferred person(a), and draws only on his own 'miserable treasure', he will in the end suffer from the same poverty and isolation as those who remain loyal to the symbolist tradition, notably Valéry, and in Spain Juan Ramón Jiménez, with their ideas of pure poetry. Against this, in agreement with Alberti and others, he urges a move towards impure poetry:

May the poetry we seek be thus, worn as by an acid, by the duties of the hand, steeped in sweat and smoke, smelling of urine and lilies, spattered by the various professions exercised within and outside the law.

An impure poetry, like a suit, like a body, with stains of food and shameful doings, wrinkled, of observations, dreams, wakefulness, prophecies, confessions of love and hatred, beasts, quakes, idylls, political beliefs, negations, doubts, affirmations, taxes.[19]

Things counter, original, spare and strange, men's 'gear, tackle and trim', the freckled variety of the world, inspired Gerard Manley Hopkins to praise of God. Through an admittedly soiled version of them Neruda reaches towards human solidarity, emphasizing just that soiled imperfection that links him with others. But in both cases there is a moral deduction. This becomes quite clear in Neruda's 'Canto sobre unas ruinas' (Song on some ruins), one of the Civil War poems, though distinguished from the rest by its generality (the ruins could be anywhere). Destruction, while ceaseless and natural, can also be wanton, and in this second case is to be abhorred because it works against man's efforts, vulnerable and puny as these may be.

> Todo ha ido y caído
> brutalmente marchito.
> Utensilios heridos, telas
> nocturnas, espuma sucia, orines justamente
> vertidos, mejillas, vidrio, lana,
> alcanfor, círculos de hilo y cuero, todo,
> todo por una rueda vuelto al polvo,

Everything is gone, has fallen, is brutally withered. Wounded utensils, noctural cloths, scum, piss just released, cheeks, glass, wool, camphor, rings of thread and leather, everything, everything put back to dust by a wheel.

Neruda's old vision of total decomposition and mutual extermination remains in this poem in the continuing admission of the intimacy between putrefaction and growth ('the flower that rises from the bone destroyed'). But his emphasis is now on man's endeavour to survive and build, his soiled tools becoming the equivalent of those 'good elements', celery, wine, of the 'Three material songs'.

It is then not so much a question of life's processes changing as of Neruda's attitude towards them. Vallejo, who incorporated everything into the self that speaks in his poems struggled hard to make them human, always aware, as we have seen, both of the perils of 'impurity' and of the fact that those who destroy, who do not overcome the animal in them, are also human. Simply by adopting a different stance Neruda is able to announce in two stanzas of 'meeting' his equivalent of Vallejo's hard-earned achievement:

> Yo de los hombres tengo la misma mano herida,
> yo sostengo la misma copa roja
> e igual asombro enfurecido
> . . .
>
> Y así reunido,
> duramente central, no busco asilo
> en los huecos del llanto:

I of men have the same wounded hand, I uphold the same red cup and similar infuriated astonishment... ¶And thus reunited, hard and central, I don't seek asylum in the hollows of weeping.

In a poem like 'Epistle to the Passers-by', Vallejo, after warring with himself, can say: 'And I myself convalesce, smiling with my lips'; and we like him can only hope that the smile is that uniquely human act and not a simian grin. Firmly 'reunited', Neruda offers himself to us with confidence, a veteran of inner anguish that is chemical sooner than zoological: 'Look at this face/newly emerged from the terrible salt/look at this bitter mouth that smiles,/look at this new heart that salutes you/with its flower overflowing, determined and golden.'

With that agility we have noted in him throughout, Neruda can do this just because he is able to present his 'I' from some ulterior position that in the last instance is immune. Vallejo could not have said 'I have of men the same wounded hand', or 'I join my wolf steps to the steps of man', because he would not admit a formal distinction on this scale between 'I' and 'they' in the first place. This in turn makes it easier for Neruda to 'explain' the new departures in his poetry, offering himself as a creature of circumstance from somewhere implicitly beyond it. In the *Third Residence* he apologizes for the mood of 'The furies and the pains', saying it was written in a previous world, by another man, placing characteristic weight on the conjunction in the phrase 'The world has changed and my poetry has changed'. And rhetorically this anticipates later 'explanations' of the whole of the *Residences* prior to 'Meeting' as a product of a sick capitalist society. Perhaps the most famous of his Civil War poems is in fact entitled 'I explain a few things'. Assuming his reader's desire to know why he is no longer obsessed with his 'poppy-covered metaphysics', he answers that surrounding reality, 'the blood in the streets' of Madrid, left him no alternative but solidarity. He appears almost as someone arguing a case on his behalf: witnesses are called, friends like 'Rafael' (Alberti) and 'Federico' (García Lorca). Other 'evidence' is circumstantial: the brute facts of the bombardment of Madrid. An accomplished attorney he concludes the poem with an impassioned appeal of increasingly urgent rhythms:

> Venid a ver la sangre por las calles,
> venid a ver
> la sangre por las calles,

venid a ver la sangre
por las calles!

Come and see the blood in the streets,/come and see/the blood in the
streets,/come and see the blood/in the streets!

By the same token Neruda 'sets the stage' for his other Civil
War poems. The geography and history of the moment are given
in accounts of specific battles (Jarama, Almería) and reports
coming in from other places.[20] The actors are similarly identified:
the people's army, the militia and the international volunteers on
the one side; the generals, the priests and the rich on the other.
In their midst, and with consummate dramatic sense, Neruda
either exhorts and comforts or curses and reviles. These poems
first reveal Neruda's huge talent for invective (fostered incidentally by his reading of Quevedo[21] while in Madrid). 'Sanjurjo in
hell', the *guardia civil*, the 'hyenas from Africa', embody a decomposition now definitely evil as the pus and pestilence of Spain
(contrast Vallejo's view of tradition), and his denunciations of
them anticipate those of González Videla in *Canto general*. Correspondingly, the tenderness of his solace for the mothers of dead
militia men, issued from his heart to theirs, matches that which
he later expressed for the natural and elemental world of his beloved and wronged America. The point is, his own position, his
human size, as Vallejo put it, is never a problem. Vallejo spoke
of the conflict between the 'yo durable, profundo' (the durable,
deep I') and the 'non-I'; Neruda asserts an I that is 'duramente
central' (hard and central'): already in 'Unidad' he had spoken of
himself as 'central', surrounded by others. There could be no
clearer contrast than that between Vallejo's 'Hymn' and Neruda's
praise of the international volunteers. Seeing them arrive in
Madrid, so far from feeling inadequate, Neruda swells with pride,
appropriate to his witness of the moment. In short he oscillates
between tenderness and outrage, pride and execration, emotions
which even if humanly contradictory are explained and justified
in the material circumstances, or to use his word, the 'contexture'
presented in his poems.

Distrusting Neruda's capacity as a performer, his rhetorical play
with his 'I' from some remoter and shielded consciousness, certain
critics have censured him for it. For them he lacks Vallejo's
rigorous and agonized sense of self and of being human, and

escapes too easily from what he 'is' in a series of dramatic personae. One of the most intelligent criticisms of this kind contrasts Neruda with Vallejo in terms of their origins and responsibilities as poets.

Neruda found in the third book of *Residencia* the key to becoming *the* twentieth-century South American poet: the revolutionary stance which always changes with the tides of time. With that recognition and its acceptance Neruda became a figure – or let us say his detachment worked. Vallejo, in spite of his travels from country to country, never could come to terms with one system, and it seems to be to his benefit, for he has produced a poetry dense in texture that holds his feelings and, in reading, releases them. . . In Vallejo the amount of physical suffering is the alteration that it seeks.[22]

Propositions such as this force us on to the problem of the sincerity, or apparent truthfulness of poetry, since, here at least, that of the poet matters only in what he creates. For his part, Vallejo does not allow us to imagine him using his poetry for anything but an exploration and a quest for faith that were as important to him as they could be to anyone else. He is so much in his language, his tone and attitudes, that for these purposes he is revealed as selfless. From *The Black Heralds* to *Spain*, he can be felt as a constant unrelenting consciousness which could be denied only bestially, or by someone of superhuman intelligence and moral certainty. And that sense of being on the very frontier of what he is and would become gives his poems their power and glory. But to say this should not mean that we censure Neruda for failing to be Vallejo. Neruda, so prolific, can be lax, a 'great bad poet' (to use the phrase Juan Ramón Jiménez used to revenge himself on Neruda). And his changes of stance 'with the tides of time' may not always be perfectly effected. But seeing him as merely circumstantial is another matter. His dramatic and rhetorical skills, better his ability to speak out of his circumstances, however difficult, is no less that of a poet. And in Neruda's case it was consummate. In his best poetry (of which there is much) he speaks on a scale and with an agility unrivalled in Latin America.[23] In *Canto general*, notably in the section 'America, I do not invoke your name in vain', he created a huge centre of energy that is both personal and continental; and in the closing sections he plunges deep enough into persona or personality for his words to be inconceivable as a histrionic act: the final art that effaces itself. And in subsequent works, like the reflective *Estravagario* (1958)[24] he operates with such subtlety and sure-footedness that he can allude without loss to just the 'defect' he has been charged with, in lines like 'I'd love to be able to press a bell and summon the real me', or 'I'm no good at being independent'. The multiple ironies of 'statements' like these belong to a poet who can also say, openly:

> Por eso no pido perdón
> Estoy en mi sitio de siempre
> Tengo un árbol con tantas hojas
> que aunque no me jacto de eterno
> me río de ti y del otoño.

So I make no excuse. I'm in my usual place. I have a tree with so many leaves that though I don't boast immortality, I can laugh at you and the autumn.

# 7. The traditions of Octavio Paz

Paz began publishing in late adolescence, in the 1930s. Since then he has travelled widely in literature and the world, and his writing has passed through several important stages, chapters of an unusually rich intellectual biography. Universalist by inclination, he has been successively affected by different cultures, philosophies and religions, of which he made 'creeds' of his own: ancient Mexican, Surrealist, Hispanic, Oriental, and so on. Of course, these stages of his creeds can seldom be separated cleanly from one another (partly because of the way he has tended and arranged his poems in recent anthologies).[1] Moreover, there are undoubted constants in his work, ideas which he comes back to again and again, and which have been well described in criticism[2]: a disrespect for inherited language, which dates from his earliest poems ('Las palabras', 'Destino del poeta'); his eroticism; his quest for primordial man; his anarchic equation of sexual with social form. However, a progression of particular enthusiasms can be seen in his writing about poetry no less than in the poetry itself. For it is on these twin testimonies[3] that his considerable authority rests, both inside and outside Mexico. As a poet–critic he is unrivalled as an interpreter of the poetry and poetic traditions of his sub-continent, even though he has admittedly been somewhat taciturn about the great figures Vallejo and Neruda.

I

An early (though hardly enduring) obsession of Paz's was with the past of Mexico, with its suppressed 'maternal' tradition. In the *Labyrinth of Solitude* (1950) he set about exposing the Mexican soul and the violently antagonistic elements which formed his nation. He saw himself and his compatriots as children of an inadmissible historical event: the Spanish rape of Indian Mexico, Cortes's murder of Cuauhtemoc and humiliation of Malinche. Neither Hispanist nor indigenist prejudice could of itself provide an acceptable national legend, the consequent dilemma being expressed in every form of Mexican life. Where pre-Hispanic belief could be incorporated into Christianity, it had been; but only at the expense of both religions. He writes with especial eloquence of the degree to which such figures as the Aztec god Huitzilopchtli and the last Aztec emperor Cuauhtemoc had become identified with Christ, but with a Christ definitively crucified, whose essence was bloody, mutilated failure. He speaks too of the Virgin, of implausible purity, who locally derived strength from such mother figures as Coatlicue, the earth goddess 'snake skirt', and her associate Itzpapalotl, 'Obsidian Butterfly'. This second goddess is evoked with extraordinary energy in his 'Mariposa de obsidiana', a prose poem from ¿Aguila o Sol? (Eagle or Sun?) of this period, when Garibay's Aztec translations were beginning to circulate in Mexico[4]. She is the withered crone whose men and children have been murdered, now 'so small and grey' that many mistake her for a pile of dust. Yet still inside her she has the power to be the 'fixed centre that moves the dance' and so recall how she tore open the clouds to make rain and planted gardens of fire, gardens of blood, in the southern sky. The man devoted or sacrificed to her can still reach 'the other side of the year' where 'you will open my body into two to read the letters of your destiny'.

Another poem, much briefer and less violent, is a response to a quartz mask of Tlaloc, an ancient god of rain and fertility. His very age guaranteed him a kind of immunity in the holocaust, and Paz makes him into a rare emblem of hope:

> Tocado por la luz
> el cuarzo ya es cascada.
> Sobre sus aguas flota, niño, el dios.

Touched by the light the quartz is now a cascade. On its waters floats, a child, the god.

Yet the career of this infant is short lived. He suffers from the start from that distancing which puts the poem in the Parnassian tradition: an object encased for inspection. Other 'pre-Columbian' pieces gathered as appropriately-named Loose Stones (Piedras sueltas, 1955) are of the same kind: cameos of the ruins at Uxmal, for example, unalterably remote from any living city. Mexican references continue to crop up in later collections, though less and less often, and never as a serious proposition. A long section of a later poem 'Salamandra' is devoted to the myth of Xolotl (an aspect of Quetzalcoatl), to telling how this god refused to sacrifice himself so that the sun might have strength and rise.

No late el sol clavado en la mitad del cielo
No respira
No comienza la vida sin la sangre
Sin la brasa del sacrificio
No se mueve la rueda de los días
Xólotl se niega a consumirse

The sun does not pulse nailed in the middle of the sky, does not breathe, life does not begin without blood, without the sacrificial brand the wheel of the days does not move, Xolotl refuses to be consumed.

The details and the old vision may be there, even down to precise quotations, in translation, from the Aztec *Legend of the Suns*; but the point is not. In fact this whole section is literally parenthetical, so much incidental information. The 'true' amphibian is the old world salamander and not its American counterpart, the axolotl; it is the 'caucasian' (Paz's word) creature who is nearer to the beginning of the life Paz is interested in. In other words, gods and myths from Mexico's Indian culture do little more than decorate Paz's poems as counterweights or exotica. When this is not true, as in the case of the fearsome Itzpapalotl, then they are as it were self-destructive, self-cancelling. The destiny to be read in her sundered body is precisely the absence of one. As he says in *Labyrinth of Solitude*, the Mexican is the child of nothing and begins in himself.

As such a child of nothing, then, Paz differs from those 'indigenist' writers who feed on the old lore of their country. Specifically, he parts company from those compatriots of his who believe in the cultural programme of the Mexican Revolution, which in the 1920s had produced murals of paradisiacal Indians, like Orozco's Malinche, the Mexican Eve. All this was false or fond, while the proposition that Mexicans should recover the customs of their American forebears, and their language (which Paz himself displays little knowledge of), seemed to him preposterous or even 'lunatic'. He would himself wish to descend from neither Indian nor Spaniard but to 'deny' them both. In his poetry this is exactly what he has done, encasing Tlaloc and rending Itzpapalotl in two. Very occasionally a phrase of his will catch an Aztec expression: the 'flowered bone' in 'Vaivén' derives from the Nahuatl lyrics in the *Cantares mexicanos*. But little more. His attitude is perhaps best drawn in his most famous 'Mexican' poem, 'Sun Stone,' 'Piedra de sol'.

This title is the name given to a large stone disc prominently displayed in the Anthropological Museum in Mexico City. Its discovery excited much attention but the full meaning of the designs carved on it remains unclear. Sunstone may well prove to be a misnomer; but there can be no doubt that it records facts of the Mesoamerican calendar and possibly correlates the magic *tonalpohualli* of the Aztecs (the divinatory count formed of 20 signs and 13 numbers), with solar and planetary cycles. Paz in fact allots to his poem the same number of lines (584) as there are days in the synodic cycle of Venus, a planet which in turn unquestionably features in many Mesoamerican myths, as the heavenly form of Quetzalcoatl and other heroes. He also makes his poem circular like the stone, by bringing us at the end back to the opening lines:

> un sauce de cristal, un chopo de agua,
> un alto surtidor que el viento arquea.
> un árbol bien plantado mas danzante,
> un caminar de río que se curva
> avanza, retrocede, da un rodeo
> y llega siempre:

A crystal willow, a poplar of water, a high jet arched by the wind, a tree well planted but dancing, a river movement which bends, advances, goes back, turns round and arrives always:

Within this circular time he sets episodes from his life, his first loves in Mexico, being in Madrid during the Spanish Civil War. His plan is to switch loves and deaths out of their separate histories into a state where 'what happened was not but is being', and in which identity itself becomes plural (like 'personal' names derived from the *tonalpohualli*); or shockingly, even a disgusting illusion:

> ¿Cuándo somos de veras lo que somos?,
> bien mirado no somos, nunca somos
> a solas sino vértigo y vacío,
> muecas en el espejo, horror y vómito

When are we really what we are?, closely considered we are not, by ourselves we never are anything but vertigo and vacuum, grimace in the mirror, horror and vomit.

The force of the poem, Paz's first major lyric, is palpable, and due in part to reliance on an arcane sense of time and personality. Yet 'closely considered', in precisely those respects, he proves to be much less an Indian sage than a late Spanish Romantic: 'fate', 'presage', 'omen' are spoken of not in the holistic terms of the *tonalpohualli* but in a nineteenth-century idiom which looks back to the Counter Reformation and the Spanish Golden Age:

> un caminar entre las espesuras
> de los días futuros y el aciago
> fulgor de la desdicha como un ave
> petrificando el bosque con su canto

A movement among the thickets of the future days and the fateful glare of misfortune like a bird petrifying the woods with his song.

While doubtless the formal context of the poem continues to create tension with this very foreign mode within it, the conflicts of such a relationship hardly suggest that the poet is wholly in control of or even very interested in them. For all his desire to collapse linear history into a moment, in a key passage about crime and evil in the world (lines 436–74) we progress through it (and through an immaculately Western version of it at that) in relentless sequence, from Cain and Abel (lines whose atmospheric sentimentality incidentally echoes Manuel Machado and Albert Samain)[5] to the death throes of Trotsky and Madero. Linear movement, from one point to another, is further enforced by the use of such etymologically resonant verbs as *disertar* ('the jackal dissertates among the ruins of Niniveh'). A last irony is the fact that though Paz would credit the ancient Mexicans with no more than a circular notion of time (into which his own is more or less loosely fitted), their codices show that they were quite aware of the problems implicit in 'Sun Stone' and of expressing them formally perhaps more satisfyingly than this poem does.[6]

In the last analysis it would probably be no less delicate a task to trace Paz's Mexican origin in his poetry than it would be to think of Vallejo or Neruda as specifically *South* American poets (though we made some effort in that direction with Neruda in chapter 3). At any rate, a Mexico of literature and personal experience was Paz's touchstone in *Labyrinth of Solitude* and *Eagle or Sun?* Before we pass on to his next phase it is perhaps worth exploring this initial sense of origin a little further by comparing him with one of the salient Mexican poets of the following generation, which he has variously inspired. José Emilio Pacheco (1939–) was one of the co-editors of Paz's own fundamental Mexican anthology *Poesía en movimiento. Mexico, 1915–66*, and his early work, *Los elementos de la noche* (The Elements of Night, 1963) and *El reposo del fuego* (The Repose of Fire, 1966), shows a certain indebtedness to Paz, who is also one of his best critics. At first sight Pacheco is a lot less 'indigenous' than the Paz of *Eagle or Sun*? We look in vain for cameos of pre-Columbian cities, evocations of ancient American gods, poetry that is in any way 'about' Mexico and its past. At the same time, in his numerous translations and his constant recourse to the classical antiquity of the Old World (above all, Heraclitus), Pacheco sustains from the start a universal erudition reminiscent of the 'foundation' poet of *Poesía en movimiento*: the great humanist Alfonso Reyes (1889–1959). When Mexico filters into Pacheco's poems it is as something irrepressible and yet all but impossible to represent in words. The following poem from *El reposo del fuego* is explicit enough on this point:

> Mexico subterráneo... El poderoso
> virrey, emperador, sátrapa hizo
> construir para sí todo el desierto.
> Hemos creado el desierto,
> las montañas
> – rígidas de basalto y sombra y polvo –
> son la inmovilidad.
> Ah, cuánto estruendo
> el de las aguas muertas resonando
> en el silencio cóncavo
>                     Es retórica,
> iniquidad retórica mi llanto.

Subterranean Mexico... The powerful viceroy, emperor, satrap had the whole desert built for himself. We have created the desert, the mountains – rigid with basalt and shadow and dust – are immobility. Ah, what a din that of the dead waters resounding in the concave silence. It is rhetoric, rhetorical iniquity my weeping.

Pacheco is wholly remarkable for never ceasing to reach towards a truer rhetoric, a voice that can express even part of that heritage and not totally destroy his other inherited culture of the West. (In this he once again resembles Reyes.) Few other poets of his generation have resisted the divisiveness of being Mexican as successfully. Tomás Segovia, for example, seemed to uphold the Old World *against* the Indian one in his collection *Anagnórisis* (1967), and it is significant that he later abandoned the style and cultural pretensions of that book entirely, out of respect for what he calls the 'forgotten abyss' of Mexico. Ostensibly on the 'other side' we find a poet like Marco Antonio Montes de Oca, whose verse has been much enhanced by the glittering strangeness of Nahuatl lyrics in collections like *Delante de la luz cantan los pájoros* (The Birds Sing Before the Light, 1959). But once again the style, brilliant as Paz (for one) has recognized it to be, does not last, and disappears under pressure from a real modern world (as we note in the following chapter). A recent poem by Pacheco in fact hints this delicately, with its untranslatable pun on 'pavo real', the peacock of Modernist poetry that is either royal or real ('Un pavo real visto por Montes de Oca'):

> En el vago jardín rubendariano
> con soberbia despliega sus vitrales
> Y en la fuente de musgo
> lanza un grito
> de pavor
> porque el agua no refleja
> sus pavoirrealidad.

In the vague Rubén-Darío-esque garden it displays its stained glass with pride. And at the moss fountain it utters a cry of terror because the water does not reflect its pavoirreality.

Interestingly, it is precisely when the pressure of modern 'reality' is greatest that Pacheco finds a way of speaking from out of his past. For example, his poem on the government's massacre of students and civilians at Tlatelolco (the site of a pre-Columbian temple in Mexico City) in 1968, draws powerfully on a Nahuatl lament ('Lectura de los Cantares Mexicanos: Manuscrito de Tlatelolco, octubre 1968', in *No me preguntes cómo pasa el tiempo*, 1969):

> Cuando todos se hubieron reunido,
> los hombres en armas de guerra
> fueron a cerrar la salidas,
> las entradas, los pasos.
> Sus perros van por delante,
> los van precediendo.
>
> Entonces se oyó el estruendo,
> entonces se alzaron los gritos.
> Muchos maridos buscaban a sus mujeres.
> Unos llevaban en brazos a sus hijos pequeños.
> Con perfidia fueron muertos,
> sin saberlo murieron.
>
> . . .

Ah yo nací en la guerra florida,
yo soy mexicano.
Sufro, mi corazón se llena de pena;
veo la desolación que se cierne sobre el templo
cuando todos los escudos se abrasan en llamas.

En los caminos yacen dardos rotos.
Las casas están destechadas.
Enrojecidos tienen sus muros.
Gusanos pululan por calles y plazas.

Golpeamos los muros de adobe
y es nuestra herencia
una red de agujeros.

Esto es lo que ha hecho el Dador de la Vida
allí en Tlatelolco.

When everyone was assembled the men with weapons of war went to close the exits, the entrances, the ways through. Their dogs go before them, precede them. ¶Then the uproar was heard, then the shouts were raised. Many husbands looked for their wives. Some carried their children in their arms. They were killed by treachery, they died not knowing it... ¶Ah I was born in the flowery war, I am Mexican. I suffer, my heart is filled with grief; I see desolation hovering over the temple when all the shields are burned in flames ¶Broken spears lie on the roads. The houses are without roofs. Their walls are reddened. Worms swarm through streets and squares. ¶We beat the walls of adobe and our heritage is a net of holes. ¶This is what the Giver of Life has done, there in Tlatelolco.

With its Nahuatl parallelisms, eerie expression of persona, and intricate tense structure, this poem echoes native accounts of the Spanish conquest ('broken spears') and of the 'flowery war' fought for sacrificial victims in ancient Mexico. And this echo is as unrelenting, necessary and continuous as Pacheco's sense of heritage, which also informs his short stories *El principio del placer*, 1972, and appears again in his most recent verse collection *Irás y no volverás* (You Will Go and Not Return, 1973), especially in the section 'Homage to Nezahualcoyotl'.

In other words, Pacheco has refused to let his complex national heritage be a phase, something to go on from, as it has been with Paz. He has also refused to let the 'inadmissible' or 'forgotten' Indian part of it either drown the rest or itself be submerged in silence. Paz has well described himself as a poet of movement, whose existence is defined by successive moments; and, as we shall see, only in much more recent and maturer verse has he integrated the epistemology of such a definition into his writing.

Pacheco by contrast is static: there is a thunderous circuit in his work which will not go away nor is urged to.

2

In most respects Paz's biggest 'Mexican' poem, 'Sun Stone', in fact belongs more properly to the collection it appeared in: *La estación violenta* (The Violent Season, 1958). Complemented by Paz's first major work of criticism, *El arco y la lira* (The Bow and the Lyre, 1956), these poems as a whole amount if anything to a certain scepticism about the idea of Mexico. At any event, he openly repudiates the indigenists and the social realists, and all forms of national concern with culture. Against these traditions he would set another, which had come to fascinate him more and more from the late 1940s onwards, that of the Surrealists. In a metaphor fundamental to all his writing, but especially to that of this period, he would break out of his labyrinth of solitude into new utterance. Out of empty constriction, in which man is fragmented socially and erotically, he would join the Surrealists in conjuring that marvellous instant when we truly 'inhabit our names'.

Paz was 'converted' to surrealism by André Breton, to whom he was introduced by Benjamin Péret in Paris after the Second World War. His essay on Breton's death in 1966[7] is passionate and brilliant, even by his standards. There he records that it was a chapter from Breton's *L'Amour fou* (the fifth) and Blake's *Marriage of Heaven and Hell* which had first opened for him 'the doors of modern poetry'. By this he meant that he came to share the Surrealists' ideas of what constituted the 'modernity' of poetry, making their line of moral and literary precursors his own: Sade (the subject of an urgently affectionate homage, 'The Prisoner'), Nerval, Novalis, Baudelaire, Rimbaud, Apollinaire. *The Bow and the Lyre*, which has a good deal to say about these writers and the 'great Romantics' in general, might be thought of as a second spiritual history written under the new tutelage of Breton; as for the poems of *The Violent Season*, they mark the high point of such European influence in his work.

Though these poems abound with epigraphs and submerged quotations from this source, Paz rarely pushes towards those extremes of traumatic distortion or fluidity which mark, say, Dali's paintings, or David Gascoyne's response to them. Nor do his poems often flash with 'absurd' humour. Figures like 'the girl who slips over the shining edge of the guillotine', and the man who descends from the moon with a fragrant bunch of epitaphs (two of the 'Masks of Dawn'), are rare visitors. It was as though, having heard the Surrealist message a little late, he felt bound to take it very seriously. There is little in *The Violent Season* which does not conform to a set of given *ideas*. For example, the poem just mentioned, 'Masks of Dawn', clearly has a lot to do with the Apollinaire of a poem like 'Zone'. There is the same location in a city (Venice, Paris) at specific times of the day, the same attention to the names and shapes of places in the city, and to the very different types of people who inhabit it. Further, both poets attribute a certain deadness in life to 'this ancient world' of Europe, driven back to Byzantium by the new spirit. But while Apollinaire's footwork is so fast and subtle (beyond the amazing effects of 'Zone's' being an *ambulatory* poem) that we could hardly identify anything as fixed as a stance or an attitude, Paz makes his closing lines into little less than a manifesto:

> Pero la luz avanza a grandes pasos,
> aplastando bostezos y agonías.
> ¡Júbilos, resplandores que desgarran!
> El alba lanza su primer cuchillo.

But the light advances in great strides squashing yawns and death agonies. Jubilant splendours that grab you! The dawn throws its first knife.

Faced with enthusiasm of such directness (or 'healthiness' as one critic has put it), we are hardly discouraged from reading the whole poem as a gloss, an earnest working out, of the single line from Apollinaire which forms the epigraph to *The Violent Season*: 'O Soleil c'est le temps de la Raison ardente'. If 'ardent reason' is an oxymoron, then these poems tend more to the second than to the first term.

Setting his experience thus in space and time, Paz effectively compartmentalizes his cosmopolitanism as a citizen of the twentieth century in a way most surrealists made a point of trying to supersede. In his 'Himno entre ruinas' (Hymn Among Ruins), the ruins (like the masks of Venice) retain that near-Parnassian solidity we noted earlier in Paz. A further separation is made into luminous positive odd-numbered stanzas in Roman type and dark negative even ones in italics; all however are subject more or less effortlessly to the 'high yellow shout' of the sun at the end and its 'impartial beneficence'. As before, the poet's psyche does not luxuriate in its own realm but flows in carefully defined stanzas, or into outbursts of unrestricted generality, in a pattern more reminiscent of Darío's 'Divagación' than of the French surrealists. The 'Mexican' stanza is the first of the italicized series:

> La noche cae sobre Teotihuacán
> El canto mexicano estalla en un carajo,
> estrella de colores que se apaga,
> piedra que nos cierra las puertas del contacto.
> Sabe la tierra a tierra envejecida.

Night falls on Teotihuacan. The Mexican song explodes in an oath, star of colours that fades, stone which cuts off our doors of contact. The land tastes of agèd land.

Here we are back in the labyrinth, the stone unenlivened by sun, with the young men of the state smoking grass and playing Spanish guitars; the old music of the 'canto mexicano' (or the Nahuatl lyric) issues only into foreign blasphemy. The word is too deeply buried and gods can no longer be made at teo-ti-hua-can ('God-making-place' in Nahuatl); as is the case in other dead cities, with their Eliotic rats and 'anaemic' sun (stanza 4). The last epithet is in fact a good clue to the way Paz is operating in this and other poems of his so-called violent season. In its context, 'anaemic' cannot but evoke the solar blood cults of Aztec and other religions, would anticipate some ritual antidote of cosmic proportions of the kind invoked by Apollinaire in 'Zone' (the blood of the 'cou coupé' at sunrise), by the Surrealist Artaud in his response to the 'primitive' rites of the Tarahumara, or for that matter by José Emilio Pacheco in his Tlatelolco and other poems. Paz prefers to be less violent than that. The very stanzaic divisions of his poem, act in this sense as safety compartments. More important, he resolves whatever tension there is in it in the 'sweet' and reasonable final image of the orange, segmented yet whole:

> ¡Día, redondo día,
> luminosa naranja de veinticuatro gajos,
> todos atravesados por una misma y amarilla dulzura!

Day, round day, luminous orange of twenty-four segments, all permeated by the same yellow sweetness!

It should be emphasized that by the time Paz had his direct knowledge of Surrealism through Breton, that movement was considered dead by most of its former advocates. Certainly Breton himself, however noble in his refusal to accommodate his faith to the politics of, say, the Casablanca Conference and their consequences in Europe and the world, was by then no longer involving himself in primary questions of literature and society with quite the passion of the early manifestos, and publications like *Le Surréalisme au service de la Révolution*. In any case he had moved steadily from that total trust in the subconscious, as the 'automatic' source of writing, painting and politics alike, towards allowing credit to such a concept as 'superior reason'. It is the latter Breton who influenced Paz the more, fostering in him 'ardent reason' sooner than total iconoclasm since that had somehow already been gone through. The way Paz has reacted to that 'revelatory' fifth chapter of *L'Amour fou* would certainly support this view. For Breton's account in that chapter of his experience with his wife in the gardens of Orotava and their ascent of the peak of Teide, in Tenerife, stands as a document of the Golden Age in the fullest sense. Indeed, inspired by Buñuel and Dali's film *L'Age d'or*, Breton draws out all that he can discover Marx and Freud to have in common, suggesting 'mad' hope for human beings who are both social and in love. These protestations could of course be understood as an attempt to make good the dilemma which had led to his break with the Communist Party and which would estrange him increasingly from the 'committed' Eluard and Aragon. Yet even as such an attempt it vastly enriches his deliberate re-writing of Genesis in *L'Amour fou*, in favour of the natural innocence of man.

Paz picks up very little on this concern. Not that he should for one moment be thought 'a-political'. He began his publishing career in the 1930s with strong Marxist sympathies; and while he did not remain orthodox for long, events like the Spanish Civil War, the US invasion of Santo Domingo, the death of Che Guevara, intrude strongly into his verse. And he repudiated the Tlatelolco massacre of 1968 more boldly than most, and resigned his post as ambassador (to India). Enthused by this and other, less tragic, desecrations of 'the temple of Capitalism', he reported feeling his poetry to be inadequate as a gesture, or even 'infamous'. What ever this ultimately may or may not say about Paz's good faith (given that 'sincerity' can be found in such matters), it is in fact hard to detect in his poems a coherent or sustained feeling for man in society. The 'golden age', as the great political postulate of Rousseau, and of course Breton, when invoked at all, is the stuff of no more than a fable:[8]

> Había milagros sencillos llamados pájaros
> Todo era de todos
>                     Todos eran todo
> Sólo había una palabra inmensa y sin revés

There were simple miracles called birds. Everything belonged to everyone Everyone was everything. There was only one word immense and without opposite.

The triteness of this expression is matched by that of a passage in 'Sun Stone' which tells of such a state in the present tense:

> y vislumbramos
> nuestra unidad perdida, el desamparo
> que es ser hombres, la gloria que es ser hombres
> y compartir el pan, el sol, la muerte.
> el olvidado asombro de estar vivos:

and we glimpse our lost unity, the exposure of being man, the glory of being man and sharing bread, sun, death, the forgotten thrill of being alive.

There is a kind of anarchic blandness here, embarrassingly exposed in what Paz goes on to say about Abelard. Poor Abelard is chastised for having not let Heloise become his whore, for having insisted on marriage; thus, Paz says, he compromised and 'yielded to the laws'. Surely just the opposite is true in Paz's own terms. The whole point of Abelard's love was that he didn't want it to be hypocritically concealed within a society which could much sooner have accepted whoredom than a belief in human love as passionate and *un*compromising as his.

This particular lapse is the more surprising in Paz given that in his whole dedication to Breton he exalted love at the expense of all the other manifestations of the Golden Age, lit with such passion in *L'Amour fou*. In fact no one could mistake in Paz the effect of special paragraphs like the following from chapter 5, whose high eroticism feeds directly on Breton's experience with his wife in Orotava:

We shall never get over these burgeonings of the golden age. Orpheus passed this way, leading the tiger and the gazelle side by side. The heavy serpents unwind and fall around the circular bench we are sitting on to enjoy the deep twilight that finds at noon the means of sharing the garden with the great light of day. I burn to call this bench, which surrounds a tree several yards thick, the bench of fevers.

With the biblical use of such verbs as 'choir' for the 'fall' of the serpents around the tree, Orotava, in sinless Eden, acquires the status of an 'immense vestibule of physical love', in a 'delirium of absolute presence', of 'curtains drawn back and caressing feline eyes piercing alone the sky with lightning'. These are phrases and visions which impressed Paz deeply, in poems like 'Broken Jar' (in *The Violent Season*):

> el día y la noche se acarician largamente como un
>     hombre y una mujer enamorados,
> como un solo río interminable bajo arcos de siglos flu-
>     yen las estaciones y los hombres,
> hacia allá, al centro vivo del origen, más allá de fin
>     y comienzo.

the day and the night caress each other at length like a man and a woman in love, like a single unending river the seasons and men flow under arches of centuries, further on, to the live centre of the origin beyond end and beginning.

At the first of origins, Adam and Eve enact a rite powerful enough to exorcise all subsequent evil in whatever form or sphere. The act of love in this panerotic creed is the mighty antidote to solitude, frustration, and emptiness (moods often caught in images startlingly similar to those of Borges' *Fictions*: the labyrinth, the abominable mirrors which like fatherhood sordidly reproduce our kind, the chaos of Babel, the dizzy geometry of the disembodied mind, and so on). The couple is the preeminent poetic and social form, superior (and here the difference from the early Breton) to all around it.

   Their integrity, enhanced in a host of mythic and 'elemental' metaphors, sun and earth, fire and water, overrides all other concern. Indeed the principal victory of love in *The Violent Season* is the reconciling of the 'enemy halves' not of any secular world, but of the body and the mind, making the Broken Jar erotically whole. This poem is full of allusions to the inner experience of such 'surrealist' visionaries as Blake, Rimbaud and Baudelaire, against which is set an appropriately (for him) unpeopled landscape ('But at my side there was no one/only the plain'). All of the three poets mentioned enrich the view of his inner eye:

> La mirada interior se despliega y un mundo de vértigo
> y llama nace bajo la frente del que sueña:
> soles azules, verdes remolinos, picos de luz que abren
> astros como granadas,
> tornasol solitario, ojo de oro girando en el centro de una
> explanada calcinada,
> bosques de cristal de sonido, bosques de ecos y respues-
> tas y ondas, diálogo de transparencias,

The inner look unfolds and a world of vertigo and flame is born in the dreamer's head: blue suns, green whirlpools, peaks of lights opening stars like pomegranates, solitary sunflower, eye of gold turning in centre of a scorched esplanade, crystal forests of sound, forests of echoes and answers and waves, dialogue of transparencies.

But the sunflower does not become the mystic centre of a warring universe as it did for Blake, any more than natural 'correspondences' are made subject to the cities of men, as they were by Baudelaire. And while Rimbaud makes the blues and greens and reds of his voyage aboard the 'Drunken Boat' the more intense and poignant for recognizing himself as the child of secular energy brilliantly and persistently misdirected (by carriers of 'Flemish wheat and English cotton'), who suspects that nostalgia for the 'old parapets of Europe' may be irremediable and that no new order in the world may even correspond to his delirium (hence the overwhelming pathos of the child at the end sadly squatting to launch a boat 'as frail as a May butterfly'), Paz, by contrast, simply and 'healthily' asserts the primary efficacy of love. For, that love can reconcile the (old Romantic) enemy halves of passion and consciousness is in itself enough; despite its etymology, sex for Paz is not fully secular, of the world and generation of man.

If Paz translates his paneroticism into any other 'zone' of active relationships, it is, then, not a human environment, unrelinquished by the early surrealists and those they recognized as precursors. (This would explain his reserve about the 'human' poetry of Vallejo and Neruda.) To language, however, this privilege is extended. Writing a poem is thus like making love, is another means to the true origin. Words are played with, teased, even tormented so that they spark across the blank page. The poem may thus 'prepare an amorous order'. For the reader not raised to the same pitch of excitement as the poet these games can prove tiresome, and erotic connection feels more like a poor pun ('simiente no miente' – 'seed does not lie' or 'if it lies it does not': 'inocencia y no ciencia' – 'innocence and not knowledge', where the last three words almost exactly echo the first one). And the references or connotations of the terms involved tend to be restricted, as in a conceit, by the exclusiveness of their situation. Against this it should be said that Paz's verse of this period can flow overwhelmingly, in psalmodic progression through half repetitions, uninterrupted and not at all abrupt, to climactic endings that carry an amazing change of conviction:

> y la conciencia-espejo se licúa,
> vuelve a ser fuente, manantial de fábulas:
> Hombre, árbol de imágenes,
> palabras que son flores que son frutos que son actos.

and mirror-consciousness dissolves, becomes again the fount, fabulous source: man, tree of images, words that are flowers that are fruit that are acts.

## 3

As if spiritual alliance with Breton had somehow given him the impetus he needed, Paz emerged from *The Violent Season* ready to explore territory around him neglected hitherto. In the books which followed this one he appropriated regions which previously his ambiguous sense of nationality, and then his strong interest in the Europe of the Surrealists, had encouraged him to skirt around. *Salamandra* (1962), and its complementary book of criticism *Cuadrivio* (1965), might well be called his Hispanic books. They involve him in a series of dialogues with poets of his language, which make clearer his points of difference with the Surrealists and help to define him specifically as a Hispanic poet.

Of course Paz could always be said to have 'belonged here', especially in his earliest collections, where his debt to the 'post-Modernist' tradition in Mexico and Latin America is obvious. But his doubts about the literary traditions of 'arthritic Spanish' had been persistent. And now he was on to something more ambitious, which in the first instance would oblige him to face squarely that other 'Golden Age' of his past: the literature of imperial sixteenth- and seventeenth-century Spain, especially the poets Góngora and Quevedo. The former had of course long been 'recognized' by the French and was to that extent more readily acceptable; however at this stage Paz notably deepens his interest in him. A poem like 'Ustica' (in *Salamander*) brings out strongly both the covert Mediterranean in Góngora, hinted at already in the epigraph to 'Hymn among Ruins' ('where foaming the Sicilian sea . . .'); and that poet's neo-Platonic or elemental view of landscape. When Paz speaks of the Sicilian island in question as a 'hard peach', a 'drop of sun petrified', he comes very close indeed to the process of distillation and immobilization at the heart of the *Solitudes*. However 'Ustica' would finally be all *against* that kind of solitude and petrification: to the extent that Paz admits Góngora against this wish he is no longer simply ignoring reactionary forces in him (also palpable in his earlier Parnassianism) that run counter to his ostensible poetica of fluidity. This admission had been made already in 'Hymn among Ruins', an uncharacteristically structured poem, but one in which, as we have seen, order and sweet reason triumph too easily. The result in 'Ustica' is a poem of extraordinary power and potential violence not least because of what Góngora taught him about the loneliness of man in nature. Paz's revaluation of Góngora's near contemporary, Quevedo, was more dramatic though it affected his poetry less profoundly. The funereal scatologist depicted in *Labyrinth of Solitude* is made in *Salamander* into the object of homage as a poet of love. Quevedo's sonnet 'Love constant beyond death' is celebrated in an extensive gloss by Paz which, whatever its own merit, declares intentions of rapprochement, especially in the closing 'Lauda'. The tercets of the sonnet point to growing 'Spanish' concerns in Paz himself:

> Alma a quien todo un Dios prisión ha sido,
> venas que humor a tanto fuego han dado,
> medulas que han gloriosamente ardido:
>
> su cuerpo dejarán, no su cuidado;
> serán ceniza, mas tendrá sentido;
> polvo serán, mas polvo enamorado.

*Soul that has been prison to all of a God, veins that have given humour to so much fire, marrow that has gloriously burned: ¶they shall leave their body, but not their care; they shall be ash, but this ash will have sense; dust they shall be, but loving dust.*

This agonized dualism, the feeling for fire's need of humour and of survival through intensity, are caught in the very title *Salaman-*

*der*. Further inquisitions into the nature of love, as *amor* rather than *amour*, and its relation to desire and to death, are made in his responses at this time to the twentieth-century Spanish poet Luis Cernuda, in both a poem to him in *Salamander* and an essay in *Cuadrivio*.[9]

'Ustica', as a poem about love and death, which sees, for example, 'desire worked by death' as 'pale calcareous lace', also strongly recalls the sensibility of Ramón López Velarde, to whom Paz devotes another of the four essays in *Cuadrivio*. There he traces intimately the effects of Spanish Counter-Reformation culture on a poet like Velarde writing in Mexico early this century (in lines like the famous question of his lover: 'Did you preserve your flesh on every bone?'). Paz's wish to uncover such traditions in Mexico, after all, becomes one of the points of the essay, and the main reason for his anthology *Poesía en movimiento. Mexico, 1915–66*. On neither occasion, of course, is he interested in national tradition as such: López Velarde, he says, has more in common with Lugones or Laforgue than with any other Mexican. But he is interested in finding corollaries, poets and poems in his own language to match those of the almost exclusively non-Hispanic European tradition of the Surrealists. And, as we have begun to suggest, in the very process of this kind of translation into Spanish, the literary traditions of that language perceptibly affect the shape of Paz's philosophy of love and his poetics. Most telling in this respect is his encounter with Rubén Darío.

Darío inspires the opening study in *Cuadrivio*, which in so far as it would vindicate Hispanic Modernism as 'modern', still stands as a landmark in Hispanic literary criticism; in formal and sub-merged quotations this poet also informs *Salamander*, in a way that could hardly be inferred from previous collections. One of Paz's strategies, in ransoming Darío as a 'Modernist', is to pillory those nationalist critics of Spain (numerous, if stupid), who, embarrassed that he was both so influential on peninsular poetry and yet only a Nicaraguan, had persistently underrated him. For Paz, Darío thus became a way of coming to terms with the Hispanic tradition from a position of strength, a further 'return of the galleons'. Darío may almost be said to be a device, enabling Paz to 'reclaim' the literary tradition of the Spanish language, in a fashion few other Latin American poets have cared to do. Paz's interpretation of Darío could hardly differ more, for example, from that of Vallejo, who (as we noted) saw in him first of all a 'cosmic' American.

In *Cuadrivio* Paz gave Darío (not always on unequivocal evidence) the place of honour in his equivalent to the Surrealists' line of 'great Romantics and Symbolists', along with Vicente Huidobro, and others. In doing so Paz stressed Darío's qualities as a profoundly religious poet who was unsatisfied by Christianity and anticipated Paz's own panerotic creed. In the last analysis his enthusiasm for Darío could be understood as something approaching covert identification with him, one who strove to implant such a creed in a culture inimical to it for good historical and even linguistic reason, and which he himself could never entirely be rid of. In this way, no less than the priapic blasphemer of 'Celestial flesh' and 'Divagation', the meditative, frustrated Darío of poems like 'Lo fatal' comes to fascinate Paz. Phrases like the following, from this last poem: 'and the horror of being dead tomorrow, and of suffering for life and for the shade' (themselves an echo of the Spanish Golden Age), deflate those moments of Paz's poetry which might previously have been sustained by some positive exhortation. The victory of 'La Raison ardente' is less assured.

At a more mundane level too, as the misunderstood cosmopolitan, the not wholly acknowledged father of free verse in Spanish, the spirit superior of his time, Darío had the curious effect of eliciting the confessional in Paz. Certainly it is hard to interpret a poem like 'Augurios' any other way. Darío's poem of the same title (from *Cantos de vida y esperanza*), on which it is based, is wholly dispeptic, from beginning to end:

> Hoy pasó un águila
> sobre mi cabeza;
> lleva en sus alas
> la tormenta
>
> . . .
> No pasa nada.
> La muerte llegó.

Today an eagle passed over my head; it carries in its wings the storm. . . ¶Nothing passes. Death came.

After erotic confidence: the memento mori, the suspicion that death is final and all-pervading. His cry as an individual trapped in 'human mud' thus becomes contemptuous of life's illusions, a self-pitying plea for at least momentary attention. Paz writes his

sequel clearly conscious of this. In fact his lines succeed each other
a little like illustrative marginalia:

> En cada cuna
> Eros y leche: digestión pacífica
> Sin pesadillas griegas;
> . . .
> Deportes y cultura para todos
> Los hijos de vecino: camporrasos
> Todos los camposantos;
> Pulgas
> Vestidas a la moda en las metrópolis.

In every cradle Eros and milk: peaceful digestion without Greek night-
mares;. . . ¶Sports and culture for every local child: graveyards bulldozed
flat; fleas dressed fashionably in the metropolis.

In fact throughout the poem he entrusts himself to a verb only
once, at the end:

> El vacío pregona
> Una filantropía que despena.

Emptiness proclaims a philanthropy that anaesthetizes.

His wit thereby is more than tainted with arrogance. He operates
on a 'higher level', not even bothering to articulate in verb relationship his own relationship with mankind, his subject. It is true
that a phrase like 'Greek nightmare' is ironic in that ancient
Greeks 'ought' not to be the source of a nightmare, but the in-
spirational (Mediterranean) force they were for Darío and are
frequently for Paz. But here his throw-away delivery undermines
any possible irony behind that in turn, so that whether we like it
or not we are left with some kind of negative statement. While
Breton endeavoured to transmute his social condition, by urging
passionate faith in the innocent heart of man, 'against all odds' as
Paz recognized, in 'Augurios' Paz could seem simply insulting,
to be 'entering matter' as one of his titles has it, in the worst of
humours. This was less true of Darío's original, where there is a
subtle interplay, in main verbs, between intimacy and formality,
and a deliberate sacrifice of personal dignity in the low-key final
lines that announce death.

One of the poems by Darío which Paz (in *Cuadrivio*) most ad-
mires is the 'Epistle to Madame Lugones' (see p. 72), which he
singles out as an 'indubitable antecedent to what would be one

of the conquests of contemporary poetry: the fusion of literary language and the speech of the city'. It is also perhaps the only poem of Darío's which resolves his painful oscillations between love and mortal despair, in a tone which can contain them both and which, significantly, locates him in various sets of relationships with other people and specific places (all being tacitly referred to the addressee of the epistle). For the poem is eminently a *dialogue*. Despite the growing importance which Paz was attaching to this concept and form, and for all his admiration of the composite language of the 'Epistle' (which at another point he also detects in 'Augurios'), Paz does not yet come near to emulating it, though he does constantly evoke, as nowhere else, the city as a place of common speech and intercourse. The city, in this sense, remains unredeemed and desert, like Eliot's London, the abstract scene of randy cats and simian panic. Except for a wishful (and private) attempt[10] to relate to it as a feminine presence, a woman ('Ciudad Mujer Presencia'), he hovers above it, dislocated and haunted by the ghost of solipsism.

The mood of frustrated coherence in *Salamander* is perhaps best represented in the title poem and 'Ustica' (which are closely akin to each other).[11] The latter is one of Paz's most powerful poems; it catches especially well that suppressed violence, the extremity of both his passion and of his fears for its meaning matched with death; further, for its survival in a groundswell of incest and ominous telluric myth. The first stanza, verbless, has the pained impatience of 'Augurios', and leaves us with similarly little hope, in this case in the eventual fate of the sun, its capacity to resist atrophy, a career to 'cooled matter'. The alliterative 's's work like an exasperated hiss ('sol', 'sucesivo', 'solo'). Then comes his view of the 'petrified' island Ustica, mentioned earlier. This initial constriction and contracting of matter makes the plight of surviving life, the sweet water of the cisterns, the more acute:

> Por las noches se oye
> El respirar de las cisternas,
> El jadeo del agua dulce
> Turbada por el mar.
> La hora es alta y rayada de verde.
> El cuerpo oscuro del vino
> En las jarras dormido
> Es un sol más negro y fresco.

At night the sound of the cisterns breathing, the panting of the sweet water perturbed by the sea. The hour is high and streaked with green. The dark body of the wine sleeping in the jars is a blacker, fresher sun.

The sea thus becomes the ambient of 'the rose of the depths', a candelabra of pink veins which can survive only down there. On land it becomes as calcareous as López Velarde's skeletons. At this point the poet first introduces himself and his companion into the text:

> Rocas color de azufre,
> Altas piedras adustas.
> Tú estás a mi costado.
> Tus pensamientos son negros y dorados.
> Si alargase la mano
> Cortaría un racimo de verdades intactas.

Sulphur-coloured rocks, tall austere stones. You are at my side. Your thoughts are black and gold. If I were to stretch out my hand, I should pluck a bunch of intact truths.

What these truths might be is left unsaid. Could they survive intact in an atmosphere so turbulent and electric, where sulphur threatens gold and the horizontal and the vertical are so violently juxtaposed? He is kept from realizing the expectations of his grasp. We focus now again on the sea, in a salt light of huge intensity, bright yet eerily phosphorescent. The sea is many-armed like its rose, but also an abyss, because its organic chemistry also decomposes. As a wholly un-innocent repository of life it recalls Baudelaire's dazzling dream of a sea of ebony:

> Abajo, entre peñas centelleantes,
> Va y viene el mar lleno de brazos.
> Vértigos. La luz se precipita.
> Yo te miré a la cara,
> Yo me asomé al abismo:
> Mortalidad es transparencia.

Below, among sparkling cliffs, the sea comes and goes full of arms. Vertigo. The light rushes down. I looked at your face, I rimmed the abyss: mortality is transparence.

Such an insight can hardly be borne. The bold love cadences of the 'Hymn among ruins' or 'Broken jar', the fruit taken that is word and act (and not the hypothetical bunch dependent on a subjunctive verb), yield to the horrific intuition that there may be no transcendence, no escape from matter, *mater–materia*, that in an Eden which is a graveyard only the helpless innocence of incest can endure:

> Osario, paraíso
> Nuestras raíces anudadas
> En el sexo, en la boca deshecha
> De la Madre enterrada.
> Jardín de árboles incestuosos
> Sobre la tierra de los muertos.

Ossuary, paradise: our roots knotted in the sex, the undone mouth of the Mother. Garden of incestuous trees on the earth of the dead.

Testing his erotic creed against a growing obsession with death and decay, Paz creates a poem of extraordinary tension and issues into a desperate form of love that is (as he is clearly aware) both prior to the first social taboo, and solipsistic the moment he ceases to be god. In this state he was readier for his next encounter: with the Orient.

### 4

Paz's acquaintance with the East began in the 1950s when he travelled to India and Japan. In 1962 he became Mexican ambassador to India, and deeply immersed himself in that country before his resignation six years later. It was there also that he got to know his second wife. The fruits of these experiences is the collection of poems which exactly spans this period: *East Slope* (*Ladera Este*). His explorations in geography and philosophy are witnessed in the very titles of the poems: 'Tanghi-Garu Pass'; 'Madurai', 'Vrindaban', 'Happiness in Herat', the trilogy on Himachal Pradesh (the part of the Western Himalayas where the Vedas were reputedly composed); the erotic pair 'Maithuna'. In the first instance the very difference of climate kept him from the devastating introspection of *Salamander*, and, for example, of Neruda's 'Eastern' poems in *Residence on Earth*. In the bar of the British Club in Madurai he rises even to the jocular, a rare mood for him. Intercalating the phrases (in italics) of a certain Sri K. J. Chidambaram into his own observations, he plays with a contrast between the holy and the commercial India, a game repeated in the second Himachal Pradesh poem. More frequently, the landscape and the lore of country demand of him less divided attention. Indeed the exterior world, in an apparent regress, can acquire the 'objectivity' of much earlier pieces:

> Montes de mica. Cabras negras.
> Bajo las pezuñas sonámbulas
> La pizarra relumbra, ceñuda.
>
> Sol fijo, clavado
> En la enorme cicatriz de piedra.
> La muerte nos piensa.

Mountains of mica. Black goats. Under the somnambulant hooves the slate gleams, rugged. ¶Fixed sun, nailed on the huge scar of stone. Death thinks us.

Scale, rare atmosphere, and the ease with which 'elements' display themselves, permit him simply to reveal them and their message. The same might be said of the forms and concepts of Buddhist and Hindu philosophy, those categories like sunyata, sansara and nirvana which in their uncommon precision can pattern a poem almost of themselves.

Reflecting on his Indian experience in 'Cuento de dos jardines' (Story of Two Gardens) and placing it in the story of his own life, Paz makes of it a beginning, of the same order as his own physical origin as a human being. One of the two gardens is in Mixcoac, his Mexican birthplace (now a suburb of the capital); there, as a child already he 'spied the feverish construction of my ruin' and learnt 'to say goodbye' to himself. The other is in India, and he enters it not as a new home but as the beginning of the Beginning, another Eden where before the huge tree, the nim, his sexual ecstasy is consecrated:

> Tú misma,
>        La muchacha del cuento,
>                      La alumna del
>                      jardín.
> Olvidé a Nagarjuna y Dharmakirti
>                      En tus pechos,
>   En tu grito los encontré:
>                      *Maithuna*,
>                      Dos en uno,
> Uno en todo,
>        Todo en nada,
>                    ¡*Sunyata*,
>   Plenitud vacía,
>                    Vacuidad redonda como tu grupa!

You yourself, the girl of the story, the pupil of the garden. I forgot
Nagarjuna and Dharmakirti in your breasts, in your shout I found them:
*Maithuna*, two in one, one in all, all in nothing, *Sunyata*, empty plenitude,
space round like your haunches!

The Indian garden, with its tree and preternatural colours, becomes an emblem of the country itself, whose vagina is 'soaked
with sap, semen, poisonous juices'; the atmosphere of the place
is every bit as electric as Breton's Orotava. The remarkable thing,
however, in this heavily autobiographical, or better, confessional
poem, is the poet's admission that, chronologically, between these
two gardens, of childhood and fruition, there were no others ('no
hubo jardines'). In other words, we are given a hint why the
intense eroticism of *The Violent Season* was not sustained and
why *Salamander* manifested a certain dispeptic dualism. If we
are to take Paz at his word, only on the 'East Slope' did he begin
to match philosophy with experience, forming of them both a new
creed that would be referred to its source only to poetic advantage.

The best poems in *East Slope*, 'Viento entero' and 'Vrindaban',
demonstrate how this might be so. In Vrindaban, the sacred Hindu
city, he both questions the sources of his belief and asserts his self
in a way hardly precedented in his poetry. From the start the poem
is (appropriately) about himself as a poet, writing and pausing,
surrounded by a darkness rich in foliage and breath. The momen-
tum of the car he was travelling in a few moments earlier sustains
the tracing of a few taut signs, black on white, a tiny garden of
letters, and leads him past commonplaces of experience and phrase
to the question: 'Do I believe in men or the stars?' He does not
answer directly. Belief is at least what is seen: 'I believe/(here, a
row of dots)/I see.' But what is seen, the phenomenal world (here,
the jasmine and the stench, the brillance and the misery, of India),
is too myriad and protean to furnish guarantee. It spreads like fire
and leaves him striving to control it like the poor mortal in Buddhist philosophy, 'mountebank, monkey of the Absolute'. At this
point he is fixed by *another* eye: a mystic looks at him from the
other bank of perfect knowledge ('prajnaparamita'), immobile in
his perennial philosophy:

> En cuclillas
> > Cubierto de cenizas pálidas
> Un sadú me miraba y se reía
> Desde su orilla me miraba

Crouching, covered with pale ashes. a sadhu was looking at me and smiling, from his bank he was looking at me.

The message from over there is a sacred chant, like the one which closes *The Waste Land*, grotesquely mixed with bowel rumblings. This sadhu may have seen Krishna herself, have been servant to her ravishing blue tree, have touched the cleft in the rock, the ultimate feminine abyss. In any case, his formless vertigo is why he lives in total abjection 'on the quay where they burn the dead'. The experience of being located in this way by another eye finally provokes Paz into one of his frankest admissions:

> Los absolutos las eternidades
> Y sus aledaños
>            No son mi tema
> Tengo hambre de vida y también de morir
> Sé lo que creo y lo escribo

Absolutes eternities and their purlieus are not my theme. I have a hunger to live and also to die. I know what I believe and what I write.

The startling directness of the statement may be due to the long time it took him to make it. The past stages of his life are implicitly recognized here, perhaps for the first time, as is a self that is not all. On the East Slope he defines his hunger as a first premise, and articulates a deeply Western need for movement and flow. But of course for such a realization to happen, in order indeed that it can be thinkable, some exterior fixity has to be there. That is why the encounter with the sadhu in Vrindaban was fortunate for more than this poem. It offered the chance of dialogue, a radical challenge to solipsism, as is the hope of the final lines:

> Nunca estoy solo
> Hablo siempre contigo Hablas siempre conmigo
> A oscuras voy y planto signos

I am never alone. I talk always with you. You talk always with me. I go in the dark and plant signs.

The high point of *East Slope* is 'Viento entero' (Whole Wind), probably Paz's finest achievement as a poet. Following the line suggested in 'Vrindaban' and elaborating further his crucial experience of India, he subsumes and transmutes the recurrent passions and ambitions of his earlier poetry. As in 'Sun Stone', he would integrate in a continuous present separate moments of time and space (the bazaar at Kabul, Paris, and 'various places and areas in northern India, West Pakistan and Afghanistan', as his notes tell us). As in 'Hymn Among Ruins', another 'major' poem, these are arranged in sections to produce an intricate pattern of echo and opposition. In this case there are nine (rather than seven) stanzas or strophes, which are not separate but hinge or turn on the refrain 'the present is perpetual'. 'Whole Wind' also presents a characteristically Paz-like view of the phenomenal world: his interest in elemental colours and textures (mountains of bone and snow, day of agate, black cloud on a black mountain in a landscape like a petrified ochre storm), and in the four humours: water, fire, earth, and the air of the title. As previously, he strives to discover in a world of such composition objective correlatives for his condition: the internal correspondences of the poem, over its considerable length, are intricate and unusually hard to describe.

However, Paz has told us how his condition was newly defined for him in Vrindaban. From the beginning of 'Whole Wind', the phenomenal world is more radically matched with its transcendental opposite, samsara with nirvana. The noise and the light of bazaar at Kabul, thus equivalent, are intercalated into silent spaces which are just as real:

> Alto fulgor a martillazos esculpido
> En los claros de silencio
>                          Estallan
> Los gritos de los niños

High glare sculptured by hammer blows in the lacunae of silence, there burst out the shouts of the children.

Later on, by the same dialectic, two or three birds 'invent' a garden out of nothing. Similarly the four humours, essences of phenomena, are made to counteract each other to suggest a reality beyond them. Rather than tie each one to a specific quality, as he had often done before, he sets them in self-cancelling contradiction. The girl who appears in the second strophe is a flame 'if water is fire'; later she is a diaphanous drop of water 'if fire is water'. Together earth and wind create the vortex which moves the poem; air perturbs matter in a persistent whirl which becomes the turning of space itself by the final strophe.

Throughout, the spiral also informs the progress of the poem through pairs of strophes which reciprocate but do not eclipse each other, and which steadily expand the circumference of reality.[12] At first he is simply the observer, of mountains and merchants:

> El presente es perpetuo
> Los montes son de hueso y son de nieve
> Están aquí desde el principio
> El viento acaba de nacer
> > > Sin edad
> Como la luz y como el polvo
> > > > Molino de sonidos
> El bazar tornasolea

The present is perpetual, the mountains are of bone and are of snow, they have been here from the beginning, the wind has just been born, ageless like the light, and like the dust turning mill of sounds the bazaar irridesces.

By contrast he dominates the second strophe, where in Paris he greets the girl, the 'you' which with him makes the 'we' that traverses with effortless intimacy 'the four spaces the three times (tenses)'. In the third and fourth strophes he and his companion are in a garden: she is naked, on a quilt. He contemplates, but with thoughts of the outside world in his head: by now the outer and the inner are more intricately mixed. A 'great flight of crows' (a line from Darío) reminds him specifically of his Latin American condition: news of the US invasion of Santo Domingo recalls in turn revolutionary spirit in Mexico, and, in an overtly Third World idiom, resistance to the imperial British in Misarag. However, rather than accentuate the opposition implicit here or erect a protective wall around the garden to make the *hortus conclusus* of earlier poems, he boldly associates the woman's bright passion (like 'wine in the glass jar') with the secular world ('el siglo'), which

> Se ha encendido en nuestras tierras
> Con su lumbre
> > > Las manos abrasadas
> Los constructores de catedrales y pirámides
> Levantarán sus casas transparentes

has been lit in our lands with its glow, their hands scorched the builders of cathedrals and pyramids will erect their transparent houses.

In strophe 4, as if exhausted by this transference, the woman's quilt turns from red to black and the sun sets in her breasts. She may be 'fruit', a 'date', but this old metaphor cannot by itself work for long either, and the dark ghost of solipsism eerily returns in the near homonym Datia, the phantom walled city in Madhya Pradesh, self-enclosing and uninhabited.

This initial exploration of his erotic and social self vastly enhances the climax of strophe 5, which is matched its turn by strophe 6. In the high, ferociously unpeopled landscape around the Salang Gorge human beings are reduced to the rush of water below, the white leap in the river that leaves their bodies 'abandoned'. In primary, elemental solitudes he comes nearer to orgasmic origin that can of itself lead only to dispersion and fragmentation. Yet the turning line of the poem continues. The transition, from strophes 5 to 6, through the alliterative refrain, is one of Paz's most compelling moments. The reverberations of the word 'white' alone are amazing, against black, hot, then phosphorescent, foam, then blank and calm, the beard of the marabout ('morabito') against the mulberry ('moral'), half echoed as 'blanco' in 'flanco' (flank), and so on:

> Tus ojos se abren y se cierran
> >               Animales fosforecentes
>
> Abajo
> >     El desfiladero caliente
> La ola que se dilata y se rompe
> >               Tus piernas abiertas
>
> El salto blanco
> La espuma de nuestros cuerpos abandonados
> >               El presente es perpetuo
> El morabito regaba la tumba de santo
> Sus barbas eran más blancas que las nubes
> Frente al moral
> >           Al flanco del torrente
> Repetiste mi nombre
> >           Dispersión de sílabas

Your eyes open and close, phosphorescent animals, below the hot gulley the wave that swells and breaks, your open legs, the white leap, the foam of our abandoned bodies, the present is perpetual, the marabout was watering the saint's grave, his beard was whiter than the clouds against the mulberry on the torrent's flank, you repeated my name, dispersion of syllables.

The sweet wholeness of the orange in the 'Hymn Among Ruins' is a far cry from here. It is half remembered perhaps in the pomegranate offered to them by the river Amu-Darya (by an adolescent with green eyes, a hallucinatory colour switch): by the grains of the fruit, ashen now for containing those dispersed syllables, the broken alphabet of the Bactrian plain and dust-covered names, he rises to the vow: 'I swear to be earth and wind/ vortex/ on your bones.'

His being would, then, be constant turbulence, the current instability confessed to at a similar juncture in 'Vrindaban' ('I am in the unstable hour'). Here however, the movement is less gratui-tous, less dependent on given fixity (the sadhu's eye), and formally even more part of the poem itself, in the spiralling images and the conflict of humours already mentioned, in the persistent end-of-line twists where verbs both conclude and refer forward, and in the refrain ('the present is perpetual') set as a half line now to the left now to the right of the page. Nowhere does he vindicate the shape of his utterance quite as he does in 'Whole Wind'. Like an undeniable turbine the poem carries him through the further pre or super human oppositions of strophes 7 and 8, the dark monsoon forests of the 'anima mundi' below the 'peak of the world', Kalaisai in the Himalayas, where Shiva and Parvati caress each other and 'each caress lasts a century for the god and for man'. Neither is denied in the time the poem has by now generated 'between heaven (sky) and earth', kept coherent by perpetual motion between the two. In his poem on 'Reading John Cage' (also in *East Slope*), Paz translated that writer's ideas of music and silence into what he had made of oriental philosophy, in the neat phrase: 'Nirvana is Samsara, Samsara is not Nirvana'. In his notes he points out that the Buddhist formula is wholly reciprocal, an all-enclosing circle (Nirvana is Samsara, Samsara is Nirvana). Refusing to subjugate self and the phenomenal world in this way he would sustain them in the widening spiral so brilliantly traced in 'Whole Wind'.

Such is the power of 'the movement in which is moulded and unmade the whole being' that the orbit of the closing strophe en-compasses both intimate memories of infancy and open space. The childhood garden half recalls that of Ustica and, by its allusion to the fairy tale 'Almendrita', the 'Story of Two Gardens':

> Llueve sobre mi infancia
> Llueve sobre el jardín de la fiebre
> Flores de sílex árboles de humo
> En una hojo de higuera tú navegas
> Por mi frente

It rains on my infancy, it rains on the garden of fever, flowers of silica trees of smoke, on a fig leaf you sail through my brow.

But since the world can by now uproot itself, the old tension, the violent vision of the 'buried mother', is released in a final 'launching':

> Gira el espacio
> Arranca sus raices el mundo
> No pesan más que el alba nuestros cuerpos
> Tendidos

Space turns, the world tears up its roots, our bodies weigh no more than the dawn outstretched.

Since his return from India Paz's poetry has entered yet another chapter. His friendship with Cage (also acknowledged in Cage's *A Year from Monday*),[13] and a lively involvement with the structuralists, commemorated in his book on Lévi-Strauss,[14] had already been corroborated in the long poem *Blanco* (1967), which Paz advises us ought to be read as a succession of signs on a single page.[15] Further: 'as the reading goes on the page unfolds in a space which in its movement allows the text to appear and which in a certain sense produces it'. His concern to relate 'temporal text to the space surrounding it was taken a step further in *Topoemas* (1968), a neologism from *topos* and *poema*. At the same time his special sense of poetic identity has underlain the experiments of *Renga*, poetry written in immediate collaboration with poets of other nationalities and languages (Charles Tomlinson, Jacques Roubaud and Edoardo Sanguineti). But this chapter of his plural career cannot yet be written about for the simple reason that it itself is still being written.

# 8. Modern priorities

When Vallejo and Neruda strove to be politically responsible as poets in the 1930s they did so in the spirit of the International, for the Civil War had made Spain the 'cockpit' of Europe and the world. In more recent decades several Latin American poets have assumed responsibility of this kind as part of a specifically 'Third World' identity, something Neruda came to hint at, though not define, in *Canto general*. Accepting, on the strength of social and economic analysis, that as a Latin American one has more in common with Africa and south-east Asia than with the Old World or other parts of America like the United States, must severely upset traditional ideas of cultural identity and loyalty. Indeed credence is extended less readily to the idea of cultural tradition itself, as it has been defended by, say, Octavio Paz, or by T. S. Eliot, when he said that a poet should write 'not merely with his own generation in his bones, but with a feeling that the whole of the literature of Europe from Homer and within it the whole of the literature of his own country has a simultaneous existence and composes a simultaneous order'.[1]

At the forefront of this Third World way of thinking are of course the revolutionaries of Cuba, Central America, the Andes, and elsewhere, whose ideas not just of culture but of the society that forms it are drawn from the works of such people as Giap, Debray and Guevara.[2] These writers, notably Debray, have in particular stressed guerrilla warfare as the formative experience of the socialist, the thing that prepares man (especially bourgeois intellectuals and artists) for the new society, in some ways more effectively than orthodox political strategies had done or were likely to do. Controversial as this emphasis is, not least among the left in Latin America, it has affected recent poetry of the sub-continent deeply and divisively. Some have accepted it passionately enough to become revolutionaries themselves, guerrilla poets. Others have expressed their sympathies less dramatically, exploring the predicament of a poet not himself revolutionary in a situation that is, in fact or in potential. Yet others have disregarded the cultural discrimination implicit in the term Third World and have reaffirmed their identity within the Western tradition.

First of all, the idea that the revolution is possible, and that the best way to achieve it is fighting against the imperialists and their agents, has inspired those engaged in the struggle to a new lyric confidence, the resilient simplicity that the fighter-poet Martí had wanted in his poems. The Guatemalan Otto René Castillo (captured and killed in 1967), or the Peruvian Javier Heraud (shot in action in his twenty-first year), can, for example, be felt to be writing out of a situation as primary and all-encompassing as that of, say, the First World War poets. The motifs of this guerrilla poetry are recurrent and urge their own power. With his existence measured by things found again to be essential, Heraud faces death with simple faith, simply stated:

> Yo no me
> río de
> la
> muerte.
> Sucede
> simple-
> mente,
> que no
> tengo miedo
> de morir
> entre
> pájaros
> y
> árboles[3]

I don't laugh at death. It's just that I'm not afraid to die among birds and trees.

Like him these birds and trees are beings of the mountains, the sierra, out of which the revolution is coming. He speaks and defends it 'with his life': in his 'Arte poética', poetry, 'a marvellous lightning', is both the 'song of the oppressed peoples' and the 'new song of the liberated', even the redemption of man. So that even without knowledge of the dramatic circumstances of his end we find in a poem like his address to the fly ('Las moscas') a necessary drive (again like Martí's) right through to the last wish for dignity:

> Sólo espero no alimentarla
> y no verla en mis entrañas,
> el día que si acaso
> me matan en el campo
> y dejan mi cuerpo bajo el sol.

I only hope not to feed you and not to see you in my entrails, the day they cut me open in the countryside and leave my body under the sun.

In Cuba after the revolution, both writers who had participated in it and those who committed themselves later tried to record their experience as something new and definitive, among them Roberto Fernández Retamar, Fayad Jamis and Pablo Armando Fernández. This last's *Libro de los héroes* (Book of the Heroes, 1963) is the result of such an endeavour, as the title suggests. 'De hombre a muerte' (From Man to Death) concentrates on the meaning of the epic of the Sierra Maestra in similar terms. In the third section of this poem he intercalates the precise and plain details of a military observer's report ('. . . at 7 a.m. a reconnaissance plane appeared') with the thoughts of a guerrilla fighter, the love that his enemy detests. The effect is remarkable in fusing personal immediacy with a common cause which even if it brings a particular death is unquestionable and cannot be gainsaid. In fact the speaker is so integrated in the guerrilla focus, shares their present sadness to such an extent, that he applies to himself a plural adjective 'expuestos' (exposed) in phrases like the following:

> Expuestos a la lluvia preguntándome cuándo
>       volveremos
> a vernos, mi niña.
> Esos hombres que nunca estuvieron en combate
> que no han peleado con amor
> que no dejaron para siempre las cruces
> no conocen la guerra.
> No vamos a morir.

Exposed to the rain asking myself when we'll see each other again, my girl. Those men who were never in combat, who haven't fought with love, who didn't leave the crosses for ever don't know war. We're not going to die.

Fernández was one of those who did not fight himself, and his poetry, at times uneven, amounts to an act of imaginative faith. Far more common, in Cuba and elsewhere, are those for whom commitment has entailed something of the awkwardness expressed by Vallejo in his 'Hymn'. This is especially true of those who recognized in Che Guevara an emblem of the Third World who by his life and martyrdom could not but implicate them. The many homages to him express a whole range of emotions, from residual hope to pained discomfort. (Though his official communism made him curiously reticent on some points, Neruda sang his praise much as he had sung the heroes of the Spanish Republic.)[4] Guevara's death in 1967 caught poets most keenly. Responses of marked intricacy came from Mexico, partly perhaps because of the intricacy of poetic traditions there,[5] as Paz and others had shaped them. In his 'Ode for the death of Che Guevara', Marco Antonio Montes de Oca,[6] for example, found that death 'distant', yet 'shared' and 'decisive'; and adds, 'for the first time I feel scant of words'. As a pure explosion of truth Guevara robs him, if only momentarily, of the brilliant flow of language, part surrealist and part ancient Mexican in the style of Paz's *Eagle or Sun?*, that characterizes his other verse. A poem by José Emilio Pacheco registers the shock yet more intimately. The hero, omnipresent, is not even named, and pulls the poet back, as he escapes, 'blinded', to a distance of dubious neutrality:

> Fue como si tratara de alejarme,
> de estar más lejos cada vez del héroe.
>
> Cegado por la luz del aeropuerto
> vi en *The Toronto Star*
> noticias vagas:
> *Rumor de que los 'rangers' lo cercaron.*
>
> Al descender en Amsterdam supimos,
> con hondo azoro incrédulo, el martirio
> y el altivo final en una abyecta
> noche de Sudamérica.
>
> Y en Heathrow Airport el *Times* decía:
> *Ha comezado la leyenda.*
> Y es cierto:
>
> ellos le dieron muerte;
> vida, los condenados de la tierra.[7]

It was as if I was trying to get away, to be ever further from the hero. ¶Blinded by the airport light I saw vague reports in *The Toronto Star*: Rumoured that the Rangers have surrounded him. ¶Coming down in Amsterdam we got to know, with deep incredulous trepidation, of the martyrdom and the proud finale in an abject night in South America. ¶And in Heathrow Airport *The Times* said: The legend has begun. And it's true: ¶they gave him death; life, the damned of the earth.

Beyond personal testimonies of this kind it is not hard to recognize revolutionary involvement in Latin America as a Third World theatre. What is more difficult is to assess the importance of such involvement in modern Latin American poetry generally. The practice of modern poets is by no means exhaustively illustrated by the five to whom the rest of this chapter is dedicated, the Nicaraguan Ernesto Cardenal, the Peruvian Carlos Germán Belli, the Chilean Nicanor Parra, the Brazilian João Cabral de Melo Neto, and the Argentinian Alberto Girri. But discussing their work necessarily brings up basic critical problems. Some of them have written apparently indifferent to the politics of their subcontinent, yet are considered reactionary for this by others. And while for some being a Christian poet, or being an 'anti-poet', will be a way of being revolutionary, for others it will be the opposite. The situation is made the more interesting by the fact that, though they have exerted powerful influence, the revolutionaries of Cuba, Allende's Chile and elsewhere, unlike those of Stalinist Russia, have not settled these critical problems for themselves, by defining what poetry, or literature in general, 'should' be like. As Castro said: 'The Revolution has to understand the real situation and should therefore act in such a manner that the whole group of artists and intellectuals who are not genuinely revolutionaries can find within the Revolution a place to work and create, a place where their creative spirit, even though they are not revolutionary writers and artists, has the opportunity and freedom to be expressed.'[8]

I

Ernesto Cardenal lives in a Christian community (Solentiname), which he founded, on an island in the Lake of San Juan in Nicaragua. He is prominent among those Latin Americans who urgently desire to reconcile Christianity and communism, in the spirit of Pope John XXIII's *Progressio populorum*, and would find common ground for social justice, if necessary outside the church and without orthodox Marxism. (At mass at Solentiname the congregation discusses passages from Guevara's writings along with the Bible.) His record of his visits to Cuba (*En Cuba*)[9] is both very alert and inspired. Despite defects freely acknowledged, statistically if necessary, he found there that 'the Vallejo-era of America had begun (the new man, and man brother of man)'. The society he found, and the poets in it (whose work is quoted at length in the book), were vindicated as a tangible object of faith, of the kind Vallejo did not live to see. We best approach Cardenal by mentioning these things because for him faith and poetry are intimately linked.

His first major work, *Hora O* (Zero Hour), and *Epigrams*, emerge from the 'tropical nights of Central America', an atmospere thick with dictators, misery and injustice. His anger and his reasons for it are comparable with Neruda's in *Canto general*. But his satire has, precisely, an epigrammatic quality and relies less on exposed feelings than on an exposing intelligence, as in his lines on the dictator of Nicaragua: 'Somoza unveils the statue of Somoza in the Somoza Stadium'. Similarly, instead of launching into invective, he documents his subject with the appearance of painstaking accuracy. The detail of occurrence in his hands acquires an absurd yet undeniable certainty, as in these passages from *Hora O*:

Cuando había dinero
y no había empréstitos extranjeros
ni los impuestos eran para Pierpont Morgan & Cía.
y la compañía frutera no competía con el pequeño cosechero.
Pero vino la United Fruit Company
con sus subsidiarias la Tela Railroad Company
y la Trujillo Railroad Company
aliada con la Cuyamel Fruit Company
y Vaccaro Brothers & Company
más tarde Standard Fruit & Steamship Company
de la Standard Fruit & Steamship Corporation:
. . .

La condición era que la Compañía construyera el Ferrocarril,
pero la Compañía no lo construía,
porque las mulas en Honduras eran más baratas que el Ferrocarril,
y "un Dibutado más bbarato que una mula"
—como decía Zemurray—
aunque seguía disfrutando de las exenciones de impuesto
y los 175.000 acres de subvención para la Compañía,
con la obligación de pagar a la nación por cada milla
que no construyera, pero no pagaba nada a la nación
aunque no construía ninguna milla (Carías es el dictador
que más millas de línea férrea no construyó)

When there was money and there were no foreign loans and the taxes weren't for Pierpont Morgan & Co., and the fruit company didn't compete with the small grower. But the United Fruit Company came with its subsidiaries the Tela Railroad Company and the Trujillo Railroad Company allied to the Cuyamel Fruit Company and Vaccaro Brothers &

Company, later the Standard Fruit and Steamship Company of the Standard Fruit and Steamship Corporation... ¶The condition was that the Company should build the railway, but the Company didn't build it, because the mules in Honduras were cheaper than the railway, and 'a deputy was cheaper than a mule' (as Zemurray would say), although it went on enjoying the tax exemption and the 175,000 acres granted to the Company, with the obligation to pay the nation for each mile it didn't build, but it didn't pay the nation anything although it didn't build a single mile (Carias is the dictator who didn't build most miles of track).

Cardenal learned to focus on his subject in this way largely through his deep knowledge of poetry in English, especially Pound's. The detailed and exterior language of the Cantos is unmistakable in *Hora O*, down to such precise techniques as quoting from magazines like *Time*. (In fact his critics have complained that his verse reads like a translation from English.) After studying at Columbia (New York) Cardenal went back to the United States in 1957 to the Trappist monastery in Kentucky where the poet Thomas Merton lived. His three years there are recorded in the collection *Gethsemane Ky.* (1961), an intimate document by one in retreat from the exterior world. His confinement in Gethsemane strengthened his inner faith to the extent that he launched on the huge undertaking of re-writing the 150 Psalms of David for the modern world. In verses like the following he prays to God as 'I' in the voice of mankind and names the new evils he faces: 'Save me Lord/from the S.S. the N.K.V.D. the F.B.I. the G.N./Save me from their Councils of War/from the rage of their judges and their guards' (Psalm 7). From there he kept up the tension between his faith and a highly-politicized sense of reality. After his *Oration for Marilyn Monroe* have come narratives of the conquest and history of Central America (*El estrecho dudoso*) and the *Homage to the American Indians*. These last two works achieve an epic tone and are worthy of comparison with *Canto general*.

Cardenal's great strength is to have allowed 'facts' of the exterior world to speak for themselves while preserving a firm centre from which to arrange them. In these more recent works the first person is in fact not often formally expressed, is sooner implicit, and powerfully so, in the whole configuration of the poem. As we noted in an earlier chapter, in his homage to the Indians he will occasionally interpret their being favourably in terms of his own faith, incorporating them as it were into his universe on slight 'evidence' (his Christianization of Nezahualcoyotl being a case in point). But this rarely seems forced in a given poem because of his talent for creating a space in which statements, from diverse sources, are cumulative and not pre-emptive. 'His is a poetry that *announces*', as Oviedo has said: 'Cardenal's poetic feat consists of making us see that the history of America is a prediction, that this utopia did once happen and that new signs announce it in the midst of the hecatomb.'[10] To make his American credo more immediate, Neruda re-shaped history and geography, placed himself in them as the voice that invokes, censures and extols, in ways that we have examined. By convincing us of the 'objective' truth of his immense erudition, the corollary of his faith, Cardenal fuses experience yet more thoroughly and strives for a specifically prophetic tone. This is especially evident in the poems which draw on the Maya prophecies, or *katuns*, which refer to both past and future from some further point; and in his verses on the death of Merton, perhaps his most fulsome profession of understanding of life and the world. The length and scale of these poems, and the multiplicity of their references (comparable to Pound's) make quotation especially hard, but here are some of his lines to Merton:

> Donde los algonquinos espíritus con mocasines espíritus
> cazan castores espíritus sobre una nieve espíritu
> 　　　　　creímos que la luna estaba lejos
> morir no es salir del mundo es
> hundirse en él
> estás en la clandestinidad del universo
> 　　　el underground
> fuera de Establishment de este mundo, del espacio tiempo
> sin Johnson ni Nixon
> 　　　　allí no hay tigres
> 　　　　　　　　dicen los malayos
> (una Isla del oeste)
> 　　　　　　que van a dar a la mar
> 　　　　　　que es la vida
> Donde los muertos se juntan oh Netzahualcóyotl
> o 'Corazón del Mundo'
> 　　　　　Hemingway, Raissa, Barth, Alfonso Cortés
> el mundo es mucho más profundo
> 　　　　　　Hades, donde Xto bajó
> 　　　　　　　　seno, vientre (Mt. 12, 40)
> 　　　　　　　　　　SIGN OF JONAS
> 　　　las profundidades de la belleza visible

donde nada la gran ballena cósmica
llena de profetas

Where the spirit Algonquin with spirit moccasins hunt spirit beavers over a spirit snow, we thought the moon was far away, dying is not leaving the world it's sinking into it, you're in the clandestine universe, the underground, outside the Establishment of this world, of spatial time, without Johnson or Nixon where there are no tigers the Malayans say (an Island in the west) that flow to the sea that is life. Where the dead gather oh Netzahualcoyotl or 'Heart of the World' Hemingway, Raissa, Barth, Alfonso Cortés, the world is much deeper, Hades, where Xto descended, breast, belly (Matt. 12, 40) SIGN OF JONAS, the depths of visible beauty, where the great cosmic whale swims full of prophets.

## 2

Among his contemporaries Cardenal is exceptional not just for having a faith of such intensity but for expressing it in terms that are politically so exuberant and accessible. Beside him a writer like the Peruvian Carlos Germán Belli seems at first sight cramped, bitter and hostile. In religious terms Belli is a last agonized Adam, addressing God only in sarcastic disbelief. Like Vallejo, he emerges reluctantly from the womb and the family (once quite rich), from pastoral innocence into a harsh Darwinian world. Unlike Vallejo, and still less like Cardenal (who performed the feat of integrating evolutionary theory into his Psalms), he seems resigned about it. But this is not the whole story.

Belli's major collection is entitled *El pie sobre el cuello* (The Foot on the Neck). The neck is the poet's. The foot belongs to his oppressors: tax, low wages, heat, and the 'cruel white masters of Peru' who just allow him to breathe and swallow, like close-fitting stocks. In his prostration he recognizes the futility of excitement, though not of resistance, and observes minutely the process of his survival, as he absorbs daily his 'alimentary pill' (which is what he himself becomes in the poem 'Bolo de pulpo') and labours with his 'sudiparous' glands uncooled by the 'austral breeze'. This is the condition he enjoys as a 'poor amanuensis of Peru'.

The grim fixity of his situation is conveyed by the steady repetition of phrases and lines: 'I see and I hate', 'stammering or cross-eyed or lame'. Lines from one poem become the title of another, and the degree of interpenetration is such that the five books gathered in *The Foot on the Neck*[11] – *Poemas* (1958), *Dentro y afuera* (Inside and Outside, 1960), *Oh hada cibernética* (Oh Cybernetic Fairy, 1962), *El pie sobre el cuello* (1964) and *Por el monte abajo* (Down the Hill, 1966) – appear as fragments of the same vast and unchanging poem. This coherence however palpably tightens over the years. The first book, *Poemas*, shows traces of the dream images of the surrealists (whom Belli knows thoroughly), as well as sudden phonetic outbursts in the style of *Trilce*. But from the start Belli also announces what becomes the distinguishing feature of his work: a diction so excruciatingly controlled that his speaking through it is the analogue of his effort to exist at all. Emotions, which given direct outlet might have seemed hysterical or self-indulgent, have to squeeze their way through the interstices of his language, so that linguistic expression in the poems becomes itself a metaphor of the condition they describe.

This diction is first of all that of the Spanish Golden Age. Belli speaks of himself, his habitat, his family and so on, in the language of Garcilaso and other pastoral poets. With his brother 'Anfriso' he labours under the 'austral breeze', searching for the shade-giving poplar or myrtle. He also adopts sixteenth- and seventeenth-century Spanish verse forms and vocabulary, working up to the syntactic complexities of Góngora (separating adjectives from nouns, for example), and the prosodic complexities of the sestina (a poem of six stanzas of six lines, each ending with the same six words each time in a different order, the six words being used all together in a final tercet). Here is an example of such a tercet, based on the words 'cojo, cuello, cepo, crudo, amo, ocio':

> pero cojo yo en fin y con mi cuello
> deste cepo cautivo, heme, ¡ay crudo hado!,
> ¡ay vil amo!, en pos siempre de un breve ocio.

But lame in short and with my neck captive of these stocks, behold me, ay crude fate!, ay vile master!, seeking always brief respite.

By these means he establishes a clear and coherent connection between Latinate poetic convention and the Latinate language of technology and science: the 'cybernetic fairy' which should release and dignify him in fact oppresses him like the Peruvian heirs of the Spanish conquistadors. Like the subject of some of Vallejo's poems he is reduced to scientific explanation of himself, as disintegrating anatomy (or 'chassis') with its sudiparous glands and 'sonorous bilial expansion'; or regresses to the form of a bear or an ant.

Belli's language, then, makes him appear an agonizedly 'Latin' American in a poem like the following ('En Bética no bella'):

> Ya calo, crudos zagales desta Bética
> no bella, mi materia, y me doy cuenta
> que de abolladuras ornado estoy
> por faenas que me habéis señalado
> tan sólo a mí y a nadie más ¿por qué?,
> mas del corzo la priesa privativa
> ante el venablo, yo no podré haber,
> o que el seso se me huya de sus arcas
> por el cerúleo claustro, pues entonces
> ni un olmo habría donde granjear
> la sombra para Filis, o a mis vástagos,
> o a Anfriso tullido, hermano mío;
> pero no cejaré, no, aunque no escriba
> ni copule ni baile en esta Bética
> no bella, en donde tantos años vivo.

I now comprehend, crude swains of this unbeautiful Betica, my matter, and I realize that I am decorated with bruises from tasks you assigned to me, only to me and no one else, why?, but I cannot have the speed peculiar to the roe before the dart, or that my brains should flee their box through the cerulean claustrum, for then there would be not a single elm to spread shade for Phyllis, or my offspring, or maimed Anfriso, brother of mine; but I will not yield, no, though I don't write or copulate or dance in this unbeautiful Betica, where I have lived for so many years.

In the sonnets of *Human Poems*, as we noted, Vallejo reduced and enhanced self-pity by deliberately formal statement. With Belli this process is carried much further. The formal constriction is such that we have almost to translate the poem to discover what is happening. 'I suffer from excessive work in Peru; I can't run away or shoot my brains out because I have dependents; but I won't give up.' Betica was the Latin name for Andalusia and southern Spain. Peru is unbeautifully southern: the climate is bad and even the directions, of sun and wind, are the wrong way round (being of the other hemisphere). Despite this he speaks to other swains, using the archaic language of the pastoral tradition and the classical tradition generally ('desta', 'faenas', 'corzo', 'venablo', 'cerúleo', 'vástago', etc.). His wife becomes Phyllis, with whom he would ideally sport in the shade; his brother Alfonso (who suffered even more than he) becomes the fine-sounding Anfriso. The effective constriction of self is extreme to the point of absurdity. The syntax is painfully contrived ('but to the roe the speed peculiar before the dart I cannot have') and crude reality is grotesquely avoided. Even bruises 'decorate' him, and when he realizes he has them he asks 'why?' quite decorously.

This being so, Belli's greatest hazard must then be that his poetry slips into parody, seems like an elaborate joke, cruel perhaps, but empty of passion once we have done the 'translation' and got the point. He in fact avoids this danger for the same reason that his poetry, in the last instance, has a strong political charge. What Ortega, in an excellent article,[12] has called Belli's 'baroque mask' and 'hyperbole' are belied in the poem above by verbs like 'copulate' at the end, which suggests a tougher man underneath. The only language that Belli found to be even nearly adequate for himself and his situation may be 'absurd', as Vallejo's often was. But, again like Vallejo, this does not finally mean that he 'gives up'. Even under the incredible load he bears and in near-mortal constriction in the 'stocks of Peru', he is not a fatalist. Although he returns incessantly to a prior happy state, as a foetus in the 'luminous cloister' of the womb, as a shepherd in a remote valley of a happier Betica, his poetry works as an amazing cauterizer of the nostalgia that feeds on the idea that such loss is irrevocable. In a poem to his wife he contrasts their lineages, his being barely human:

> Porque prójimos no éramos nosotros,
> y en horma yo lucía de cuadrúpedo,
>     del hocico a la cola,
>     exactamente un bruto.

Because we were not close, and in form I stood out as a quadruped, from the snout to the tail, exactly a brute.

But the fault, apparently genetic (according to that old reactionary explanation) is really social:

> Tal estado ¿qué? Por los dioses no,
> ni en el materno claustro fue jamás,
>     sino a la orilla fiera
>     del Betis que me helaba.

Such a state, how? Not because of the gods, nor was it ever in the maternal cloister, but on the fierce bank of the Betis which froze me.

Just because of the self-imposed restriction of his verse, when he gives precise and actual details of this 'fierce bank' the accusatory effect is doubly forceful. The gentle shepherd turns suddenly active, catching us by surprise:

> pues en cada linaje
> el deterioro ejerce su dominio
> por culpa de la propiedad privada,
> que miro y aborrezco;

For in every lineage deterioration exercises its power through the fault of private property, which I see and hate.

With similar intensity he sees and hates 'these chiles, perus and ecuadors'. When these places, as political and social realities, have been changed, when Lima ceases to be the 'Lima la horrible' of César Moro (the Peruvian surrealist quoted in an epigraph) or of Salazar Bondy (author of a book of that title), then just possibly he can rise from his cramped foetal posture. In the title poem of 'Down the hill', where exceptionally he speaks in the first person plural, he discovers, in the very thoroughness with which he has been reduced while others ascend, 'buoyant', a final term that makes of every survival a potential resistance:

> Bien si poquillos seres no más somos,
> el final punto no es ser cosa chica,
> que por el mundo tantas hay dispersas,
> pues nuestro caso grave más se torna
>            por tales agrias cuestas.

Even if we are just tiny beings the final point is not to be a small thing, for over the world there are so many dispersed, since our case becomes graver down such rough slopes.

The importance of this ultimate fact of survival emerges again in 'Bolo de pulpo' (Octopus Bolus), where having been digested he navigates the ends of the intestines to say: 'I remember myself not as a mediocre shepherd, but as a leader, enthroned in the splendid valley.' Though this is clearly ironic the significant word is 'remember'. It indicates that beneath his sarcastic use of classical conventions of the Spanish Golden Age lies some faith in the ideals, social and human, from which those conventions originally derived. The deterioration of the world he inhabits is, then, that of the language he describes it in. So that, within his poems, the intimation of recovered stature, of 'perennial ardent love', has definite historical and political overtones.

3

Like other Chileans of his generation, Nicanor Parra has faced
the large problem of how to write at all and avoid the overwhelming influence of Neruda.[13] This explains in part the acrobatic
assertiveness of his first major book *Poemas y antipoemas* (Poems
and Antipoems, 1954). The opposition in the title is not fully
reflected in the work, which mostly exposes what he calls the vices
of the modern world, among them the prevalence of dream over
common sense. A poem like 'Paisaje' (Landscape) may be un-
adulteratedly surreal:

> ¡Véis esa pierna humana que cuelga de la luna
> Como un árbol que crece para abajo
> Esa pierna temible que flota en el vacío    ·
> Illuminada apenas por el rayo
> De la luna y el aire del olvido!

Can you see that human leg hanging from the moon like a tree growing
downwards. That fearsome leg that floats in space barely illuminated by
a moon-beam and the air of oblivion.

But it has the feel of an exercise. More characteristically, he
speaks corrosively and conversationally, and continuously refers
to the listener's common sense. 'But why dig deeper into these
disagreeable matters'; 'Consider, lads'; 'I am the one who expresses himself badly'; 'I spent my nights at my desk absorbed in
the practice of automatic writing'. He is thus an anti-poet by being
an ante-poet, in a prior or external position:

> Un alma que ha estado embotellada durante años
> En una especie de abismo sexual e intelectual
> Alimentándose escasamente por la nariz
> Desea hacerse escuchar por ustedes.

A soul which has been bottled up for years in a kind of sexual and
intellectual abyss, feeding itself thinly through the nose, desires to be
listened to by you.

In this and later collections he in fact shows himself hypersensi-
tive to his readers' reactions, and matches sentimentality and self-
indulgence with caustic self-awareness. He confesses ironically
that he is 'contemporary with silent film'. Or he will say that the
rite of self-possession demands that

> Cierro los ojos para ver mejor

> Y canto con rencor
> Una canción de comienzos de siglo.

I close my eyes to see better, and I sing with rancour a song of the turn of the century.

With the first line an echo, indeed rancorous, of the Spanish Modernist Manuel Machado, this is ironic because we can sense Parra acting thus as a character exiled from himself, as Ortega has keenly observed.[14] When this 'period gentleman' rejoins Parra the result is a self-deprecatory 'Consultorio sentimental':

> Caballero de buena voluntad
> Apto para trabajos personales
> Ofrécese para cuidar señorita de noche
> Gratis
>     sin compromisos de ninguna especie
> A condición de que sea realmente de noche.
>
> Seriedad absoluta.
> Disposición a contraer matrimonio
> Siempre que la señorita sepa mover las caderas.

Gentleman, well intentioned, suitable for personal work, prepared to look after young lady at night, gratis, without obligation of any kind, on condition that it really is at night. ¶Completely responsible. Disposed to matrimony provided the lady knows how to move her hips.

Parra's *Versos de salón* (Drawing-room Verses, 1960), since they are shockingly not that, could indicate that his attack on gentlemanly sentiment is at the root of his anti-poetry. While others write in French, he says (i.e. are polite), he writes in 'Araucanian and Latin', 'grating verses' that are original. He spies through the keyhole and uncovers the absurdities that underlie bourgeois hypocrisy and the poetry it engenders. In 'El pequeño burgués' (The Petit Bourgeois) he wittily goes through the abilities demanded of anyone who wants to be acceptable: 'to distinguish a viola from a violin', 'to receive visitors in pijamas', 'to prevent loss of hair', 'to swallow quantities of saliva' (this last phrase runs through the poem and denotes the achievement of not being a peasant who simply spits). Defining his anti-poet as a *persona non grata* who concedes to himself the right to say anything, he remarks that he may shake the foundations of 'decadent and out-dated institutions'. And it is this kind of irreverence that attracted the Beat generation of the US to him in the 1950s, notably Ferlinghetti and Ginsberg.[15] But this by no means makes him a revolutionary.

A more pointed definition of what an anti-poet is can be found in the poem 'Test', where the reader is asked to underline whichever phrase he considers correct, from a list which includes:

> Un bailarín al borde del abismo?
> Un narciso que ama a todo el mundo?
> Un bromista sangriento
> Deliberadamente miserable?
> Un poeta que duerme en una silla?
> Un alquimista de los tiempos modernos?
> Un revolucionario de bolsillo?
> Un pequeño burgués?
> Un charlatan?
>             un dios?
>                         un inocente?
> Un aldeano de Santiago de Chile?

A dancer on the edge of the abyss? A narcissus who loves everyone? A cruel joker who is deliberately wretched? A poet asleep in a chair? An alchemist of modern times? A pocket revolutionary? A petit bourgeois? A charlatan? a god? an innocent? A native of Santiago, Chile?

Parra does not himself indicate which is right; and he is certainly not anti-bourgeois in the name of another ideology, in the way that Neruda, or a younger Chilean like Fernando Lamberg[16] manifestly are. The colloquial humour and songs of another collection of Parra's, *La cueca larga* (1958; the cueca being a national folk dance), encouraged some critics to see in him the champion of popular solidarity. Parra no doubt has this sympathy and desire, but they cannot nearly account for him as a poet (one of the 'vices of the modern world' was the exaltation of folklore into a spiritual category). Above all he is the individual as he announced at the start (in the poem 'I am the Individual') and repeated in 'Acta de independencia' (Declaration of Independence):

> Independientemente
> De los designios de la Iglesia Católica
> Me declaro país independiente.
>     . . .
> Que me perdone el Comité Central.

Independently of the designs of the Catholic church I declare myself an independent country. . . . ¶May the Central Committee forgive me.

In other words, wrily apologetic, he is prepared to take the consequences of exposing the absurdities of life anarchically, beyond
the designs of systems, Christian or Communist.

As an individual poet his one loyalty is in fact to poetry, which
however has its own rules. Behaviour towards it (her, in Spanish)
is like behaviour towards a woman. It (she) can be impossibly
demanding, a 'viper' ('La víbora'):

> Apasionada hasta el delirio no me daba un instante de tregua,
> Exigiéndome perentoriamente que besara su boca
> Y que contestase sin dilación sus necias preguntas
> Varias de ellas referentes a la eternidad y a la vida futura
> Temas que producían en mí un lamentable estado de ánimo,
> Zumbidos de oídos, entrecortadas náuseas, desvanecimientos prematuros
> Que ella sabía aprovechar con ese espíritu práctico que la caracterizaba
> Para vestirse rápidamente sin pérdida de tiempo
> Y abandonar mi apartamento dejándome con un palmo de narices.

Deliriously passionate, she didn't give me an instant's peace, peremptorily
demanding I kiss her mouth and answer her stupid questions without
hesitation, several of them referring to eternity and the future life, subjects
which produced in me a lamentable state of mind, buzzing in my ears,
fitful nausea, premature fainting which she knew how to take advantage
of with that practical spirit that typified her in order to dress quickly
losing no time and to leave my flat having slapped my face.

The difficulties of this relationship can lead to the realization that
'Poetry has finished with me': 'What do I gain by saying/I have
behaved well/and she has behaved badly/when they know that
I'm to blame.' There is an implicit appeal for sympathy here, that
in turn has its irony. If the guarantees of life are, as he says, en-
joyment of it and a sense of humour, it is a question of seeing how
far you can take them. And this is what happens when you behave
badly and go too far: the end of poetry, which is still however a
poem, a paradoxical proof of his 'gallant' method. Parra's poems
are full of this kind of 'testing'. He will evince the will to total
power, as in 'Cambios de nombre' (Changes of Name):

> Mi posición es ésta:
> El poeta no cumple su palabra
> Si no cambia los nombres de las cosas.
>
> ¿Con qué razón el sol
> Ha de seguir llamándose sol?
> ¡Pido que se le llame Micifuz
> El de las botas de cuarenta leguas!
>
> . . .

> Bueno, la noche es larga
> Todo sujeto que se estime a sí mismo
> Debe tener su propio diccionario.
> Y antes que se me olvide
> Al propio dios hay que cambiarle nombre
> Que cada cual lo llame como quiera :
> Ese es un problema personal.

My position is this : the poet doesn't keep his word if he doesn't change the names of things. ¶Why should the sun go on being called sun? I request that it be called Micifuz, the one with the forty-league boots!... Well, the night is long. Every person who respects himself ought to have his own dictionary. And before I forget, God too must have his name changed, let everyone call him what he will : that is a personal problem.

But of course it is only the manic ambition that is a 'personal problem'. Parra is showing that for him at least etymology, the truth of words, resists manhandling, is unfortunately after all sooner the dictionary's than the individual's, words being locked in what *is*, in a life we can otherwise do little about ('The world has always been this way, that is, absurd'). The line 'that is a personal problem' is a good example of the life-saving agility, of the sudden twists that become more marked in later collections (*Canciones rusas*, Russian Songs, 1964; *Ejercicios respiratorios*, Breathing Exercises, 1966). The poem 'Montaña rusa' (Switchback) is itself what it describes :

> Durante medio siglo
> La poesía fue
> El paraíso del tonto solemne.
> Hasta que vine yo
> Y me instalé con mi montaña rusa.
>
> Suban, si les parece.
> Claro que yo no respondo si bajan
> Echando sangre por boca y narices.

For half a century poetry was the paradise of the solemn fool. Until I came along and settled in with my switchback. ¶Climb aboard, why not. Of course I'm not responsible if you come down bleeding through mouth and nose.

The rules of the game are the subject of another poem that begins with disarming free advice :

> Escriban lo que quieran.
> En el estilo que les parezca mejor.
> Ha pasado demasiada sangre bajo los puentes

Para seguir creyendo
Que sólo se puede seguir un camino.

En poesía se permite todo.

A condición expresa
          por cierto
De superar la página en blanco.

Write what you want. In the style you find best. Too much blood has
flowed under the bridges to go on believing that only one road should be
followed. ¶In poetry everything is permitted. ¶On the express condition,
of course, that the blank page is improved on.

It is significant that many of Parra's poems are ostensibly 'after
the event', or posthumous: 'What the Dead Man Said About
Himself', 'Memories of Youth', 'In the Cemetery' (two poems),
'Funeral Address'. This allows him momentary respite in the game,
a pause in the anarchic struggle with absurdity. He takes this
procedure to what must be its limit in 'Me retracto de todo lo
dicho' (I Take Back Everything I've Said). Poet and anti-poet, he
asks the reader to allow him this last request because 'words took
revenge' on him, making him say what he didn't mean. In a confession that may be treacherous or genuine, and in a retraction and
gesture of independence that may now seem to intimate solidarity,
he says:[17]

Perdóname lector
Amistoso lector
Que no me pueda despedir de ti
Con un abrazo fiel:
Me despido de ti
Con una triste sonrisa forzada.

Puede que yo no sea más que eso
Pero oye mi última palabra:
Me retracto de todo lo dicho.
Con la mayor amargura del mundo
Me retracto de todo lo que he dicho.

Forgive me reader, friendly reader, for I can't take my leave of you with
a faithful embrace: I take leave of you with a sad forced smile. ¶Maybe
that's all I am, but hear my last word: I take back everything I've said.
With the greatest bitterness in the world I take back everything I've said.

## 4

The Brazilian João Cabral de Melo Neto has also called himself an
antipoet. His *Poesias completas*[18] (edited so as to extend back-

wards in time from *Educação pela pedra* (Education Through
Stone, 1965), to *Pedra do sono,* (Stone of Sleep, 1941) are dedicated to Manuel Bandeira as 'esta antilira'. And a work of 1946,
his 'Fable of Amphion' (evocative of Mário de Andrade's persona
in *Hallucinated City*), is followed by an 'antiode', against poetry
said to be profound. But his opposition to 'poetry' is of quite a
different order from Parra's.

If Parra is close to the Beats in being irreverently anti-poetry,
Cabral shares the self-critical austerity of Marianne Moore, whom
he congratulates for making a 'clear scar' with her poetic scalpel.
Though he probably distrusts lyric conventions as much as Parra,
being anti-poetry does not lead Cabral to attack it directly as a
bourgeois or individualist excess. Rather he advises soberly what
should and may be done with words in poems that exemplify the
advice. In one of his switches Parra suggests how changing the
dictionary meaning of a word is and is not a 'personal problem'.
Cabral with steady logic disengages words from their 'dictionary
situation', as he puts it, revealing the power they have of their
own. As a demonstration he transforms words that are 'poetically
impossible' (a recurrent phrase) before our very eyes (and ears).
This is what he does in 'A palavra sêda' (The Word Silk):

> A atmosfera que te envolve
> atinge tais atmosferas
> que transforma muitas coisas
> que te concernem, ou cercam.
>
> E como as coisas, palavras
> impossíveis de poema:
> exemplo, a palavra ouro,
> e até êste poema, sêda.
>
> E certo que tua pessoa
> não faz dormir, mas desperta;
> nem é *sedante*, palavra
> derivada da de sêda.

The atmosphere that envelopes you includes such atmospheres that it
transforms many things that concern you, or surround you. ¶And like
things, words impossible in a poem: example, the word gold, and up to
this poem, silk. ¶It's true that your person doesn't induce sleep, but
awakens; nor is it a sedative, a word derived from the word silk.

In a further series of propositions he reaches the conclusion that
under the 'false academic surface' said to be 'like silk' there is

something 'muscular, animal, carnal, panther, feline, of feline substance or its manner', etc., which persists in the 'thing silk' ('na coisa sêda').

In this kind of play with the surfaces and meanings of words Cabral owes a great deal to Carlos Drummond de Andrade. In contrast to the Modernists who immediately preceded him, Carlos Drummond was a highly reflective poet and his best poems are often about poetry. His advice in 'Procura de poesia' (Search For Poetry),[19] doubtless directed at the Modernists of São Paulo or regional Brazil, makes a point more widely applicable:

> Não cantes tua cidade, deixa-a em paz.
> O canto não é o movimento das máquinas nem o segrêdo
>     das casas.
> Não é música ouvida de passagem; rumor do mar nas
>     ruas junto à linha de espuma.
> O canto não é a natureza
> nem os homens em sociedade.
> Para êle, chuva e noite, fadiga e esperança nada significam.
> A poesia (não tires poesia das coisas)
> elide sujeito e objeto.
>
> Não dramatizes, não invoques,
> não indagues. Não percas tempo em mentir.
> Não te aborreças.

Don't sing your city, leave it in peace. Song is not the movement of machines nor the secret of houses. It's not the music heard in passing; murmur of the sea in the streets near the line of foam. Song is not nature, nor men in society. For it, rain and night, fatigue and hope mean nothing. Poetry (don't draw poetry out of things) elides subject and object. ¶Don't dramatize, don't invoke, don't state. Don't waste time lying. Don't hate yourself.

This is what he says should be done instead:

> Penetra surdamente no reino das palavras.
> Lá estão os poemas que esperam ser escritos.
> Estão paralisados, mas não há desespêro,
> há calma e frescura na superfície intacta.
> Ei-los sós e mudos, em estado de dicionário.
> Convive com teus poemas, antes de escrevê-los.
> Tem paciência, se obscuros. Calma, se te provocam.
> Espera que cada um se realize e consume
> com seu poder de palavra
> e seu poder de silêncio.

Enter the kingdom of words unobtrusively. There are the poems that wait to be written. They are paralized, but there's no desperation, there's calm and freshness on their intact surface. Look at them alone and mute, in a dictionary state. Live with your poems before writing them. Be patient if they're obscure. Calm if they provoke you. Wait for each one to be realized and fulfilled with its word power and its silence power.

Cabral could hardly have followed this advice more closely. We cannot help noticing in him that same interest in the state or situation of words, in the great importance of how to approach them, of allowing them to exert their own powers. Exactly echoing Drummond, Cabral says he 'lives with certain words, domestic bees'; these are those 'twenty words, always the same' of which he knows 'the function, the evaporation, the density less than that of air'. Cabral took this 'Poetry lesson' (Lição de poesia) most seriously in *Uma faca só lâmina* (A Knife Only Blade, 1955). It is a sizeable poem which however relies principally on only three word-images: bullet, clock and blade. These, coaxed, tried and tested with calm intelligence, become themselves surgical instruments to perform the delicate operation of eliding subject and object, of making reality into literature.

In subsequent collections, like *Serial* (1961) and *Education by Stone*, words are similarly tested and brought out through sheer effort of concentration. A paradigm case is 'Coisas de cabeceira, Recife' (Title-page Items, Recife), in this last collection:

> Diversas coisas se alinham na memória
> numa prateleira com o rótulo: Recife.
> Coisas como de cabeceira de memória,
> a um tempo coisas e no próprio índice;
> e pois que em índice: densas, recortadas,
> bem legíveis, em suas formas simples.

Various things line up in memory, on a shelf with the label: Recife. Things as if from the title-page of memory, at once things and in their own index; and since in an index: dense, clear-cut, quite legible, in their simple forms.

The second part of the poem gives us some of these words. Initially they might be thought to be either material ('combogo', 'telhados') or abstract ('paralelipipedo'). In Cabral's poem they all acquire a new quality of being *both* concrete ('dense') and conceptual ('in their own index'). How much this is altogether part of a deliberate procedure on the poet's part is brought home when we turn from this piece 'about' Recife to another 'about' Seville. This opens with an identical first two lines, except for the substitution of the appropriate place name. The 'things' in this poem are in fact idiomatic Andalusian phrases (printed in Spanish). Cabral's overall method is such however that we accept them on the same terms and feel in them the same power as we do in the things of Recife.

An increasingly common feature of Cabral's poetry, notably since *A Knife Only Blade*, has been this kind of formal interchangeability, the insistence not just on certain words but on whole sentences appearing and re-appearing as part of an argument that is both logical ('anti-poetic') and hypnotic. In this the textures he creates come to resemble Belli's. There is the same patient reliance on a reduced vocabulary and set repeated phrases, the same censoring of personal emotion, and of cognitive statements 'about' another supposed reality outside the poem. But with Belli the whole exercise may be understood as metaphorical: that is, the choice of Latinate diction, at once archaic and scientific, can be understood to indicate how sadly diminished the reality and exterior values have become which once inspired such diction. With Cabral, moral or political messages are yet harder to read, as we shall see.

The language of Cabral's poems is in this sense ostensibly normal, even mathematically neutral; or to use his words, 'it shows only the indifferent perfection of geometry, like magazine reproductions of Mondrian, seen from a distance'. Take for example the balanced, paralogical propositions of 'O mar e o canavial' (The Sea and the Canefield):

> O que o mar sim aprende do canavial:
> a elocução horizontal de seu verso;
> a geórgica de cordel, ininterrupta,
> narrada em voz e silêncio paralelos.
> O que o mar não aprende do canavial:
> a veemência passional da preamar;
> a mão-de-pilão das ondas na areia,
> moída e miúda, pilada do que pilar.

What the sea does learn from the canefield: the horizontal eloquence of its verse; the string georgic, uninterrupted, narrated in parallel voice and silence. What the sea doesn't learn from the canefield: the passionate vehemence of high-tide; the pounding of the waves on the sand, damp and minute, thoroughly pounded.

Completing the symmetry, the poem goes on to tell what the canefield does and does not learn from the sea. Earlier, in 'The Word Silk', we were presented with an especially telling example

of Cabral's power of apparently reasoned argument: we accept
that the word in question ('sêda') derives from the same root as
'sedante', against what we know to be true (the two having nothing
to do with each other etymologically). Cabral does not assert such
truths as his own dictionary out of wit or desperation, as Parra
might have done, but out of the profoundest respect for 'the
genuine' in poetry, as Marianne Moore put it, and as Drummond
de Andrade had focused on it. That is, the strength a poet can
draw out of the irreducible reality of words, their sounds, shapes,
contours, presences, absences and logical connections.

We are led then to ask whether there is any essential difference
between Cabral and those Concrete poets[20] (in Brazil notably
Haraldo and Augusto Campos) whose work consists of word ar-
rangements on a page. With them, as with Octavio Paz's *Topoemas*, the arrangement highlights structural qualities that Cabral
is undoubtedly interested in, but little else. For example:

```
solo  sombra
sol  sombra
so  sombra
   sombra  so
 sombra  sol
sombra  solo
```

(the words involved mean 'alone', 'shadow', 'sun' and 'only').
What distinguishes Cabral from the Concretists is not so much
word arrangement as the fact that his verse continues to allow us
to presuppose that it is suppressing or resisting something else.
Cabral may be 'unemphatic, impersonal', but he is not unhuman
or unplaced. In an early poem to Paul Valéry he openly questions
the function, the 'no' in this sense, of his poetry: 'Is it the devil
in the body/or the poem/that causes me to spit/on my hygenic
no?' Valéry's pure poetry is 'the sweet tranquility/of the statue
in the square/among the flesh of men that grows and breeds'. But
this sweet calm is also that of the man 'on the shore', reduced by
implacable forces:

> o calor evapora,
> a areia absorve,
>
> as águas dissolvem
> os líquidos da vida;
> e o vento dispersa
> os sonhos, e apaga

a inaudível palavra
futura, – apenas
saída da bôca,
sorvida no silêncio.

the heat evaporates, the sand absorbs, ¶the waters dissolve the liquids of
life; and the wind disperses dreams and stifles ¶the inaudible future word
– no sooner out of the mouth than absorbed in the silence.

Cabral could hardly have said better how he speaks himself in
later poems as a man from north-east Brazil: the *sertão*, the
*caatinga*, the relentless sun, the terrible droughts, the elemental
colours and materials which form the substance of Graciliano
Ramos's brilliant 'north-eastern' work of the 1930s, *Vidas secas*
(Barren Lives). In his poem to Ramos, Cabral does actually open
into an 'audible' address; but his speech is rigorously limited to
the man who knows the experience deeply enough to know it is
unspeakable. The four sections (each of two stanzas) of the
poem begin, respectively, with the phrases 'I speak only with
what I speak', 'I speak only of what I speak', 'I speak only on
behalf of whom I speak' and 'I speak only for whom I speak'
('com que', 'do que', 'por quem', 'para quem'). The someone
'exists in these climates', 'in caatinga conditions'. The something
is 'the same twenty words turning round the sun which cleans
them of everything that is not a knife'. The something also 're-
duces everything to prickles, toast or simply leafage, luxuriant
leaf, full-leafed, where fraudulence can hide'. The fraudulence
consists of imagining precisely that you can talk about such things
descriptively, leafily, when in fact you can at best 'cultivate what
is synonymous with diminution'.

If then his poetry is not just for the sake of words and self-
sufficiency, but is also synonymous with or analogous to a specific
experience of a specific (Latin American) reality, we may after all
admit that parallel with Belli. But while Belli codes his poems so
that we decode the moral, Cabral, with his 'same twenty words'
invites us to a more intense linguistic discovery. As an anti-poet,
having revealed the 'density of words', Cabral may draw a moral
lesson from the exercise, only to suggest that the terrible strength
of the reality that oppresses them and lies irremediably, pre-
didactically, beyond.

Uma educação pela pedra : por lições;
para aprender da pedra, freqüentá-la;

captar sua voz inenfática, impessoal
(pela de dicção ela começa as aulas).
A lição de moral, sua resistência fria
ao que flui e a fluir, a ser maleada;
a de poética, sua carnadura concreta;
a de economia, seu adensar-se compacta :
lições da pedra (de fora para dentro,
cartilha muda), para quem soletrá-la.

Outra educação pela pedra : no Sertão
(de dentro para fora, e pré-didática).
No Sertão a pedra não sabe lecionar
e se lecionasse, não ensinaria nada;
lá não se aprende a pedra : lá a pedra,
uma pedra de nascença, entranha a alma.

An education through stone: by lessons; in order to learn from stone, frequent it; capture its unemphatic, impersonal voice (through that of diction it starts off the schoolroom). The moral lesson, its cold resistance to what flowed and to flowing, to being handled; the poetic lesson, its concrete flesh; the economic one, its compact denseness: lessons of stone (from outside inwards, a blank page), for whoever can read it. ¶Another education through stone: in the Sertão (from inside outwards, and predidactic). In the Sertão, stone doesn't know how to give lessons, and if it did it wouldn't teach anything; there you don't learn from stone: there stone, a stone from birth, is the soul's core.

By showing two kinds of education, this poem has the apparent symmetry and internal balance of others. But the symmetry is only apparent; the immense charge of the second stanza is unmatched and forces us 'out' into a reality beyond it. Ramos, a communist, was the least obviously 'political' of novelists. For similar reasons, Cabral, also from the north-east, commits himself as austerely as he does.

## 5

For many Argentinian writers, notoriously Borges, being Latin American implies the idea of being an exile. The reality of the place may be 'predidactic' as it is for Cabral (or, much earlier, was for Andrés Bello); may be grotesquely degraded and diminished, as it is for Belli: [21] but unlike any poet discussed so far, and at the opposite pole to Cardenal with his Third World faith, the Argentinian Alberto Girri is specifically a *displaced* witness, nostalgic and elegaic. In his first collections[22] *Playa sola* (Beach Alone, 1946) and *Coronación de la espera* (Coronation of Waiting, 1947), he raises the 'declaration of his skin' as it 'ages, alone', in an attempt to say that the 'West is sick with matter and irony'. His desire for coherence, a live civilization, is insatiable, and unsatisfied. His exasperated intellect allows him neither rationality nor to relinquish rationality. He refuses to 'grow tender', flees 'deceiving faith' with the full realization that 'order, order of whatever kind is forbidden to me'. Neither Christianity, as he understands it, nor the political creeds that spread in Latin America after the Second World War can relieve him of an overwhelming sense of the degeneration of his culture, if not of mankind as a whole. Man, the species that excels in destroying and maiming itself, is gripped by endemic evil, and rehearses the same senseless acts in successive avatars. Contemplating an old postcard from his mother he says 'every faculty is recreated in vain actions': 'Neither have been born nor is she dead.' In the collection *El ojo* (The Eye, 1964) this pessimism is given more overt sexual expression. The great genital metaphor of the eye in a triangle prompts the will to castration, to becoming a eunuch in the human line, this being an antidote to the 'poison' carried in menstruation. In the phrase of Richard Wilbur (the North American poet he has translated[23] and in some respects resembles), Girri might have said 'I am a sort of martyr, as you see'. But true to his ethic he will not find a way out in individual martyrdom. The worst disorder is that of the 'disordered one who puts everything in himself and in himself puts and gives his laws to anything he pleases', as he says in the title poem of *La condición necesaria* (The Necessary Condition, 1960).

These are large (and chilling) statements, but do not appear as such in Girri's poems because of the sobriety of his manner. Sooner than make himself the protagonist of this awful drama he often reflects on its plot, resignedly and obliquely if necessary. 'Comentario' (Commentary) is an important piece in this and other respects. In it he comments on the cluster of myths which served as the focus for J. G. Frazer's *The Golden Bough*. Our only sure way of knowing this comes in two lines over half way through which are a summary of the 'facts', and are enclosed in quotation marks: 'Attis, shepherd of Phrygia, deceived Cybele,/ who punished him by turning him into a pine tree'. Attis was to Cybele, an ancient Asiatic goddess of fertility, what Virbius was to Diana, the goddess who was at the centre of the cult at Aricia studied by Frazer. And in historical times both males, mortal devotees of goddesses, were represented by a line of priests known as kings of the Wood, guardians of the sacred tree (of the golden bough), each winning the title (*rex nemorensis*) by killing off his predecessor, only to be killed in turn by his successor. Now Girri proposes, reasonably, that the senses of a shepherd (Attis) should 'be in agreement' with the notion that being seduced by a goddess 'who is movement, fertility, the multiple breasts of the earth', is less tedious than sitting around pastorally anaesthetized by the heat of noon. He also supposes that the consequent ennobling, the becoming king of the wood, would inspire dreams of future fame and immortality (if only in the form of marble statues), even though, as we ought to know, such dreams are illusory, assassination or castration being more likely fates. The fate of mortals generally is murder by a successor, or, in Attis's case castration (being turned into a pine tree). Girri then goes on to attack certain kinds of poetry that has been made out of the story. An anti-poet in his own style, he deflates those pastoral illusions perpetrated by Ovid and Catullus. However hurtful, the truth of the matter is sooner 'the odious truth of the tribe', the instinct by which we go on rehearsing the myth, condemned to our 'necessary condition' as mortals.

'Commentary' is remarkable for the fullness of meaning conveyed in a level tone and ordered syntax. (In any case it is a plainer response to the golden bough myth than Eliot's in *The Waste Land*, or Pound's in the Pison Cantos.) This effect alerts us to another important quality of Girri's writing, which he has well described in 'Libro' (Book). There he recognizes the sovereign power expressed by words as signs and formulae, but also states the 'maximal law,/the immutable exigency/of not conserving the arcane in writing,/of transmitting it only confidentially'. Having confidence in the poet, faith in and *with* him, becomes indispensable to the degree that Girri moves perceptibly from his role of witness or commentator to that of guide. In all cases he himself still sees himself as alone, 'like a mirror without echo' (a clear allusion to Narcissus). Or again alone, 'despite Virgil'. Yet it is Virgil's working of that myth of the golden bough which brings out his larger ambition in another poem, in the collection *Examen de nuestra causa* (Examination Of Our Cause, 1956). The epi-

graph and the final lines of this poem, entitled 'Palomas' (Doves),
are a quotation from Book VI of the Aeneid: 'Este duces, o, si qua
via est' (Guide me, if there is a way). This is Aeneas about to
descend into the underworld, in search of secrets, as he says, as
arcane as the golden bough, entreating the doves of Girri's title.
We note that elsewhere Girri opposes these birds (the 'aves
maternas' of Virgil, an omen) to the crows, who grew black because of their bad faith as guides: in 'Commentary' Ovid's
pastoral poetry about Attis is called a crow. In this set of clues,
which may be scattered or erudite, but are wholly lucid, Girri
suggests that there may be or have been 'a way', that he is not
just the examiner of but martyr to 'our cause' (a term of deliberate
ambiguity), and then by asking to be guided he would initiate us
as a guide. Closely echoing the Aeneid, even in phonetic detail
(paredes/per duras, for example), Girri shows he is much less
interested in the pastoral or georgic than in the imperial Virgil,
with his large ambition and agony:

> y como Eneas imploró, suplico
> que en sus vuelos me señalen
> allá abajo, detrás de las paredes,
> en la espesura del asfalto,
> quién oculta, dónde languidece,
> la dorada rama, amor y sésamo,
> para arrancarla de cuajo
> y azotarme hasta aventar la borra,
> las emanaciones que el espejo devuelve,
> figuras y arbitrios
> de mi buscar certezas
> y no querer posarme en ellas,
> de mi dejarme consumir apeteciendo
> retener algo que  supere todo cambio
> aunque sólo en lo que ya no es
> se demore lo mejor de mí.

And as Aeneas implored, I beg that in their flights they show me here
below, behind the walls, in the thickness of the asphalt, who is concealing,
where the golden bough is languishing, love and sesame, so I may tear
it down and lash myself till I get rid of the chaff, the emanation that the
mirror returns, figures and taxes of my seeking certainties and not wanting
to settle in them, of my letting myself be consumed yearning to retain
something which is superior to all change although only in what no longer
is does the best part of me reside.

From what has been said it will be clear that there will be no
straight answer to the question: where, in the past, does that

best part reside? Except perhaps, not the America of Bello (Bello having accepted the georgic America as a substitute for the imperial). Girri has encouraged us to think of his poems as a 'universal fragment'; and they have, notably in later collections, a wide cultural reference (Lao Tse and Eastern mysticism; European romanticism, and so on). However in *Elegías italianas* (Italian Elegies, 1962), a remarkably coherent collection, he literally guides us round the scene of a dominant passion in him. The physical presence of places intimately linked with the Graeco–Roman past which so interests him (Rome, Venice, Ravenna, Salerno) makes his attitudes and allegiances quite specific. Visiting the estate of Tiberius, once the refuge of early Christians, he opens by almost spitting out the etymology of the place-name, the word acting as a quick conductor of latent feeling.

### SPERLONGA

Es
una corrupción del latín spelunca,
significa cueva, caverna,
cavidad natural
entre el mar y la montaña,

Sperlonga is a corruption of the Latin spelunca, means cave, cavern, natural cavity between sea and mountain.

He goes on to say what Sperlonga 'means'·in history, and what that history means to him. His dictionary, quite different from Parra's or Cabral's, is pointedly relied on, and its authority is importantly Latin. This authority is openly reinforced in his Venetian elegy. Though each stanza is entirely elliptical and lacks a main verb, he manages to insert into the poem statements as 'direct' as the following: 'Attila is returning – will the genius of the Roman be enough to build us a refuge today?' This is Girri's 'confidential' poetry: it relies as narrowly on given sympathies as say Eliot's footnotes to *The Waste Land*, if taken seriously. If the reader happens not to feel included in the term 'us', and less of an exiled son than Girri, the poem must suffer.

For this reason perhaps his most effective elegy of an Italy 'that no longer is' is one where he matches such cultural prejudice with the admission of what he is doing: 'Elegia de la costa' (Elegy of the Coast). Nostalgic and elegaic he evokes the flowers on the coast at Paestum, the roses famous in Augustan times, as an emblem of what has been lost: the imperial yet incipiently 'ᵗian' Roman genius of Virgil's major poetry. The fortune cᵢ culture itself becomes an analogue for his own understanding oᵢ life: according to its laws Attis or Aeneas were carried from pastoral sleepiness to proud guardianship of the arcane, but proved mortal. Corroborated on this scale Girri moves to quite uncharacteristic lyrical humility

> Dos veces al año
> mi hogar entre rosas, oh presencia
> de un hogar que tus dioses borraron.
> Dos veces
> la nostalgia
> ensombreciendo, aplastando rosas.
>
> ¿Te disminuye, tibia Paestum,
> que este sea mi pago? ¿Tomarás el poema
> como algo menos efímero
> que el momento de dejarte?

Twice a year my home among roses, oh presence of a home that your gods obliterated. Twice the nostalgia darkening, flattening roses. ¶Does it diminish you, tibia Paestum, that this should be my place? Will you take the poem as something less ephemeral than the moment of leaving you?

His Argentineness comes through in that most gaucho of words 'pago'. With this conditon the only saving dignity may be to leave, to go back into American exile. A century and a half after Independence, in the case of the Latin American Girri the emphasis is strongly, if unhopefully, on the first term of the epithet.

The refusal in this book to let 'Latin American' be simply *an* epithet may at times have seemed insistent or contrived. If any good has come of it, that means we have got closer to poets conscious of Spanish and Portuguese (and French) as not the only poetic languages of the sub-continent (from Anchieta and Sor Juana to Oswald de Andrade and Ernesto Cardenal); to those conscious of having or needing a separate American identity (from Bello to Neruda); and to those concerned primarily that American poetry should have its own identity (the Modernists). Of course, what really matters is 'poetry itself', and not what it may represent or tell us *about*. Yet if the prejudices of traditional criticism are a guide then certain poets and certain qualities in them tend to get overlooked or underestimated in the absence of a perspective such as ours. Bello would be an obvious case in point. The scope and precision of some of his lines are unrivalled, but little known. Again, it is a truism that the Modernists of Spanish America and Brazil were the 'founders' of Latin American poetry. Yet few have convincingly pinpointed what earned them that reputation, what special poetic virtue there is in, say, Darío's 'Divagation' or Mário de Andrade's *Hallucinated City*.

Clearly, this is no one's fault, least of all the poets', who are hardly under an *obligation* to tell us how to look at their work. Still, the 'founders', the Latin American Modernists, were less helpful than they might have been, and certainly lacked the strategies of Eliot or Pound. The Spanish American Modernists were in fact terrible critics, with the single exception of José Enrique Rodó (who was not a poet). Darío, for example, found imitating Catulle Mendès more important than translating the ambitions of his poetry into prose. The Brazilians were much better, though nationally restricted. Only later was much critical sense made of the 'situation' of the Latin American poet, by Pedro Henríquez Ureña in his magnificent book *Literary Currents in Hispanic America* (which includes Brazil), by Octavio Paz in his essays, and by some of the younger critics we have mentioned.

Even so, beyond a certain point it is less useful to define that 'situation'. In approaching the work of Latin American poets we have relied on the meaningfulness of a number of linguistic, cultural, political and geographical terms. But if there's anything happening in a poem at all, then there comes a moment when such terms enter a larger reality. Only with this in mind can we hope to grasp the paradoxes in Girri, or Belli. Finally, and most important, only thus can we sense what 'American-ness' may be in Neruda and Vallejo: Atlantean still, the one; the other, planetary.

# Notes

## 2. VERNACULAR AMERICAN

1 The carols (*villancicos* and tocotins) which she composed in Aztec are in her *Obras completas* II, Mexico 1952. She is one of the few writers of the Colonial period of international standing.

2 From the sixteenth-century manuscript in Portuguese, Castilian, Latin and Tupi edited by M. de L. de Paula Martins as *Poesia*, São Paulo 1954, p. 552.

3 See E. C. Hills, 'The Quechua Drama "Ollanta" ', *Romanic Review*, v, 126–76; P. E. Means, *The Ancient Civilization of the Andes*, New York 1931, p. 440ff.; S. Salazar Bondy, *Ollantay*, Lima 1953 and 1957.

4 From *Tupac Amaru Kamaq Taytanchisman. Haylli-Taki. A Nuestro Padre Creador Tupac Amaru. Himno-Canción*, Lima 1962. Arguedas, perhaps better-known as a novelist, edited several anthologies of Quechua literature in the original and in translation, among them: *Canto Kechwa*, Lima 1938 (in English as *The Singing Mountaineers*, University of Texas Press); *Canciones y cuentos del pueblo quechua*, Lima 1949; *Poesía quechua*, Buenos Aires 1966. Tupac Amaru, an ancient Andean god, was also the name of an Inca emperor, and of the leader of the rebellion against the Spanish in 1781, whose supporters were referred to derisively by the Spaniards as *tupamaros* (whence the name of the guerrilla movement in modern Uruguay).

5 For notes on modern poets publishing in Guarani, see N. González, 'La poesía guaraní', *América indígena*, XVIII, p. 67ff.

6 Lorenzo Boturini Benducci left a mass of published and unpublished work; his *Idea de una nueva Historia General de la América Septentrional*, Madrid 1746, has been sadly unrecognized. It established for the first time the right of Americans to a history of their own, with its own heroic past independent of the Old World. The Italian G. B. Vico first suggested this way of thinking in his *Scienza nuova*, 1725.

7 See my article 'An Indian Farewell in Prescott's *Conquest of Mexico*', *American Literature*, 45 (1973), pp. 348–56.

8 See my article 'Inca Hymns and the Epic-Makers', *Indiana* (Berlin), i, pp. 199–212.

9 His collection *Las comarcas* (1962) includes a 'Huayno', and *Simple canción* (1950) a 'Yaraví'; there is a 'Canción quechua' in Mistral's *Ternura* (1924).

10 See my article 'Ubirajara, Hiawatha, Cumanda: National Virtue from American Indian Literature', *Comparative Literature Studies*, ix, pp. 243–52. J. G. Herder greatly interested himself in 'primitive' and ancient song and poetry and anthologized it on a world-wide scale in his *Stimmen der Völker in Liedern* and elsewhere.

11 'Carta ao Dr Jaguaribe', appended to *Iracema* in J. Alencar, *Obra completa*, Rio 1965 (2nd ed.), vol. III.

12 In the essay 'On Cannibals', which of course Shakespeare drew on in *The Tempest*. Montaigne quotes such a song in his essay and shows his characteristically modern intelligence by taking it seriously and comparing it to classical Greek poetry, against the conventions of his age.

13 *Poesía precolumbina*, Buenos Aires 1960.

14 These are to some extent documented in my notes to the Penguin volume *Ernesto Cardenal. Selected Poems*, 1975, edited by Jean Franco.

15 In *Las aztecas. Poesías tomadas de los antiguos cantares mexicanos*, Mexico 1854; on this see M. Menéndez y Pelayo, *Historia de la poesía hispanoamericana* (Madrid 1948), i, p. 139, and my article 'Nezahual-coyotl's Lamentaciones and their Nahuatl Origins', *Estudios de cultura náhuatl*, x, 392–408.

16 'Carta a Margarita Villka', *Quiero escribir, pero me sale espuma*, Havana 1972.

17 *Voyage of a Naturalist*, chapter 8.

18 In their excellent anthology *La poesía gauchesca*, Mexico 1955, 2 vols.; this is the source of quotations here.

19 There is a useful collection of contemporary reviews, by Juan María Gutiérrez, Vicente Fidel López and others, in the Sopena (Buenos Aires) edition of *Santos Vega*.

20 The suggestion that the poem was epic was first made by the Spaniard Miguel de Unamuno.

21 The disowning has gone so far by now that a modern edition of *Martín Fierro* like E. F. Tiscornia's (Buenos Aires 1969), actually refers to gaucho language as 'uncultured' and 'incorrect'.

22 There is a good selection of poems by these and other early writers in I. Pereda Valdés's *Antología de la poesía negra americana*, Montevideo 1953. Pereda Valdés has also edited the anthology *Lo negro y lo mulato en la Poesía Cubana*, Montevideo 1970, which has a copious introduction.

23 *Antología de la poesía negra hispanoamericana*, Madrid 1935 and *Mapa de la poesía negra*, Buenos Aires 1946.

24 Carpentier also disowned his first novel *Ecué-Yamba-O*, an 'Afro-Cuban' work.

25 Moraes has recounted to Selden Rodman how experience of the slums (*favelas*) of Rio in 1945, in the company of Waldo Frank, changed him from being 'a citizen of the Upper Middle Class, pre-pared by their priesthood to be a good Rightist', and explained in these terms the transition in his poetry from the early *Forma e exegese* (1935) to his famous 'Balada do mangue' and the *Black Orpheus* lyrics.

26 Quoted by Jean Franco in *The Modern Culture of Latin America*, London 1967, p. 125, in the excellent chapter on 'The Indian, the Negro, the Land'.

27 See G. R. Coulthard, *Race and Colour in Caribbean Literature*, Oxford University Press 1962.

28 Guirao edited *Orbita de la poesía afrocubana, 1928–37*, Havana 1938.

29 Compare 'Hazaña y triunfo americano de Nicolás Guillén' in *Orbita de J. Marinello*, Havana 1968, 102–13; and E. Martínez Estrada, *La poesía afrocubana de Nicolás Guillén*, Montevideo 1965, which makes a stimulating comparison between the Cuban Guillén and the Andalusian García Lorca as fellow rebels against the oppressive orthodoxy of Castile.

30 *Ferrements*, Paris 1960. His *Cahier* is available in Penguin, translated by John Berger and Anna Bostock, as *Return to My Native Land* (1969). A good introduction to earlier French–American literature is A. Viatte, *Histoire littéraire de l'Amérique française des origines à 1950*, Quebec/Paris 1954.

### 3. THE GREAT SONG OF AMERICA

1 As it has been studied, for example, by Roy Harvey Pearce in *The Continuity of American Poetry*, Princeton 1965, though he stops short of Olson.

2 Bello's poems are well edited and introduced in the first volume of his *Obras completas*, Caracas, 1952, which is the source used in this chapter.

3 In J. J. Olmedo, *Poesías completas*, Mexico 1947. See above, p. 9, and E. C. Hills, *The Odes of Bello, Olmedo and Heredia*, New York 1920.

4 In his poem, and his notes to it, Olmedo in fact appealed for support to both Homer ('the Maeonian muse') and the Pindaric Ode (*Poesías completas*, pp. 131 and 125).

5 Mentioned in J. C. Ghiano's useful study 'Andrés Bello y su poema *América*', *Cuadernos del idioma* (Buenos Aires), iii, pp. 27–66.

6 First published in *El canto errante*, 1907, included in his *Poesías completas*, Madrid 1961, the source used here.

7 This point is more fully discussed in my edition of *Ariel*, Cambridge University Press 1967.

8 Adopting the same strategy in his sonnet to Whitman (in *Azul . . .*), Darío, like certain contemporary US poets, endeavoured to make of him not a 'democrat' but an 'Olympian' patriarch, with 'the proud face of an Emperor'. He uses Whitman's cry 'Oh captain! Oh my captain' as the first line of his heroic funeral Ode to the Argentine president Bartolomé Mitré (who died in 1906).

9 Rodó's essay on Darío, one of his best pieces of criticism, is of 1899 and appears in his *Obras completas*, Madrid 1957.

10 Martí's prose writing, notably the famous essay 'Nuestra América', views Latin America no less severely than Darío's 'A Colón', but intimates a new democratic spirit that was anathema to most Modernists. By a device not unlike Yeats's in 'Easter 1916', Darío, in his

portrait of Martí in *Los raros* (1905), all but apologizes for the Cuban's 'rebellion' against Spanish authority.

11  In his *Obras completas*, Mexico 1954.

12  Published in two volumes by Losada, Buenos Aires 1955, and commented on by F. Riess, *The Word and the Stone: Language and imagery in Neruda's 'Canto general'*, London 1972.

13  Especially in sections like 'Educación del cacique'.

14  Darío's 'Canto épico a las glorias de Chile' (1887) was dedicated to Balmaceda .

15  It is worth noting that Rivera, being like the other Mexican muralists more indigenist than Neruda, chose to illustrate the only lines from the whole of *Canto general* which suggest that America had reached a high point of culture and intellectual development *before* the European conquest. Rivera's painting picks out the details of these lines (I, vi, pp. 53–60), about the Maya:

> Los trabajos iban haciendo
> la simetría del panal
> en tu ciudadela amarilla,
> y el pensamiento amenazaba
> la sangre de los pedestales,
> desmontaba el cielo en la sombra,
> conducía la medecina,
> escribía sobre las piedras

Industriousness produced the symmetry of the honeycomb in your yellow fortress, and thought threatened the blood of the pedestals, it disentangled the sky at night, guided medicine, wrote on the stones.

16  This and many other important facts are noted by Emir Rodríguez Monegal in *El viajero inmóvil. Introducción a Pablo Neruda*, Buenos Aires 1966.

17  In the introduction to Nathaniel Tarn's translation *The Heights of Macchu Picchu*, London 1966, quoted above.

18  In his *Wandlungen und Symbole der Libido*, which focuses on *Hiawatha*.

#### 4. MODERNISM AND RUBEN DARIO

1  See for example G. Díaz Plaja, *Modernismo frente a 98*, Madrid 1951, and J. R. Jiménez, *El modernismo*, Mexico 1962.

2  See Juan Marinello, *Martí, escritor americano*, Mexico 1958, and *Sobre el modernismo: Polémica y definición*, Mexico 1959; both modified in 'Rubén Darío: meditación del Centenario', *Orbita de Juan Marinello*, Havana 1968. Also M. P. González's responses to him in *Notas en torno al modernismo*, Mexico 1958. More general statements include: F. de Onís, *Antología de la poesía española e hispano-americana*, Madrid 1934; M. Henríquez Ureña, *Breve historia del modernismo*, Mexico 1962 (2nd edition, used for quotations

here); R. Gullón, *Direcciones del Modernismo*, Madrid 1963; I. A. Schulman, 'Reflexiones en torno a la definición del modernismo', *Cuadernos americanos*, cxlvii; N. J. Davison, *The Concept of Modernismo in Hispanic Criticism*, Boulder, Colorado 1966.

3    Quoted by M. Henríquez Ureña, *Breve*. . . p. 158.

4    For example, in 'Sinfonía color fresa con leche' (Fraise au Lait-coloured Symphony), where he mocks the synaesthetic ambitions of the 'decadent colibrís'.

5    In *Epístolas y poemas*, Managua 1885. This and other quotations are from his *Poesías completas*, edited by A. Méndez Plancarte, Madrid 1961, amended where necessary from first editions.

6    See E. K. Mapes, *L'Influence française dans l'oeuvre de Rubén Darío*, Paris 1925.

7    'Responso', *Prosas profanas*.

8    From 'Leconte de Lisle', one of the sonnet 'Medallions' added to *Azul*. . .in 1890; de Lisle is thus explicitly distinguished from the kind of precious and minor Parnassianism of J. J. Palma, the subject of another of the sonnets.

9    See P. Grases, *Sección constante*, Mexico 1955.

10   See especially his preface to *El canto errante* (1907).

11   'José Martí', *Los raros* (1896), Buenos Aires 1952.

12   So called by I. M. Altamirano in a letter to Gutiérrez Nájera, quoted in José Emilio Pacheco's excellent *Antología del modernismo, 1884–1921*, Mexico 1970, 2 vols., i, p.5. See also I. A. Schulman, *Génesis del modernismo (Martí, Nájera, Silva, Casal)*, Mexico 1966. A similar policy was adopted later in Peru by Manuel González Prada: see my anthology *Spanish American Modernista Poets*, Oxford 1968.

13   In another of the Medallions in *Azul* . . .: this was in the style of 'Sursum' and 'A Gloria', published by Justo Sierra. After a spell in prison for homicide, Díaz Mirón went on to publish 'Idilio', a remarkable synthesis of French naturalism with the pastoral, and the stoical poems of *Lascas* (1901). See A. Castro Leal's edition of his *Poesías completas*, Mexico 1966.

14   His homage to native resistance in Cuba is mentioned by M. Henríquez Ureña, *Breve* . . . p. 116. See also J. M. Monner Sans, *Julián del Casal y el modernismo hispanoamericano*, Mexico 1952.

15   Hérédia, a Cuban by birth, invoked his American ancestry in the sonnet 'Les conquérants' (1868) and in 'La Défaite d'Atilba', a late unfinished work in which, characteristically, he planned to account for the epic history and vast geography of the continent in a succinct sequence of sonnets.

16   Who later compiled the useful *El archivo de Rubén Darío*, Buenos Aires 1943.

17   See M. Henríquez Ureña, *Breve* . . ., p. 100.

18   He displayed that 'tourist' attitude of de Lisle, Barbey d'Aurévilly and Merimée to archaic and medieval Spain *a fortiori* in his 1901 additions to *Prosas profanas*, 'Dezires' and 'Layes' in the style of Johan de Torres and others.

19 Of homosexuality, in 'Parsifal' (a line of which is quoted in Eliot's *The Waste Land*). On this period in general see A. Marasso's *Rubén Darío y su creación poética*, Buenos Aires 1954. Darío quotes Wagner's reputed remark to his pupil Augusta Holmes in the preface to *Profane prose*: 'Above all, don't imitate anyone, especially me.' Judith Gautier was associated with the 'cult' *Revue wagnérienne* in Paris in the late nineteenth century.

20 I have discussed this poem (as well as the prosodic innovations of the Modernists) in *Manuel Machado*, Cambridge University Press, 1968.

21 See I. A. Schulman, 'Reflexiones en torno a la definición del modernismo', *Cuadernos americanos*, cxlvii, and D. L. Shaw, 'Modernism: A Contribution to the Debate', *Bulletin of Hispanic Studies*, xliv, pp. 195–202.

22 On the poets mentioned below see Jorge Luis Borges, *Leopoldo Lugones*, Buenos Aires 1955; J. C. Ghiano, *Lugones, escritor*, Buenos Aires 1955; J. B. Gicovate, *Julio Herrera Reissig and the Symbolists*, Berkeley and Los Angeles 1957 and J. E. Pacheco's *Antología*.

23 This comparison is worth developing. With Eliot there is an intimate connection between the emasculated gallant Prufrock and the archetypically neuter Tiresias of *The Waste Land*, his Laforguean vocabulary and phraseology being essential to his impotent sentimentality. With Lugones, Laforgue's language certainly helps to undercut the easier emotions of a moonlit night ('farmaceutico', 'isócrono' etc.), but it does not compromise the speaker in the same way, when he comes on the scene 'in pijamas', burly and uncomplicated, an American more in the style of Darío than of Eliot.

24 *Antología*, II, p. 128.

25 Darío's career has been described in these terms, though somewhat reductively, by Pedro Salinas, *La poesía de Rubén Darío*, Buenos Aires 1948.

26 The references are to Darío's 'Hondas' (*El canto errante*) and to Pacheco's 'Declaración de Varadero', *No me preguntes como pasa el tiempo*, Mexico 1969.

## 5. BRAZILIAN MODERNISM

1 J. Nist, *The Modernist Movement in Brazil*, University of Texas Press, Austin/London, 1967; Mario da Silva Brito, *História do Modernismo brasileiro*, I, *Antecedentes da Semana de Arte Moderna*, São Paulo 1958; Wilson Martins, *The Modernist Idea: A Critical Survey of Brazilian Writing in the Twentieth Century*, translated by J. E. Tomlins, New York 1971. Mário de Andrade, *O Movimento Modernista*, Rio 1942 and Raul Bopp, *Movimentos Modernistas no Brasil* (1922–1928), Rio 1966, are both first-hand accounts. Manifestos from the main magazines of the Modernists, *Klaxon*, *Terra Roxa*, *Antropofagia*, *Verde Amarelo*, *Anta* and others, were repro-

duced in *Revista do Livro*, Rio, no. 16 (1959). An easily available anthology with an introduction in English is G. Pontiero's *An Anthology of Brazilian Modernist Poetry*, Pergamon Press 1969.

2 From the volume of that title published in São Paulo in 1917 after early collaboration with Oswald de Andrade, and before the founding of the review *Klaxon*. Subsequently in Italy, Marinetti and the Futurists issued a manifesto with the same title ('Noi') to the fascist government there in 1923.

3 By J. E. Tomlins, Vanderbilt University Press 1968, a bi-lingual edition.

4 The Modernists' desire to register spoken Brazilian in poetry, especially marked in the later collections of Manuel Bandeira (see below), is discussed by L. C. Lessa, *O Modernismo Brasileiro e a Língua Portuguesa*, Rio 1966.

5 Translated into English as *Epitaph of a Small Winner*, Penguin 1968.

6 In the preface to *Paulicéia desvairada*, and in the series of articles *Mestres do passado* published in the *Journal do Comércio*, São Paulo 1921.

7 The connection is noted briefly by G. de Torre in *Historia de las literaturas de vanguardia*, Madrid 1965, p. 579.

8 A Spanish translation by Francisco Villaespesa, *Toda la América*, was published in Madrid in 1930 and would have been easily available to Neruda during his stay there.

9 The manifesto is also reprinted in A. Cándido and J. A. Castello, *Presença da literatura brasileira*, São Paulo 1967 (2nd edition), III, pp. 66–72.

10 Much of his writing was explicitly opposed to what he considered the crypto-fascism of Modernists like Picchia.

11 'Canção do exilio, 1843', which has an epigraph from Goethe's 'Kennst Du das Land'. Incidentally, Goethe figures as a *bête noire* in Oswald's Manifesto, along with Cornelia, mother of the Gracchi, and João VI (father of Pedro I of Brazil).

12 As, in his way, had Oswald. An idea of the depth of the traditional conflict between cities like Rio and São Paulo and the interior is given by Euclides da Cunha's classic *Os sertões* (*Rebellion in the Backlands*, 1892).

13 For example, in his 'Nota preliminar' to *Libertinagem* in Manuel Bandeira, *Poesia completa e prosa*, Rio 1967 (2nd edition), taken from his *Aspectos da literatura brasileira*, Rio 1943.

14 Quoted by J. Nist, p. 80.

15 He talks about this and other poems in 'Itinerário de Pasárgada', *Poesia completa*, p. 102.


6. PRECEDENT, SELF AND COMMUNAL SELF: VALLEJO AND NERUDA

1 'Contra el secreto profesional', *Variedades* (Lima), 7 May 1927, collected in César Vallejo, *Literatura y Arte*, Buenos Aires 1966.

2    He made an instructive comparison between Chocano and Darío in another essay of the same year (22 October 1927): 'Rodó said of Rubén Darío that he was not the poet of America no doubt because Darío did not prefer, as Chocano and others have done, the deliberately American theme, artistic materials and subject in his poetry. Rodó was forgetting that in order to be a poet of America, the American sensibility was enough for Darío, the authenticity of which, through the cosmopolitanism and universality of his work, is evident and no one can cast doubts on it.' ('Los escollos de siempre', *Literatura y Arte*, p. 47.)

3    Notably in Enrique Díez Canedo's anthology of translations *La poesía francesa moderna*, Madrid 1913.

4    See for example his *Vie de Jésus* (Paris 1893, 22nd edition), with its idealized view of Galilee.

5    In 'Alfonso, estás mirándome, lo veo', in *Poemas humanos*, written as a letter from Paris to this Peruvian friend. A *cholo* is the son of a white father and an Indian mother; the term is often used pejoratively.

6    See A. Spelucín, 'Contribución al conocimiento de César Vallejo y de las primeras etapas de su evolución poética', *Aula Vallejo*, 2, pp. 29–104, and A. Coyné, *César Vallejo*, Buenos Aires 1968. The poem was originally called 'Noche en el campo'.

7    'Truenos' is one of the sections of *The Black Heralds*.

8    Apart perhaps from one late-Romantic and noticeably juvenile poem 'Oración', which deals with the degradation of the prostitute in the city.

9    So translated by W. S. Merwin, London 1969, a bi-lingual edition.

10    On this see A. Coyné, *op. cit.*, who following J. Espejo (*César Vallejo. Itinerario del hombre*, Lima 1965) suggests the following sequence: LXXI LI XLII XV XXXIV XLVI VI X LVI LXXVI VIII LXXIV XXXV XLIX LXII XL XVI XXXVII LVII LXXII XXI LXVII. See also L. M. Schneider, 'Comienzos literarios de Vallejo' (in *Aproximaciones a César Vallejo*, New York 1971, edited by A. Flores, 2 vols., I, pp. 137–85) which documents the revisions made to poems before they were included in *Trilce*.

11    This point is elegantly made by D. Gallagher in his essay on Vallejo in *Modern Latin American Literature*, Oxford University Press 1973.

12    In his *El viajero inmóvil*, Buenos Aires 1966, an indispensable work for Neruda's poetry from its beginnings to that date, which also takes into account all important existing criticism. Monegal also makes the point that the first two sections of Neruda's *Third Residence* are organically part of the first two *Residences*.

13    *El monismo agónico de Pablo Neruda*, Mexico 1971. See especially chapter 5, 'De la destrucción y la reintegración de la materia', which includes a line by line commentary on 'Galope muerto'.

14    In the first issue of a magazine which he founded on his return to Chile, *La aurora de Chile* (see Monegal, *El viajero*, pp. 98–9).

15  See her *Apuntes biográficos sobre Poemas en Prosa y Poemas humanos*, Lima 1968. *Trilce* had contained prose poems, LV for example.

16  In his 'Autopsia del Surrealismo' (*Variedades* 26 March 1930, also in *Literatura y Arte*), Vallejo offers a Marxist critique of Surrealism, Freudian psychology and modern culture generally.

17  In *Rusia en 1931* Vallejo said: 'I think of the unemployed. I think of the 40 million hungry people which capitalism has thrown from their factories and fields. Fifteen million workers idle and their families! What is to become of this army of poor people, unprecedented in history?' (Quoted by James Higgins in his useful *César Vallejo: An Anthology of his Poetry*, Pergamon Press 1970.)

18  The titles are as follows: *Odas elementales* (1954), *Nuevas odas elementales* (1957), *Tercer libro de las odas* (1957), *Navegaciones y regresos. Cuarto libro de las odas* (1959); all published in Buenos Aires.

19  'Sobre una poesía sin pureza', in the *Caballo verde para la poesía*, Madrid, October 1935, and reprinted numerous times since.

20  In 'Como era España', Neruda makes poetry out of a list of Spanish place names, incidentally echoing the sonnet of Unamuno's which begins 'Avila, Málaga, Cáceres'. (For a pointed commentary on this sonnet see O. Paz, *Traducción: Literatura y literalidad*, Barcelona 1917, p. 11.)

21  The title 'Las furias y las penas' is from Quevedo. Neruda edited the anthology *Cartas y sonetos de la muerte, de Quevedo*, Madrid 1935. In an interview with Selden Rodman Neruda acutely compared Gabriela Mistral's *Los sonetos de la muerte* (1916), her best work, with Quevedo's sonnets.

22  Clayton Eshleman in his introduction to *Poemas humanos/Human poems* (a bi-lingual edition), London 1969, p. xv. He develops the point further in his incisive review of Robert Bly's *Neruda and Vallejo: Selected Poems*, 'In Defense of Poetry', *Review* (New York), Spring 1972, pp. 39–47.

23  Neruda continued to publish up to his death in 1973. His later collections apart from those mentioned elsewhere, include *Los versos del capitán* (Buenos Aires 1953), *Cien sonetos de amor* (Buenos Aires 1959), *Plenos poderes* (Buenos Aires 1962), *Memorial de Isla Negra* (Buenos Aires 1964, 5 vols.).

24  Translated by Alastair Reid as *Estravagaria*, London 1972, a bi-lingual edition. See my note in *Stand* 14, no. 2.

### 7. THE TRADITIONS OF OCTAVIO PAZ

1  *Libertad bajo palabra* (*1935–1957*), Mexico 1967 (2nd edition); *La centena* (*Poemas: 1935–1968*), Barcelona 1972 (2nd edition, used for quotations here, except where noted).

2  See Claire Céa, *Octavio Paz* (Poètes d'aujourd'hui, no. 26), Paris 1965; J. M. Cohen, *Poetry of this Age*, London 1966, pp. 228–33;

D. Gallagher, *Modern Latin American Literature*, London 1973, pp. 67–81; R. Xirau, *Tres poetas de la soledad*, Mexico 1955, pp. 39–70 and *Poesía hispanoamericana y española*, Mexico 1961, pp. 45–55. R. Phillips, *The Poetic Modes of Octavio Paz*, Oxford University Press 1972.

3 See E. Rodríguez Monegal, 'Octavio Paz: Crítica y poesía', *Mundo nuevo*, 21, pp. 55–62.

4 For example in A. M. Garibay K., *Poesía indígena*, Mexico 1952 (2nd edition).

5 In the poems 'Abel' and 'La peau de bête', respectively: the emphasis is very much on a bloody sunset and an empty ashen plain, signs that something has gone terribly wrong.

6 Notably in the sequence in the Vienna Codex (p. 48), where the terrestrial Quetzalcoatl is joined by and to Quetzalcoatl as Venus. See K. Nowotny, *Tlacuilolli*, Berlin 1961.

7 'André Breton', *Mundo nuevo*, 6, pp. 59–62. Paz is the chief presence in Stefan Baciu's *Antología de la poesía surrealista latinoamericana*, an uncompromising and 'rigid' selection, in the words of the editor; other poets included are Tablada, Huidobro, César Moro, and Magloire Saint-Aude, whom Breton knew in Haiti.

8 'Fábula', *Semillas para un himno*, Mexico 1954.

9 For example, he makes an elaborate distinction between love and eroticism (*Cuadrivio*, p. 195), unstated as such in earlier works.

10 Which takes him into what Darío called 'el reino interior': see specifically the poem 'Interior', also in *Salamander*.

11 See E. Caracciolo, 'Salamandra de Octavio Paz', *Amaru*, March 1969, pp. 81–3. It is worth remarking that in this second, highly erotic poem Paz again follows Darío in going back to the *Song of Songs* (see p. 68): compare the lines quoted below with: 'A garden inclosed is my sister, my spouse; a spring shut up, a fountain sealed.'

12 Julio Ortega has made a valuable study of this aspect of the poem in 'Un poema de Octavio Paz', *Figuración de la persona*, Barcelona 1971, pp. 219–34.

13 The title of this book in fact stemmed from a conversation with Paz: see Cage's Foreword, p. x and Afterword, p. 163 (London edition, 1968).

14 *Claude Lévi-Strauss o el nuevo festín de Esopo*, Mexico 1967.

15 The best part of Gallagher's essay on Paz (*Modern Latin American Literature*, pp. 78–81) deals with this poem.

## 8. MODERN PRIORITIES

1 *Selected Essays*, London 1951 (1st edition 1932), p. 14.

2 See R. Debray, *Revolution in the Revolution?*, Penguin 1968 (Debray draws heavily on Giap), and Ernesto (Che) Guevara, *Man and Socialism in Cuba*, London 1969.

3 See Javier Heraud, *Poesías completas y homenaje*, Lima 1964, and the anthologies *Poesía revolucionaria del Perú*, ed. A. Molina, Lima

1955, and *Our Word*, ed. E. Dorn and G. Brotherston, London 1968. See also D. Tipton's *Peru, The New Poetry*, London 1970.

4   In *Canción de gesta*, Havana 1960.

5   Which this study does not do justice to. See in the first instance O. Paz's anthology *Poesía en movimiento* (mentioned in chapter 7), which exists in English, in sadly truncated form, as *New Poetry of Mexico*, London 1972.

6   In *Pedir el fuego*, Mexico 1968.

7   'En lo que dura el cruce del Atlantico', in *No me preguntes como pasa el tiempo*, Mexico 1969.

8   From Castro's 'Words to the Intellectuals', June 1961, quoted by J. M. Cohen in his useful anthology of translations *Writers in the New Cuba*, Penguin 1967. As Cohen remarks, this policy has not been consistently adhered to, and appeared to be openly flouted in the trial and imprisonment of the poet Herberto Padilla in the late 1960s.

9   Buenos Aires 1972.

10  J. M. Oviedo's highly perceptive review of the *Homenaje* in *Amaru* (Lima) is quoted by Pablo Antonio Cuadra (a notable Guatemalan poet in his own right) in his prologue to Ernesto Cardenal, *Antología*, Buenos Aires 1971. The Cuban Casa de las Américas has also published *Poemas de Ernesto Cardenal*, Havana 1967.

11  Montevideo 1967.

12  Julio Ortega, *Figuración de la persona*, Barcelona 1971, pp. 129–36. There is a short biographical and critical note on Belli in *Mundo nuevo* 8, pp. 84–7.

13  He later published a book jointly with him, however: *Discursos*, Santiago 1962. Neruda is credited with having driven his near contemporary Pablo de Rokha to suicide.

14  Julio Ortega, *op. cit.*, pp. 253–62. On Parra's early work see also Mario Benedetti, 'Nicanor Parra descubre y mortifica su realidad', *Letras del continente mestizo*, Montevideo 1967.

15  Allen Ginsberg and Lawrence Ferlinghetti are among his translators in *Poems and Antipoems*, New York 1967, an expanded version of *Antipoems*, previously published by City Lights, San Francisco. A recent collection of translations is *Emergency Poems*, New York 1972.

16  See for example his *Señoras y señores*, winner of the Casa de las Américas poetry prize, Havana 1973.

17  Parra speaks of his sense of social reality, and of antipoetry as a 'poetry of commitment', in an interview with Patricio Lerzundi, *Review*, Spring 1972, pp. 65–71.

18  Rio 1968.

19  From the volume *A Rosa do Povo*, Rio 1945. Michael Hamburger lucidly discusses Drummond's 'anti-poetry' in the chapter 'A New Austerity' of his *The Truth of Poetry*, London 1969, where he also deals with Marianne Moore. Drummond came in turn to be influenced by Cabral: his *Lição de poesia* (1962) owes much to Cabral's *A*

*Knife Only Blade* and to his *Duas aguas* (Two Waters, 1956). See Elizabeth Bishop's *An Anthology of Twentieth-Century Brazilian Poetry*, over half of which is devoted to Drummond and Cabral; also L. Costa Lima, *Lira e antilira: Mário, Drummond, Cabral*, Rio 1968.

20   Their work is available in the magazine *Noigandres*, published in São Paulo in the 1950s and early 1960s. See especially no. 5 (1962), an anthology of ten years' work by the *Noigandres* group. Edwin Morgan's essay 'Concrete Poetry' (in B. Bergonzi's *Innovations*, London 1968) touches on the Brazilian movement.

21   With whom Girri incidentally shares Italian origin.

22   *Poemas elegidos*, Buenos Aires 1965, is a useful anthology of his poems to that date.

23   In his *Quince poetas norteamericanos*, Buenos Aires 1966.

# Bibliography

These lists are meant as a general guide; more detailed references can be found in the chapter notes.

## I. GENERAL WORKS AND ANTHOLOGIES
### (a) *Latin America*

Baciu, S., *Antología de la poesía surrealista latinoamericana*, Mexico 1974.

Burnshaw, S., *The Poem Itself*, Harmondsworth 1964. Commentaries on poems by Bandeira, Lima, Vallejo, Meireles, Neruda.

Cohen, J. M., *Poetry of this Age, 1908–65*, London 1966.

Caracciolo-Trejo, E., *The Penguin Book of Latin American Verse*, Harmondsworth 1971.

Coulthard, G. R., *Race and Colour in Caribbean Literature*, Oxford 1962.

Fitts, D., *Anthology of Contemporary Latin-American Poetry*, New York 1947. Bi-lingual.

Franco, J., *The Modern Culture of Latin America: Society and the Artist*, London 1967.

Hamburger, M., *The Truth of Poetry. Tensions in Modern Poetry from Baudelaire to the 1960s*, London 1969.

Henríquez Ureña, P., *Las corrientes literarias en la América hispánica*, Mexico 1964 (3rd ed.). Deals with Brazil, despite its title. English version: *Literary Currents in Hispanic America*, New York 1963 (2nd ed.).

Paz, O., 'Latin American Poetry', *Times Literary Supplement*, 14 November 1968.

Pereda Valdés, I., *Antología de la poesía negra americana*, Montevideo 1953.

Rodman, S., *Tongues of Fallen Angels*, New York 1974. Conversations with and commentaries on Neruda (and Parra), Paz, Moraes, Cabral de Melo Neto.

Torre, G. de, *Historio de las literaturas de vanguardia*, Madrid 1965.

*Books Abroad* (Norman, Oklahoma), *Review* (New York) and *Tri-Quarterly* (Evanston, Illinois) are useful guides and sources of documentation, and have published special Latin American issues.

### (b) *Spanish America*

Anderson Imbert, E., *Historia de la literatura hispanoamericana*, Mexico 1954 (4th ed.), 2 vols.

Aridjis, H., *6 poetas latinoamericanos de hoy*, New York 1974. General and individual introductions in English to Huidobro, Vallejo, Neruda, Borges, Paz and Parra.

Ballagas, E., *Mapa de la poesía negra*, Buenos Aires 1946.

Bandeira, M., *Literatura hispanoamericana*, Rio 1960 (2nd ed.).

Benedetti, M., *Letras del continente mestizo*, Montevideo 1957. Essays on Darío, Vallejo, Neruda, Parra, Cardenal, Belli and others.

Benedetti, M., *Unstill Life: an Introduction to the Spanish Poetry of Latin America*, New York 1969.

Benedetti, M., *Los poetas comunicantes*, Montevideo 1972. Interviews with Parra, Cardenal, Fernández Retamar and others.

Benson, R., *Nine Latin American Poets*, New York 1968. Translations of Gorostiza, Huidobro, Neruda, Palés Matos, Paz, Pellicer, Storni, Vallejo and Villarrutia.

Borges, J. L. and Bioy Casares, A., *La poesía gauchesca*, Mexico 1955, 2 vols.

Brotherston, G., *Spanish American Modernista Poets. A Critical Anthology*, Pergamon Press 1968.

Caillet-Bois, J., *Antología de la poesía hispanoamericana*, Madrid 1965 (2nd edition).

Castillo, H., *Antología de la poesía modernista hispanoamericana*, Waltham, Mass. 1964.

Cohen, J. M., *Writers in the New Cuba*, Harmondsworth 1967.

Franco, J., *An Introduction to Spanish-American Literature*, Cambridge 1969.

Gallagher, D. P., *Modern Latin American Literature*, Oxford 1973.

González, M. P., *Notas en torno al modernismo*, Mexico 1958.

Gullón, R., *Direcciones del modernismo*, Madrid 1963.

Henríquez Ureña, M., *Breve historia del modernismo*, Mexico 1962 (2nd edition).

Menéndez y Pelayo, M., *Historia de la poesía hispano-americana* [1910], Santander 1948, 2 vols.

Onís, F. de, *Antología de la poesía española e hispano-americana*, Madrid 1934.

Ortega, J., *Figuración de la persona*, Barcelona 1971. Essays on Vallejo, Moro, Belli, Paz, Parra, Pacheco, Arguedas and others.

Oteiza, E., *Poesía argentina*, Buenos Aires 1963. An anthology.

Pacheco, J. E., *Antología del modernismo 1884–1921*, Mexico 1970. Poems of Mexican Modernists, with an extremely full introduction.

Paz, O., *Anthology of Mexican Poetry*. Translated by Samuel Beckett. Preface by C. M. Bowra. London 1958.

Paz, O., *Cuadrivio*, Mexico 1965.

Paz, O., *Poesía en movimiento, Mexico 1915–66*, Mexico 1966. An abridged English version: *New Poetry of Mexico*, London 1972.

Paz, O., *Las peras del olmo*, Barcelona 1971. Essays on Sor Juana Inés de la Cruz, Tablada, López Velarde, Gorostiza and others.

Pellegrini, A., *Antología de la poesía viva latinoamericana*, Barcelona 1966.

Schulman, I., *Génesis del modernismo* (Martí, Nájera, Silva, Casal), Mexico 1966.

Tarn, N., *Con Cuba. An Anthology of Cuban Poetry of the Last Sixty Years*, London 1969. Bi-lingual.

Tipton, D., *Peru. The New Poetry*, London 1970.

Yurkievich, S., *Fundadores de la nueva poesía latinoamericana*, Barcelona 1971. Essays on Vallejo, Huidobro, Borges, Neruda and Paz.

Zaid, G., *Leer poesía*, Mexico 1972.

### (c) Brazil

Bishop, Elizabeth, *An Anthology of Twentieth-Century Brazilian Poetry*, Middletown, Connecticut, 1971.

Costa Lima, L., *Lira e antilira: Mário, Drummond, Cabral*, Rio 1968.

Martins, W., *The Modernist Idea: A Critical Survey of Brazilian Writing in the Twentieth Century*, translated by J. E. Tomlins. New York 1971.

Nist, J., *The Modernist Movement in Brazil*, Austin/London 1967.

Pontiero, G., *An Anthology of Brazilian Modernist Poetry*, Pergamon Press 1969.

## II. WORKS OF INDIVIDUAL POETS, AND COMMENTARIES ON THEM

Andrade, Mário de, *Poesias completas*, São Paulo 1972 (3rd edition).

*Hallucinated City (Paulicéia desvairada)*, translated by J. E. Tomlins, Vanderbildt U.P. 1968. Bi-lingual.

*Cartas de Mário de Andrade a Manuel Bandeira*, Rio 1958.

*Mário de Andrade por êle mesmo*, São Paulo 1971.

Costa Lima, L., see I(c) above.

Grembecki, M. H., *Mário de Andrade e l'Esprit nouveau*, São Paulo 1969.

Bandeira, Manuel, *Poesia completa e prosa*, Rio 1967 (2nd edition).

Moraes, E. de, *Manuel Bandeira: análise e interpretação literária*, Rio 1962.

Belli, Carlos Germán, *El pie sobre el cuello*, Montevideo 1967.

*Sextinas y otros poemas*, Santiago 1970.

Benedetti, M., see I(b).

Ortega, J., see I(b).

Bello, Andrés, *Obras completas*, Caracas, I, 1952.

Ghiano, J. C., *Análisis de las Silvas Americanas de Bello*, Buenos Aires 1967.

Grases, P., *Doce estudios sobre Andrés Bello*, Buenos Aires 1950.

Rodríguez Monegal, E., *El otro Andrés Bello*, Caracas 1969.

Cabral de Melo Neto, João, *Poesias completas, 1940–65*, Rio 1968.

Costa Lima, L., see I(c).

Nunes, B., *João Cabral: nota biográfica, introdução crítica, antologia, bibliografia*, Petropolis 1971.

Rodman, S., see I(a).

Cardenal, Ernesto, *Antología*, Buenos Aires 1971.

*El estrecho dudoso*, Madrid 1966; Buenos Aires 1972.

*Homenaje a los indios americanos*, León, Nicaragua 1969; translated by Monique and Carlos Altschul as *Homage to the American Indians*, Baltimore and London 1973 (English only).

*Canto nacional*, Buenos Aires 1973.

*Selected Poems*, edited by Jean Franco, Harmondsworth (in press).

*En Cuba*, Buenos Aires 1972.
Benedetti, M., see I(b).
Casal, Julián del, *Poesías completas*, Havana 1965.
Monner Sans, J. M., *Julián del Casal y el modernismo hispano-
americano*, Mexico 1952.
Schulman, I., see I(b).
Chocano, José Santos, *Obras completas*, Mexico 1954.
Rodríguez-Peralta, P. W., *José Santos Chocano*, New York 1970.
Darío, Rubén, *Poesías completas*, Madrid 1961.
*Selected Poems*, Austin 1965.
Anderson Imbert, E., *La originalidad de Rubén Darío*, Buenos
Aires 1967.
Ghiano, J. C., *Análisis de Prosas profanas*, Buenos Aires 1968.
Ghiraldo, A., *El archivo de Rubén Darío*, Buenos Aires 1943.
Giordano, J., *La edad del ensueño. Sobre la imaginación poética de
Rubén Darío*, Santiago 1971.
Mapes, E. K., *L'Influence française dans l'oeuvre de Rubén Darío*,
Paris 1925.
Marasso, A., *Rubén Darío y su creación poética*, Buenos Aires 1954.
Mejía Sánchez, E., ed., *Estudios sobre Rubén Darío*, Mexico 1968.
Paz, O., 'El caracol y la sirena', *Cuadrivio*. See I(b).
Rodó, J. E., 'Rubén Darío', *Obras completas*, Madrid 1957.
Salinas, P., *La poesia de Rubén Darío*, Buenos Aires 1948.
*Rubén Darío Centennial Studies*, ed. M. González-Gerth and G. D.
Schade, Austin 1970.
Díaz Mirón, Salvador, *Poesías completas*, Mexico 1966 (5th edition).
Almoina, J., *Díaz Mirón. Su poética*, Mexico 1958.
Drummond de Andrade, Carlos, *Poesia completa e prosa*, Rio 1973.
*In the Middle of the Road. Selected Poems*, translated by J. Nist,
Tucson, Arizona 1965. Bi-lingual.
Costa Lima, L., see I(c).
Mendonça Teles, G., *Carlos Drummond de Andrade: a estilística
da repetição*, Rio 1970.
Girri, Alberto, *Poemas elegidos*, Buenos Aires 1965.
*Envíos*, Buenos Aires 1966.
*En la letra, ambigua selva*, Buenos Aires 1972.
*Poesía de observación*, Buenos Aires 1973.
Gonçalves Dias, António, *Poesia completa e prosa escolhida*, Rio 1959.
Ricardo, C., *O indianismo de Gonçalves Dias*, São Paulo 1964.
Guillén, Nicolás, *Patria o Muerte! The Great Zoo and other poems*,
translated by R. Márquez. New York/London 1972. Bi-lingual.
Augier, A., *Nicolás Guillén. Notas para un estudio biográfico-
crítico*, Havana 1964–5, 2 vols.
Couffon, C., *Nicolás Guillén*. Poètes d'aujourd-hui, Paris 1964.
Martínez Estrada, E., *La poesía afrocubana de Nicolás Guillén*,
Montevideo 1966.
Tous, Adriana, *La poesía de Nicolás Guillén*, Madrid 1971.
Gutiérrez Nájera, Manuel, *Poesías completas*, Mexico 1953, 2 vols.

*Crítica literaria*, I, Mexico 1959.
*Cuentos; y Cuaresmas del Duque Job*, Mexico 1963.
Schulman, I., see I(b).
Hernández, José, *Martín Fierro*, ed. E. Carilla, Barcelona 1972.
*The Gaucho Martín Fierro*, translated C. E. Ward, Albany, New York 1971. Bi-lingual.
Borello, R., *José Hernández: poesía y política*, Buenos Aires 1973.
Carilla, E., *La creación del Martín Fierro*, Madrid 1973.
Hughes, J. B., *Arte y sentido de Martín Fierro*, Madrid 1970.
Herrera y Reissig, Julio, *Poesías completas*, Madrid 1961 (2nd edition).
Gicovate, B., *Julio Herrera y Reissig and the Symbolists*, Berkeley and Los Angeles 1957.
Huidobro, Vicente, *Poesía y prosa*, Madrid 1957. Includes an essay on Huidobro's *creacionismo* by A. de Undurraga.
Barry, D., *Huidobro, o la vocación poética*, Granada 1963.
Caracciolo Trejo, E., *La poesía de Vicente Huidobro y la vanguardia*, Madrid 1974.
Jaimes Freyre, Ricardo, *Poesías completas*, La Paz 1957.
Carilla, E., *Ricardo Jaimes Freyre*, Buenos Aires 1962.
López Velarde, Ramón, *Poesías completas*, Mexico 1963 (2nd edition).
Murray, F. W., *La imagen arquetípica en la poesía de Ramón López Velarde*, Madrid 1972.
Paz, O., 'El camino de la pasión', *Cuadrivio*: see I(b).
Phillips, A. W., *Ramón López Velarde, el poeta y el prosista*, Mexico 1962.
Lugones, Leopoldo, *Obras poéticas completas*, Madrid 1959 (3rd edition).
Borges, J. L., *Leopoldo Lugones*, Buenos Aires 1955.
Ghiano, J. C., *Lugones escritor*, Buenos Aires 1955.
Martí, José, *Obras completas*, Havana 1936–47.
*Versos*, ed. E. Florit, New York 1962.
González, M. P., *Fuentes para el estudio de José Martí*, Havana 1950.
Marinello, J., *José Martí, escritor americano: Martí y el modernismo*, Mexico 1958.
Onís, J. de, *The America of José Martí*, New York 1953.
Schulman, I., see I(b).
Montes de Oca, Marco Antonio, *Poesía Reunida*, Mexico 1971.
*Presentado por sí mismo*, Mexico 1967.
Brotherston, G., 'Montes de Oca and the "Splendour of this world" ', *Books Abroad*, XLV, 36–40.
Paz, O., 'Montes de Oca', *Puertas al campo*, Mexico 1966, pp. 122–7.
Neruda, Pablo, *Obras completas*, Buenos Aires. Various editions.
*Selected Poems*, translated by Ben Belitt, New York 1961.
*Neruda and Vallejo: Selected Poems*, ed. Robert Bly, Beacon Press 1971.
*The Early Poems*, translated by D. Ossman and C. B. Hagen, New York 1969.
*Twenty Love Poems and a Song of Despair*, translated by W. S. Merwin, London 1969.

*Residence on Earth and other poems*, translated by Angel Flores, Norfolk (Connecticut) 1946.

*Residence on Earth*, translated by Donald Walsh, New York 1973.

*The Heights of Macchu Picchu*, translated by Nathaniel Tarn, London 1966.

*Let the Rail-Splitter Awake and other poems*, translated by J. M. Bernstein, New York 1951.

*Elementary Odes*, verse translation by C. Lozano, New York 1961.

*We are many*, translated by Alastair Reid, London 1967.

*Estravagaria*, translated by Alastair Reid, London 1972.

    Aguirre, M., *Genio y figura de Pablo Neruda*, Buenos Aires 1964.

    Alazraki, J., *Poética y presencia de Pablo Neruda*, New York 1965.

    Alonso, A., *Poesía y estilo de Pablo Neruda*, Buenos Aires 1966 (3rd edition).

    Concha, J., *Neruda, 1904–36*, Santiago 1972.

    Jiménez, J. R., 'América sombría?', *La corriente infinita*, Madrid 1961.

    Lellis, M. J. de, *Pablo Neruda*, Buenos Aires 1959 (2nd edition).

    Lozado, A., *El monismo agónico de Pablo Neruda. Estructura, significado y filiación de Residencia en la tierra*, Mexico 1971.

    Riess, F., *The Word and the Stone: Language and Imagery in Neruda's Canto general*, London 1974.

    Rodríguez Monegal, E., *El viajero inmóvil. Introducción a Pablo Neruda*, Buenos Aires 1966.

Olmedo, José Joaquín, *Poesías completas*, Mexico 1947.

    Hills, E. C., *The Odes of Bello, Olmedo and Heredia*, New York 1920.

Pacheco, José Emilio, *Los elementos de la noche*, Mexico 1963.

*El reposo del fuego*, Mexico 1966.

*No me preguntes cómo pasa el tiempo*, Mexico 1969.

*Irás y no volverás*, Mexico 1973.

*Tree Between Two Walls*, translated by Ed Dorn and G. Brotherston, Los Angeles 1969. Bi-lingual.

    Ortega, J., see I(b).

    Zaid, G., see I(b).

Parra, Nicanor, *Obra gruesa*, Santiago 1969.

*Discursos* (with Pablo Neruda), Santiago 1962.

*Poems and Antipoems*, London 1968.

*Emergency Poems*, New York 1972.

    Benedetti, M., see I(b).

    Montes Brunet, H., 'La antipoesía de Nicanor Parra', in *Nicanor Parra y la poesía de lo cotidiano*, Santiago 1970.

    Morales T. L., *La poesía de Nicanor Parra*, Santiago 1972.

    Ortega, J., see I(b).

    Rein, M., *Nicanor Parra y la antipoesía*, Montevideo 1970.

Paz, Octavio, *Libertad bajo palabra (1935–57)*, Mexico 1967 (2nd edition).

*La centena (Poemas 1935–68)*, Barcelona 1972 (2nd edition).

*Selected Poems*, translated by Muriel Rukeyser, Bloomington 1963. Bi-lingual.

*Sun Stone*, translated by Muriel Rukeyser, New York 1963.

*¿Aguila o sol? Eagle or Sun?*, translated by E. Weinberger, New York 1970. Bi-lingual.

*Configurations* [*Ladera este*], London 1971. Bi-lingual.

*Labyrinth of Solitude*, translated by L. Kemp, London 1967.

*The Bow and the Lyre*, New York 1973.

*The Other Mexico* [*Posdata*], translated by L. Kemp, New York 1972.

*Renga. A Chain of Poems*, New York 1972.

Céa, Claire, *Octavio Paz*, Poètes d'aujourd'hui, Paris 1965.

Ivask, I., ed., *Octavio Paz. The Perpetual Present. The Poetry and Prose of Octavio Paz*, Norman 1973. Several articles on Paz, and a full bibliography.

Ortega, J., see I(b).

Phillips, R., *The Poetic Modes of Octavio Paz*, Oxford 1972.

Xirau, R., *Octavio Paz. El sentido de la palabra*, Mexico 1970.

Silva, José Asunción, *Poesías completas* [in fact not], Madrid 1963.

García Prada, C., *José Asunción Silva. Prosas y versos*, Mexico 1942.

Schulman, I., see I(b).

Vallejo, César, *Obra poética completa*, Lima 1968.

*César Vallejo: An Anthology of his Poetry*, edited by J. Higgins, Pergamon Press 1970.

*Twenty Poems*, translated by Robert Bly, The Sixties Press 1962.

*Neruda and Vallejo: Selected Poems*, ed. Robert Bly, Beacon Press 1971.

*Selected Poems*, translated by Ed Dorn and Gordon Brotherston, Harmondsworth 1975. Bi-lingual.

*Ten Versions from Trilce*, by Charles Tomlinson and Henry Gifford, San Marcos Press 1970.

*Poemas humanos, Human Poems*, translated by Clayton Eshleman, London 1969.

*Literatura y arte*, Buenos Aires 1966.

Ballón Aguirre, E., *Vallejo como paradigma*, Lima 1974.

Coyné, A., *César Vallejo*, Buenos Aires 1968.

Escobar, A., *Cómo leer a Vallejo*, Lima 1973.

Espejo Asturrizaga, J., *César Vallejo. Itinerario del hombre*, Lima 1965.

Flores, A., ed., *Aproximaciones a César Vallejo*, New York 1971, 2 vols.

Franco, Jean, *César Vallejo*, Cambridge (in press).

Higgins, J., *Visión del hombre y de la vida en las últimas obras poéticas de César Vallejo*, Mexico 1970.

Monguió, L., *César Vallejo (1892–1938). Vida y obra. Bibliografía. Antología*, New York 1952.

Ortega, J., see I(b).

# Index